T0293532

LEADERSHIP TEAM ALIGNMENT

LEADERSHIP

TEAM ALIGNMENT

FROM CONFLICT

TO COLLABORATION

Frédéric Godart and Jacques Neatby

STANFORD BUSINESS BOOKS
STANFORD UNIVERSITY PRESS
STANFORD, CALIFORNIA

Stanford University Press
Stanford, California

Special discounts for bulk quantities of Stanford Business Books are available to corporations, professional associations, and other organizations. For details and discount information, contact the special sales department of Stanford University Press by emailing
sales@www.sup.org.

Printed in the United States of America on acid-free, archival-quality paper

Cataloging-in-Publication Data available upon request.
Library of Congress Control Number: 2022050293
ISBN: 9781503630826 (cloth), 9781503636590 (ebook)

Cover designer: Jason Anscomb
Cover photograph: iStock

To Viktor,
who may one day decide to navigate the waters of the business world

To Anne-Marie and Gabrielle,
who proved to be invaluable in-house contributors

CONTENTS

ACKNOWLEDGMENTS

The number of people we want to recognize is not inconsequential for two reasons. The first is that many CEOs, executives, and colleagues—some of whom we are fortunate to also call friends—devoted their very scarce time to share their leadership team experiences or engaged in the backbreaking work of providing feedback on chapters—or both.

Another reason is that this book is the culmination of over twenty years of reading and reflecting on issues of power, networks, and dynamics at the top of organizations. Our reflection has been informed by executives and scholars who may only now discover that we sat atop their shoulders as we wrote this book.

But if the list seems long, it is, in truth, far too short, covering only a small percentage of those who contributed to it. We apologize in advance to those whose contribution we could not bring to our readers' attention due to faulty memory retrieval systems.

Although this book's primary audience is executives, we begin by thanking our university colleagues whose support and ideas permeate our work. At INSEAD, Charles Galunic, collaborated with both of us individually before we ever met. Many of the ideas explored in his book *Backstage Leadership: The Invisible Work of Highly Effective Leaders*, find echo in our own pages. Jose-Luis Alvarez and his coauthor, Silviya Svejenova, whose *The Changing C-Suite: Executive Power in Transformation* (2021) offers the most solid account of the transformation of leadership teams we have come across. Maria Guadalupe developed extensive and cutting-edge academic research on the key topic of our book. Andrew Shipilov manages to build bridges among various managerial disciplines, notably strategy and organizational behavior, and his thinking about networks is unique. Finally, it would be impossible to write about multinational leadership teams without acknowledging the challenges of leading across cultures that Erin Meyer has written about so lucidly.

At HEC Paris, we must thank Catherine Tanneau, who hired us to teach about executive power and thus enabled us to meet. There we also encountered Emmanuel Coblence, Paul Delahaie, and Rodolphe Durand, whose curiosity and incisive thinking gave us new perspectives on our chosen topic.

At HEC Montréal and McGill University, we thank Alain Gosselin, Réal Jacob, and Louis Hébert. Their wisdom lies just beneath the surface of many of our chapters. We are also grateful to Caroline Aubé, whose knowledge of the team literature proved invaluable over the years and whose thoughts also find their way into these pages after we spent hours collaborating on articles cowritten with Phanie Rioux who must also be saluted. Finally, we thank Éloi Lafontaine Beaumier, as well as Alaric Bourgoin for his contribution to Chapter 1.

At Bocconi University, we thank Paola Cillo and Isabella Pozzo whose thinking about how multiple forms of leadership (creative, business) interact is so rich.

We thank London Business School professor Herminia Ibarra, one of the planet's great executive coaches, whose work on the challenges of transitioning to the C-suite has influenced our teaching of aspiring and current executives. The counsel of Thomas Roulet at the University of Cambridge proved critical in getting our project off the ground.

This book's value stems in large part from the direct and indirect contribution of the hundreds of executives whose thoughts and actions are reflected in these pages. Those we mention next have titles affixed to them that are not always those they carry today but are ones they held when we crossed paths with them at one time or another.

Two CEOs we are particularly grateful to are Frank Piedelièvre of the Bureau Veritas Group, the global number 2 player in the testing, inspection, and certification industry, and Yves Masse, who was leader of a ridiculously complex public health services organization when we first met. Their vastly different styles show that great team stewardship comes in many guises.

Other CEOs we worked with and whom we often pestered to reveal the secrets of their craft were Roman Oryschuk of the General Electric Company (United Kingdom), Geoffrey Close and Yves Caprara of Prayon (Belgium), Marcel Cobuz at Holcim (Irak, Morocco), Yves Devin of the Montreal Casino (Canada), and Pierre Deleplanque at Heracles Cement (Greece).

Other CEOs we worked with and subjected to particularly fruitful grillings include Kamil Beffa at Louis Dreyfuss Armateurs (France), Emilio Imbriglio at RC Grant Thornton (Canada), Helmut Herold at Telesystem Energie (Germany), and David Redfern of Holcim (Canada).

The following CEOs are ones we learned from mostly by watching them in action: Thomas Buberl of the AXA Group (France); Alan Bollard of the APEC Secretariat (Singapore); Luc Beaudoin, chief of police in Gatineau (Canada); Pascal Casanova at LafargeHolcim (France); Matthieu de Tugny of the Bureau Veritas Group Marine Division (France); Kevin O'Brien of the Bureau Veritas Consumer Products Division (United States), Madeleine Paquin of Logistec Corporation (Canada); and Carine Paumier-Hub at Vapor Rail and Vapor Stone Rail System (United States/Canada).

The executives who taught us valuable lessons as we observed them include Magali Anderson, chief sustainability and innovation officer at Holcim (Switzerland); Arnaud André, executive vice president of human resources and organizational development of the Bureau Veritas Group (France); Lisa Bate, senior vice president of the Americas at Element Materials Technology (United States); André Beaulieu, senior vice president of corporate services at BCE (Canada); Philippe Bertin, chief human resource officer (CHRO) at Prayon (Belgium); Marc Blanxart, head of building at LafargeHolcim (Switzerland); Éric Drouin, vice president of strategy at Promutuel Insurance (Canada); Marc Ducharme, chief administrative officer at Fasken LLP; Caroline Luscombe, executive vice president at Sanofi (France); Stephanie McDonald, chief human resources officer at Ontex (Belgium); Philippe Platon, chief financial officer at WeMaintain (France); Chantal Gaemperlé, group executive vice president of human resources at LVMH Moët Hennessy-Louis Vuitton (France); Lubomira Rochet, chief digital officer at L'Oréal (France); Frédérique Saint-Olive, corporate human resources vice president, bioMérieux (France); and Florence Verzelen, executive vice president of industry, marketing and sustainability at Dassault Systèmes Group (France).

Executives who explicitly shared their insights include Pascal Bécotte, member of the global executive committee at Russell Reynolds Associates; Annie Brisson, chief human resources officer of the Jean Coutu Group (Canada); Julie Lévesque, executive vice president of technology and operations at National Bank (Canada); Kathy Megyery, vice president of global affairs at Sanofi North America (United States); Pierre Neatby, vice president of worldwide marketing at Ambatovy (Madagascar); Roger-Ketcha Ngassam, global head of strategic operations at Novartis (Switzerland); Jim Rosenberg, chief of staff at Jewish United Fund (United States); Sandrine Talbot Lagloire, vice president of sales at Bossard Group (Canada/United States); and Chris Wade, global head of internal communications, the Adecco Group (Switzerland).

Special mention must go to the following individuals. First is Andrea Bogusz, head of talent and learning at the GEA Group (Germany), whose practical understanding of power and politics is truly remarkable. The insights of François Trudel, chief human resources officer at Randstad (Canada), and Philippe Redaelli, managing director of chain market data at Kaiko (France) on leadership at the top, have had a greater impact than they probably imagined. We also thank Antoine Tirard, global head of talent acquisition and management at LVMH Moët Hennessy-Louis Vuitton.

Unsurprisingly, we received tremendous support from several consultants, many of whom have also toiled as executives. Their insights over the years proved invaluable. They include Jad Bitar, managing director of Boston Consulting Group in Dubai; Madeleine Chenette, Canadian ambassador to the Organization of Economic Cooperation and Development; Philippe Frizon, vice president of strategy at Desjardins General Insurance Group; Frédéric Gascon, chief operating officer at PayFacto; Philippe Mauchard of McKinsey & Company in Belgium; Kevin O'Brien, head of international markets at WeightWatchers; and Aurèle Thériault at Interlocus. Finally, Henry Zinglersen, president of MindLab (Denmark), is one of the world's great cross-cultural experts, who, with Mark Aspinall of the United Kingdom, deserves much of the credit for the Purpose-Outcomes-Process (POP) framework discussed in Chapter 6.

Mere thanks to our family and friend are a poor reward for the time and intelligence Nicole Neatby and Bronwen Griffiths applied in reading chapter drafts. We also thank David Chemla whose experience as an executive and eye for detail served us well. Extra special thanks are extended to Lisa Yarmoshuk whose efforts and insights, married to an exceptional and unique mix of competencies, so greatly improved the final book that we were blessed to have her support.

At Stanford University Press, thanks to the entire team and especially to Cindy Lim and senior editor Steve Catalano. We could not be more grateful for how they expertly shepherded us through the process and engaged in the content with us, often waking up very early so that it would be convenient for Montréal-based Jacques and Paris-based Frédéric. The way they prodded us to submit drafts to meet tight deadlines offered lessons in leadership that may well find their way into our next book.

For those who were wondering, the red weight hanging from a metal thread on the cover of the original Stanford University Press edition of this book is a plumb line, carrying at its end a weight known as a plumb bob. This device has been used for centuries to check that a structure or wall is perfectly vertical or that it slopes at the correct angle. In other words, it is used to ensure something is aligned and thus seemed appropriate for this book's cover.

LEADERSHIP TEAM ALIGNMENT

INTRODUCTION

Why This Book, Who It's For, and What's in It for You

Why This Book

"You were speaking about us, weren't you."

So said a CEO who walked up to us after a presentation we gave at a leadership team conference years ago. He first expressed his thanks for our address and then leaned in, almost whispering the words quoted above. We soon learned he was alluding to a conflict we had described onstage that he believed had been taken from his own leadership team's experience, a team we knew well.

It was not, but it could have been.

Why? Because the conflict in question afflicts almost all leadership teams (LTs), something this CEO had not realized. He had assumed the conflict was specific to his team.

This story highlights something about LTs we have observed after years of studying and working with them: the vast majority suffer from a common set of generic dysfunctionalities, but these are not always easy to distinguish from those that are team specific. As a result, LT issues are often misdiagnosed, and consequently the wrong remedies are applied.

This book will help you correctly diagnose issues affecting your LT and propose appropriate remedies to deal with them. These remedies are practices designed for, and successfully implemented by, actual LTs. Along the way, we address the questions CEOs ask us most often:

- How can I minimize power and politics on my LT?

- What do I do about silos?

- How do I get my team members to put the organization's success ahead of their own?

- Who should sit on my team, and is it too big now?

In providing answers to these questions, we tackle two pressing LT issues. The first is why conflicts are so prevalent on LTs and what CEOs can do to manage them so they can spend their time doing something other than mediating disputes. The second is why it is difficult to create an environment where LT members take their role as organizational leaders seriously and are invested in decision making that addresses issues outside their immediate area of responsibility. As one newly named CEO once complained to us:

> My whole career, I've been a team player. I don't *want* to make decisions by myself. But getting [my team members] to pitch in on topics that don't impact them directly is like pulling teeth. I ask a question and what do I get? Crickets.[1] So I end up making a lot of decisions by myself but then they criticize me for it! I'm not complaining but, you know, it really is lonely at the top sometimes.

While this is not a self-help book intended to cure such loneliness, it will help you increase your LT's alignment, a critical dimension of LT effectiveness.

You may already believe that improving your LT's effectiveness and alignment is important. However, it is worth highlighting five reasons why all leaders and board members should be paying more attention to their LT:

1. *Alignment: Critical but difficult to achieve.* An organization's misaligned LT inevitably leads to misalignment and dysfunctionality at the levels below, which makes LT misalignment more than a team issue. It is an organizational problem.

This is hardly news to CEOs, which is why so many are concerned with their executives' alignment.[2] Unfortunately, most CEOs' efforts to achieve and maintain alignment are less successful than many would hope. In an article tellingly entitled "No One Knows Your Strategy—Not Even Your Top Leaders,"[3] the authors report that only slightly more than 50 percent of LT members in the typical organization they surveyed agreed on their organization's strategic priorities. A study by McKinsey & Company paints a similar picture: while executives agreed that being aligned on their purpose was critical, only 60 percent of them reported that they were.[4]

Our experience has been no different. Whenever we begin an LT engagement, we ask team members to name their organization's top strategic priorities. After nearly two decades, we have come across few LTs with full agreement among its members on more than one or two. Nevertheless, many CEOs and team members believe they are very much aligned as they unknowingly pull in opposite directions.

2. *More turbulence outside, more turbulence inside.* The second reason organizations need to pay more attention to their LTs is the growing turbulence in most industries. While every decade sees commentators declaring that turbulence has increased, the argument that it has increased significantly in recent years is compelling.[5] For example, on the economic front, one can point to international trade issues arising out of geopolitical tensions between old and new superpowers and to the COVID-19 pandemic, which has had companies everywhere rethinking their supply chains, among other things.[6] With increased turbulence in the external environment, internal alignment at the top becomes more difficult to achieve, provoking a ripple of conflicts at the levels below.[7]

3. *The diversity imperative.* In the social sphere, the underrepresentation of women and minorities in senior leadership positions has put pressure on organizations to diversify their top teams. This is a long-overdue priority that offers many benefits, including increased creativity.[8] Yet we must recognize that diversity means aligning more perspectives, which may lead to more conflict. LTs already manage a significant amount of conflict. But since few can boast of doing it well, diversity poses a significant challenge. Working out how LTs can deliver the benefits of diversity while maintaining alignment is critical.

> *Working out how LTs can deliver the benefits of diversity while maintaining alignment is critical.*

4. *A trust deficit in an increasingly virtual world.* When we started this project, COVID-19-related disruptions were spurring an increase in virtual contacts between LT members. We do not expect this to change in coming years given rapidly improving videoconferencing technologies and concerns over climate change. The result is fewer face-to-face LT member meetings, which in the past were always assumed necessary for building trust. This makes it imperative that executives understand what measures can be taken to build trust as in-person contact between LT members drops off.

5. *A grossly underused value creation lever.* Finally, as many CEOs admit, an effective LT is the main lever they possess to influence their organization

and achieve their goals.[9] Given how critical this lever is, developing your LT team's effectiveness may be the most potent value creation mechanism at your disposal since it requires little financial investment and, unlike organization-wide improvement initiatives, does not necessitate buy-in from hundreds of people. Why would you choose to overlook it?

The Small Sample Factor: Why So-Called LT Best Practices Are Rarely Best

That almost 50 percent of CEOs admit that developing their LT is challenging should not come as a surprise.[10] A lot of mystery surrounds how effective LTs really work. Why this is the case is worth considering because it explains why many LT practices viewed as best are rarely that.

First, few CEOs make a habit of seeking help when they wish to improve their team's effectiveness because many perceive their LT issues as rooted exclusively in interpersonal conflicts rather than in dynamics common to all LTs.[11] Accordingly, the practices they choose to meet these issues, whether good or bad, are rarely publicized. A second, and more important, reason for the shortage of true LT best practices is how few people have had in-depth exposure to a wide range of LTs.

> *Executives generally have a very small sample of high-performing LTs from which to derive good practices.*

Consider the *executives* who sit on LTs. Rare are those we meet who have sat on more than a handful of LTs. Rarer still are those who say they have sat on *effective* LTs. Thus, executives generally have a very small sample of high-performing LTs from which to derive good practices.

The same is true for *consultants*. Many may work alongside LTs, but few get to observe LTs as they go about their everyday business. The reason is simple: LTs do not like to air their laundry, dirty or otherwise, in front of strangers. Even when consultants do get to watch an entire LT at work, it is usually when they are facilitating a session on a project they are entrusted with or they are at an offsite meeting where time is spent on "team-building" activities. In such artificial environments, LT members know it pays to be on their best behavior lest the consultant tell their CEO that they are "poor team players."

The LT dynamics that consultants perceive are further distorted by savvy executives who try to co-opt them. As one executive once confided, "I always invest time helping our consultants and giving them my opinion on our team. In that way, they take my side when they talk to my CEO."

Finally, we have *LT scholars*. Although many have delivered significant insights, they are the first to admit that obtaining permission to observe LTs is challenging, a well-known issue across social scientists studying such elites. The reality is that gaining access to LTs is "extremely difficult if not virtually impossible for most researchers."[12] This is understandably so, as CEOs see little benefit, and much risk, in letting scholars eavesdrop on strategic discussions, especially when their company is publicly traded.

Our Experience with LTs

That much LT advice rests on limited firsthand knowledge of LTs is something we want to remedy with this book.

The insights and ideas you will find here are based on over eight hundred hours of direct observation of fifty-six LTs in eighteen different industries over two decades. We spent countless more hours with CEOs and individual members of these LTs assessing their team's challenges and implementing solutions to address them.

Of the fifty-six teams, thirty-three were based in North America, eighteen in western or eastern Europe, and the remaining five in Asia-Pacific. Of the five in Asia Pacific, four were based in Asia proper. However, it is important to note that these organizations were business units of American and European companies.

The types of engagements we performed for these LTs can be classified in the following manner:

- 34 percent were straight LT coaching engagements where a CEO wanted support to increase their team's effectiveness.

- 28 percent were senior leadership offsites like those that thousands of organizations hold annually.

- 20 percent were strategic planning engagements.

- 9 percent were to assist the client organization in a corporate restructuring.

- 9 percent were to provide support in a postmerger integration context.

Our work is also informed by exchanges with the more than fifteen hundred

TABLE 0.1. Breakdown of LTs by industry.

Industry	Number of Leadership Teams
Aerospace / transport	2
Cargo handling	4
Chemical	2
Construction	10
Education	1
Energy	3
Entertainment	3
Financial services	4
Hospitality/travel	3
Human resources services	2
Law enforcement	1
Marine services	5
Professional services	2
Public health	3
Shipping	2
Telecom	1
Testing, inspection, and certification	7
Trade	1
TOTAL	56

CEOs and senior executives of some of the world's top companies who attended our executive education classes in Europe and North America during which they shared their LT challenges.

Finally, our fieldwork is complemented by an in-depth study of the literature applying to LTs from a wide array of fields (e.g., management, sociology, politics, negotiations) as a means of testing and validating the insights gained through our contacts with LT leaders and members.

References to this literature are found throughout this book, and the details are in the Notes and References. This is to promote ease of reading but also to give precedence to the real-world experience of executives because of the gap between the way LTs are described in some of the literature and how they operate in the field. For example, some LT literature ignores the power and politics prevalent at the top and so promotes practices meant for an environment that hardly resembles the one in which executives work. Other writings promote practices emerging from nonexecutive team research despite it being widely acknowledged that such teams vary appreciably from LTs.[13] Thus, the adage. "In theory, theory and practice are the same. In practice, they are not," often applies to LTs.[14]

If we recommend a practice in this book, it is because we have seen it implemented by an actual LT. If we have not, we say so.

Who This Book Is For

LT Leaders, Our Primary Audience

Because LT leaders are afforded less and less time to achieve results before being shown the door, they need to build and develop their LT quickly.[15]

For simplicity, we label these leaders chief executive officers (CEOs), but they also include regional and business unit managers in large and medium-sized organizations. For example, the company depicted in Figure 0.1 has four LTs: the one under the CEO, as well as one under each of the three regional VPs: Europe, Asia, and America. (Note: we only represented two of these LTs in full).

We show the details of the European vice president's team to illustrate how it qualifies as an LT, notably because it has a mix of executives with operational and functional responsibilities. In contrast, the chief human resource officer's (CHRO) team is not an LT for the purposes of this book because it does not have such a mix.

Secondary Audiences: Executives and Board Members

After CEOs, we target two other audiences who have an interest in well-functioning LTs. First are the executives who sit on LTs, many of whom tell us their colleagues are the greatest obstacles to their success. While that may be true at times, a more common reason executives struggle once they reach the top is that they do not immediately grasp the implicit rules of the game. By making those rules explicit, we enable executives to better contribute to their organization's success and to their own.

Next are **board members**. We add our voices to those who believe boards should play a more proactive role in supporting CEOs to assess their teams.[16] Although board members we meet agree that an effective LT is critical, the majority admit they have never considered assessing their organization's LT *as a team*. They may assess LT members *individually*, for example, by using

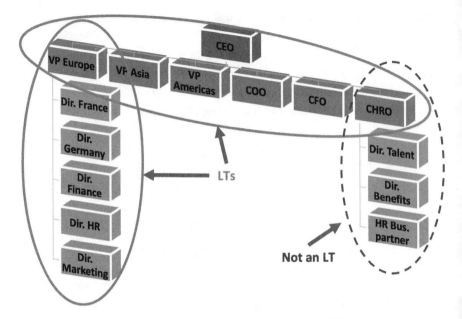

FIGURE 0.1. What an LT is, and Is Not, For the Purposes of This Book

360-degree-feedback tools, but these are not designed to assess team dynamics. At best, they indicate if LT members get along, but that hardly qualifies as a team assessment because, as we shall see, there is no evidence linking LT effectiveness to LT members getting along. In fact, LT members who get along too well should raise a red flag.

Last But Not Least

We hope our book will also help **consultants** who advise LTs and are looking for a sound framework to diagnose LT dysfunctions and remedies to address them, just as we hope some of our insights may help **LT scholars** since many of their insights have helped us.

Last, at the risk of giving this book an "appropriate for everyone" label, it may also be of interest to those concerned with corporate governance issues. Given the important role that public and private organizations play in our economy, we hope that gaining a better understanding of how they work and are governed proves useful.

Two Ways to Read This Book
and How It Is Structured

The two of us grew up on different sides of the Atlantic, and as we discovered, this has shaped the way we read business books:

- Frédéric prefers the classic, front-to-back approach.

- Jacques prefers jumping straight to the topics that most interest him and might skip the others.

To facilitate both approaches, chapters are divided into sections and subsections, each titled to identify the issues they address. Whichever approach you adopt, here is what you will find in this book:

In Part I, we single out three differences between LTs and nonexecutive teams that largely explain why commonly used practices to improve LT alignment and effectiveness are rarely successful.

In Chapter 1, we address the dual role of LT members. An LT member wears two hats: the first as leader of their unit, by which we mean a business unit or function (e.g., human resources, information technology) and the second as leader of the organization. Much of the conflict and misalignment on LTs stems from the difficulty LT members have in reconciling their responsibilities under both hats.

Chapter 2 addresses the saliency of power games on LTs. Many observers denounce such games as if this were sufficient to make them disappear. Meanwhile, new LT members are bewildered to hear their CEO say there is no place for power and politics in their organization but then notice that those who succeed are colleagues who are most adept at power games and who enter their CEO's inner circle. In this chapter, we explore why power games are inevitable and what effective CEOs we have met do to minimize their impact.

In Chapter 3 we address why many LTs get stuck in Hub-and-Spoke mode whereby CEOs interact one-on-one with LT members who live in silos, interacting very little with colleagues outside LT meetings.

At the end of each of these three chapters, you will find an "Actionable Insights" section that presents practices to meet the challenges raised in the chapter. You will also find "The Chapter in a Nutshell" section summarizing the chapter's key concepts. Figure 0.2 highlights some of the misconceptions each of these chapters address.

Part II addresses how to improve specific aspects of your LT. We have taken

Chapter 1	Chapter 2	Chapter 3
The Dual Role of LT Members	*Power Games at the Top*	*Of Hubs, Spokes, and Silo Busting*
Misconceptions • LT conflict is *interpersonal* or the result of executives putting their interests ahead of the organization's. **Reality** • Most LT conflict is *structural*: LT members are defending strategic imperatives, just as they should.	**Misconceptions** • Only ambitious, poor team players engage in power games. • Power games on LTs can be eradicated. **Reality** • Power games are unavoidable: they can be mitigated but never eradicated. • Ignoring the power games of powerful executives makes them more powerful.	**Misconceptions** • Hub-and-Spoke functioning and silos are the CEO's fault. • Hub-and-Spoke functioning is always a problem. **Reality** • LT members are chief instigators of Hub-and-Spoke mode. • Hub-and-Spoke mode is not a problem. Getting *stuck* in Hub-and-Spoke mode is. • CEOs need to learn how to lead in Hub-and-Spoke mode.

Chapter 4	Chapter 5	Chapter 6
Who Really Sits on Your LT, and What Is Its Role?	*Getting your LT's Size and Composition Right*	*Assess Your LT and Fix It*
Misconceptions • All LT members need to be involved in all strategic decisions. • LT meetings are where strategic decisions get taken. **Reality** • Effective decision making requires excluding certain LT members. • Taking decisions before an LT meeting is not a sign of dysfunctionality. • Alignment is the overlooked yet critical LT role.	**Misconception** • There is an optimal LT size. • You need to add a new position to your LT to show you are taking an issue seriously. **Reality** • There is no optimal LT size. • Succumbing to the latest executive position fad only hinders LT effectiveness.	**Misconception** • Traditional approaches to fixing LTs can have lasting effects. • An LT meeting is just a meeting. **Reality** • Traditional team-building approaches rarely create lasting team habits. • The science of habit formation can be leveraged to produce lasting effectiveness. • POP can improve LT effectiveness inside of meetings and, more important, *outside* as well.

FIGURE 0.2: Overview of Chapters 1 to 6

into consideration that LTs vary according to myriad factors, such as size (their own and that of the organization they belong to), the nature of their organization (e.g., public, private, family owned), and the profile of its members. We have chosen to focus only on solutions that can be applied universally.

Chapter 4 seeks to dispel three misconceptions about an LT's role in strategic decision making and address what may be the most critical role LTs are meant to play but rarely play well.

Chapter 5 focuses on the principles that will help you determine your LT's optimal structure, including its size and membership, considering your organization's strategy and its business model.

Chapter 6 addresses how to assess your LT by outlining the three dimensions you should be paying attention to. We then propose a tried-and-true approach to improve your LT's alignment and effectiveness more rapidly than other often advocated approaches.

These three chapters in Part II also end with "Actionable **Insights**" and "The **Chapter in a Nutshell**" sections and Figure 0.2 highlights misconceptions addressed in chapters 4, 5 and 6.

Protecting the Innocent

This book offers many cases, and except where noted, all come from organizations we know firsthand. To protect the innocent (and the not-so-innocent), the names of protagonists have been modified unless the events recounted are in the public domain.

Now all that is left for us to do is to let you read on. We hope you find the answers you seek. If you have any questions that are not raised in this book, we encourage you to share them by writing to us at leadershipteamalignment@insead.edu.

We will respond to as many as we can and may well address those that occur repeatedly in our future work.

PART I

EMBRACING LEADERSHIP TEAM REALITY

THE DUAL ROLE OF LEADERSHIP TEAM MEMBERS

"Because he's not a team player. I care about our company, but all he cares about is his bonus."

That is how Leslie, legal affairs leader of a North American multinational we worked with, explained why Sam, her counterpart in sales, had signed a customer contract that put the company at risk. When we asked Leslie why she felt Sam would do this, she replied, "It's simple. Sam's a typical salesperson: he's a cowboy. He doesn't care he's putting the entire organization at risk."

When we questioned Sam about the situation, he scoffed at Leslie's concerns. In his opinion, the contract posed no risk whatsoever.

"So why would Leslie be so upset about it?" we asked.

"Because Leslie doesn't understand the business," said Sam. "She's a lawyer. She's only concerned about covering her [backside]."

If this seems like a caricature of a dispute between LT colleagues, sadly, it is not. On more than one occasion, we have been asked to mediate similar disputes between executives from sales and legal services. Only the names were different.

But such disputes, where both parties are convinced they are defending the organization's interests against a colleague who is (a) selfish and/or (b) incompetent, and/or (c) does not understand the business, are not restricted to sales and legal executives. Such conflicts regularly affect all LT members.[1]

Understanding why is critical to explaining why so many nonexecutive team best practices rarely work when applied to LTs. The reason lies in the strategic dualities that pit LT members against one another.

Strategic Dualities: The Root
Cause of Most LT Conflicts

A strategic duality describes the tension between two *seemingly* contradictory strategic objectives. Like yin and yang in Taoist symbolism, these objectives are two interdependent halves of a whole that must be kept in harmony.[2] For executives, this is easier said than done. We use three examples that show why strategic dualities are a principal source of conflict on many LTs:

- Duality no. 1: Top line versus bottom line

- Duality no. 2: Exploration versus exploitation

- Duality no. 3: Growth versus risk management

We chose these dualities because they are the source of conflict—sometimes minor, sometimes not—in almost every organization we worked with. The odds are that at least one of them has had an impact in yours.

Three Classic Strategic Dualities and the LT Conflicts
They Inevitably Lead To

The first classic duality, **top line versus bottom line**, opposes the growth objective (the *top line*)—often defended by the head of sales—and the profitability objective (the *bottom line*), typically upheld by the chief financial officer (CFO).

Even if these two executives in your organization know (or ought to know) that they should work together to balance growth and profitability, they may still struggle to do so. The reason? The functional hat each one wears encourages them to plead the case of their respective unit.[3]

As counterintuitive as it may appear to those unfamiliar with LTs, there is nothing inherently wrong with this. Indeed, as a CEO, you should be worried if your CFO does not defend the bottom line. Similarly, you have cause for concern if your sales executive does not fight to build the top line.

However, the conflicts begin when their focus on the strategic objective they are defending blinds them to the objective their colleague is upholding, rendering them unable to balance both for the good of your company.

The second duality, the so-called **exploration versus exploitation** duality, pits the innovation objective (*exploration*), championed by your head of R&D, against the productivity objective (*exploitation*), typically promoted by your head of operations. This duality explains why these two executives butt heads at budget time.

For operations leaders, the need for funding to meet short-term operational targets often makes them lose sight that long-term survival depends on well-financed R&D. Meanwhile, the pressure to deliver game-changing innovations may blind your head of R&D to the fact that such innovations are pointless if a shortfall in operations funding means the company goes under in the short term. But when the pressure is high, both instinctively claim the lion's share of the budget. The result? Your head of R&D complains that their counterpart in operations is "a dinosaur who can't see that R&D is the future of this company!" while the head of operations retorts that they hardly need a lesson from a colleague who has never rolled up their sleeves to do "real work."

The third strategic duality, **growth versus risk management,** opposes the growth objective with the risk management objective. While growth is critical, if it is achieved without a concern for risk, your organization eventually pays a price. This duality is at the heart of the dispute at the start of this chapter between Sam in sales (whose job is to grow the top line) and Leslie in legal (whose job is to limit risk by ensuring sales contracts include protective clauses).

Unfortunately, Sam and Leslie made the mistake many sales and legal executives commit: they viewed their feud exclusively as an *interpersonal* conflict and began attacking each other's character. Had they realized they were caught in a *structural* conflict opposing sales and legal executives everywhere, their conflict would have been much easier to resolve, as we explore in this chapter.

Why Strategic Duality Conflicts Are Often Misdiagnosed as Interpersonal Conflicts

If strategic dualities are the cause of classic LT conflicts, the root of such conflicts may well lie in what Stanford professor Lee Ross and fellow psychologist Andrew Ward call "naive realism", a human tendency whereby:

- People believe they see the world objectively and without bias.

- They expect that others with access to the same information will come to the same conclusions so long as they are rational.

- Those who do not share their views must be ignorant, irrational, or biased.[4]

Another explanation why strategic dualities cause conflict is that they generate anxiety by obliging executives to reconcile objectives they view as contradictory. They adopt an *either/or* **mind-set** rather than a *both/and* **mind-set** and simply defend the objective that aligns with their unit or function's interests.[5]

Some go further and lash out at their "opponent" because, as mediation expert Cheryl Picard[6] points out, they see their colleague's actions as threatening to their values and interests.[7]

This helps to explain why executives embroiled in such conflicts often add a personal layer atop their dispute by, for example, going around telling their side of the story—and *only* their side—to anyone who will listen: their CEO, their team, their spouse, the barista at Starbucks. No one is safe.

In such circumstances, an executive on your LT may even go so far as to misattribute a colleague's words and deeds hoping to discredit their "adversary" and gain allies against them. However, once their poisoned words get back to their colleague, as they inevitably do, their relationship sinks to a new low.[8] Furthermore, it sows animosity within the LT because many feel obliged to pick sides.

It is because such disputes pick up a personal dimension that the CEOs who come to us with such disputes often misdiagnose LT conflicts. They see them as purely *interpersonal* and fail to see their *structural* causes that are rooted in the strategic objectives the protagonists are defending.

On Top of It, LT Members Have "Clients"

That LT members are expected to be spokespersons for different strategic objectives has long been recognized.[9] In this sense, LT members are not unlike lawyers defending their case before the LT "court." These members also resemble lawyers in that they have "clients": their staff, who expect them to defend their budgets and their jobs.[10] If executives are unsuccessful in defending their staff, they cannot be assured of the latter's allegiance for long.

This is the lesson the CFO at an engineering firm we worked with learned the hard way. Hired because his predecessor had let the finance department grow overly large and dysfunctional, our newcomer took immediate steps to slash his department's head count by 15 percent. Although the decision was the right one, his staff believed the cuts had gone too far and that the CEO would have accepted 10 percent.

One year later, the CFO was gone, ostensibly fired by the CEO for underperformance but, for all intents and purposes, fired by his staff who undermined him at every turn for having failed to defend them adequately.

Consequences of LT Members
Being Spokespersons

Because LT members are spokespersons for different strategic objectives or causes, three consequences arise. Keep these in mind when you decide to improve your LT's effectiveness.

Consequence No. 1: LTs Are Designed for Conflict

"Teamwork would be great … if it wasn't for my teammates."

This saying often elicits a laugh from executives whose experience with their LT colleagues is not always the happy collaborative adventure it is cracked up to be. That experience involves friction, and for good reason: LTs are designed for conflict. We mean that conflict in LTs is not only inevitable but also desirable, a feature of LT dynamics that must be managed as such.[11]

Many who hear this jump to the conclusion that we are saying that life on an LT must be one long *Game of Thrones* or *House of Cards* episode.[12] While certain executives wish to perpetuate this brutal stereotype of life at the top, that is not at all what we mean.

Instead, what we are saying is that because LT members are given a responsibility to defend strategic objectives, they predictably clash with their colleagues. We gave three examples previously when describing strategic dualities. But as Table 1.1 makes clear, those examples are the tip of the iceberg.

When such conflicts are treated as exceptional or, worse, as evidence of dysfunctionality, they end up being suppressed rather than managed, based on the mistaken assumption that teammates should not fight.

As a result, a common error is to tell an LT member involved in a conflict to be a "good team player" and to "sacrifice their unit's interest for the greater good." While this appears to make sense, the consequences can be disastrous when executives take this to heart. Thus, we have seen a head of legal services who stopped putting up a fight whenever her counterpart in sales signed a new customer contract without legal's oversight. When your legal team ceases to pester sales to review such contracts before they are signed, they become legal time bombs waiting to explode.

When all LT conflicts are treated as exceptional or, worse, as evidence of dysfunctionality, they end up being suppressed based on the mistaken assumption that teammates should not fight.

TABLE 1.1. Common Strategic Dualities and the LT Members They Oppose

Positions or Functions involved	Strategic Duality	Examples from Real LTs
Corporate headquarters vs. business units	Integration and harmonization to promote synergies vs. local specification and autonomy to respond to market needs	• Ex 1: A group CFO enacted a policy seeking to harmonize the financial reporting of all business units, thus creating a dispute with the heads of those units, who argued that they could not monitor their unit's performance appropriately because their different business models required they follow different metrics. • Ex 2: A group CHRO imposed a standard recruitment process to professionalize hiring practices across the entire group, which led to a dispute with an Asian business unit leader who claimed that the recruitment process was not adapted to the cultural specificity of her market.
Finance vs. sales	Cost control and profitability focus vs. top-line growth and market share capture	• Ex 1: A CFO systematically refused to reimburse entertainment expenses incurred by the sales team because she deemed them frivolous at a time when the company needed to tighten its belt because of a recession. This led to a dispute with the head of sales who was under pressure to make his targets despite the recession and who believed that entertaining clients would provide a competitive advantage to close deals because competitors had stopped taking clients out. • Ex 2: Sales spent money every year on a kiosk at an industry trade show because "clients expected them to be there." For her part, the CFO thought the trade fair was more of a paid vacation for the sales team than a true sales opportunity and asked sales for a detailed plan to justify the expenditure. • Ex 3: A dispute erupted on the LT of a North American manufacturing firm between the CFO and the head of sales over the pricing strategy that sales was implementing in Asia. The strategy consisted of selling product at below cost to gain market share. This had a negative impact on the firm's profitability, prompting the CFO to accuse his sales counterpart of running the company into the ground. Sales retaliated by claiming that the CFO "understood nothing about strategy."
HR vs. operations	Staff engagement and well-being vs. staff efficiency and productivity	• Ex 1: The CHRO ordered that staff not come back to the office until the end of 2021 for health reasons tied to the COVID pandemic. This created a conflict with business unit heads who believed that staff productivity would drop if they did not receive direct, in-person supervision. • Ex 2: Operations, believing that staff were disengaged and leaving the company because they were underpaid, put pressure on HR to loosen its compensation and benefits policy to give raises to a few star performers. HR, as guardian of the policy, refused and implied that engagement and staff attrition might be

Positions or Functions involved	Strategic Duality	Examples from Real LTs
Marketing vs. sales	Differentiation and medium-term innovation vs. short-term growth and revenue generation	• Ex 1: In a multinational software company, sales complained that marketing sent them client leads that led nowhere because the clients that marketing had identified were not yet ready to buy. Marketing retorted that those in sales were being shortsighted and were mistaken to expect marketing to deliver clients who already had a pen in hand to sign a deal. In marketing's opinion, sales needed to make the effort to educate these clients to help new lines of business grow. • Ex 2: In a European technology company, marketing had spent months educating a client about the benefits of an innovative new product. Sales eventually got the client to sign a contract after adapting the product to meet the client's specifications. Neither sales nor marketing wanted to give each other any credit for the new contract because credit could not be shared at bonus time.
Legal affairs vs. sales	Risk management and rule conformity vs. growth and agility in negotiations	• Ex 1: A company's general counsel insisted that the head of sales insert the company's standard limited liability clause into a contract that sales has just signed with a new client. Sales believed that any attempt to do so would reopen negotiations with the client and that the contract might be lost. • Ex 2: The head of sales complained to the CEO about a policy requiring that legal affairs be consulted before signing every contract. Sales alleged that none of the lawyers were at the office when the sales team needed them because "my salespeople work 24/7 while the legal team gets to go home at 6:00 p.m. every day." General counsel countered that sales staff purposefully waited until all lawyers had left the office before reaching out to them so there would be no obstacle to their signing contracts that were extremely risky.
Sales vs. operations	Made-to-measure and customer service vs. quality and respect for production standards	• Ex 1: To make a sale, the sales team presented a soon-to-be developed product to a client because it answered the client's needs. But sales informed operations of this only when the deal had been signed. Operations refused to deliver the product saying it did not have the money or the resources to set up a new production line to deliver a product that would meet its quality standards. • Ex 2: Sales promised a client it would deliver an order by the following week because the client had threatened to buy from a competitor if it did not. Sales did not want to tell operations about the order until the deal had been signed because they did not want to cry wolf. Upset at not having been told, operations said they could not produce a safe product in the given time frame, even though sales suspected they could have "if they had really wanted to" and if they had understood how important the deal was for the company.

TABLE 1.1. Common Strategic Dualities and the LT Members They Oppose (continued)

Positions or Functions involved	Strategic Duality	Examples from Real LTs
R&D vs. marketing	Innovation and new product push vs. adapting to client needs and product pull approach	• Ex 1: R&D boasted it had invented the "greatest new product in the world" and asked marketing to start promoting it. Marketing refused to do so, claiming that it was not what clients were asking for and was far too complex to interest clients anyhow. R&D thought marketing was too lazy to bother promoting their new idea while marketing believed R&D needed to "return to planet Earth." • Ex 2: Marketing asked R&D to work on product ideas that marketing had developed after listening to clients discuss their issues. R&D refused, saying that marketing's ideas would not work and that marketing did not understand that true innovation was not about asking clients what they wanted but foreseeing what they needed. R&D quoted Henry Ford, car maker of the early 1900s, "If I'd asked clients what they wanted, they would have asked for a faster horse."
Creativity vs. finance	New product design vs. commercial viability	• Ex: This duality is perfectly illustrated by the case of designer Raf Simons who, after a stellar performance at Christian Dior, struggled to achieve similar status at Calvin Klein (CK). When he was appointed CK's "chief creative officer" in 2016, CK's parent company clearly underestimated the roadblocks and how long it would take to transform the brand, which had become overly dependent on licensing deals and lacked stylistic coherence. CK clung to a past that glorified the human body; Simons sought to create a less body-centric, more gender-fluid image. But to change a brand requires patience and funding. While Simons assumed he had infinite resources and time, the board had run out of both by 2018.[1]

1. https://publishing.insead.edu/case/can-creativity-and-commerce-ever-be-reconciled-raf-simons-calvin-klein. Frederic Godart, Manon Frappier, and Brian Henry, "Can Creativity and Commerce Ever Be Reconciled? Raf Simons at Calvin Klein," INSEAD case study 6582 (2020).

Other examples of "giving in" we have witnessed include a CFO who stopped scrutinizing his colleagues' expenses for fear of being branded a killjoy and a human resources VP who stopped insisting that HR be involved when operational managers hired candidates to ensure hiring mistakes were avoided.

The consequences of such giving in are as dire as when LT members adopt an overly confrontational approach. Indeed, as a CEO, you should be grateful when your LT members take seriously their job as guardians of their strategic objectives because your entire organization may suffer if they step back to avoid conflict.

It is when clashes between members of your LT are accepted as part of the LT "game" that the best interests of your organization are served—if they are well managed. Managing such clashes well begins with recognizing when their source is a classic strategic duality. In Table 1.1, we lay out eight strategic dualities that manifest themselves in most organizations, along with examples from real LTs so you can recognize then more easily.

This list is by no means exhaustive, and we invite you to share others from your own experience at leadershipteamalignment@insead.edu.

Consequence No. 2: Fostering Alignment Is More Difficult on LTs Than on Nonexecutive Teams

Once one accepts that LTs are structured for and by conflict, it should come as no surprise that aligning them for organizational success is challenging for CEOs. This is because LT members, in their role as spokespersons for their unit, view organizational success from different angles.

To illustrate, we take a case study from the Canadian Broadcasting Corporation (CBC).[13] This is one of the few instances in this book where we use the real name of a protagonist. We do so because the case is in the public domain, although the interpretation of the case remains our responsibility.

The CBC is Canada's national radio and television broadcaster, and, much like the BBC, its British equivalent, its brand is strongly associated with independent journalism. Thus, its credibility, and some would say its very survival, are deeply rooted in the principles of independent journalism that promote news coverage that is perceived as balanced and fair.

Louis Lalande, leader of one of its main business units at the time of this case, had little difficulty in getting his LT members to agree that independent journalism was central to the organization's success. But that did not prevent his executives from having their own interpretation of what "independent journalism" required.

This became readily apparent when the CBC's top line experienced rapid decline as ad revenues migrated from radio and television to Facebook and other social media. To offset the losses, the organization had to decide whether to accept "advertorials" — content written by advertisers to promote a product but presented in the style of an editorial or seemingly objective journalistic article — on their platforms.

- For the *head of sales*, tasked with finding new sources of revenue, organizational success dictated the CBC embrace advertorials to feed a starving top line. Doing so, he argued, would fund the independent journalism that made the CBC one of the most trusted brands in the country.

- The *head of news services*, responsible for the integrity of CBC's journalism, saw things quite differently. Advertorials, he felt, were unethical. They were written to mislead viewers into thinking products featured in the advertorials had been subjected to an objective assessment by the CBC.

- The *head of communications* was also concerned that the organization's success would be impaired by advertorials, but for different reasons. She believed that the CBC's success rested in protecting its brand, which might be jeopardized if it became associated with products that were later tainted by scandal.

No matter which of these three executives you agree with, this case illustrates that asking executives to act in the best interests of their organization is rarely sufficient to create alignment because each LT member perceives the organization's success through their own unit's lens. They are the embodiment of Miles law, coined by Rufus E. Miles Jr., an assistant secretary to three US presidents, which posits that a person's position dictates—often unconsciously—their opinion on issues.[14] It is often expressed with the adage, "Where you stand depends on where you sit."

To summarize, LT alignment is difficult to achieve because each LT member inexorably defines organizational success differently. *This is unlike a nonexecutive team (e.g., a sports team), where the team's success, or end goal, is readily identified and agreed on.* On an LT, each member's role and incentives have them aiming for a different goal, even if they are kicking in the same direction (see Figure 1.1). In doing so, each LT member is fully convinced that their goal is *the* goal. They are surprised—no, offended!—when they are told the goal they

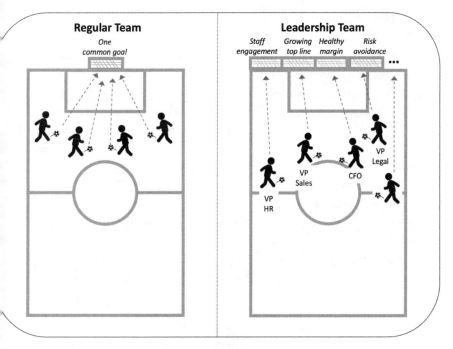

FIGURE 1.1. Regular Team versus Leadership Team

are pursuing is merely a reflection of self-interest, although this never prevents them from leveling this accusation at colleagues.

Accordingly, trying to maintain alignment by reminding LT members to be "good team players" and to work in their organization's interests is rarely effective. All LT members think they already are, even when their CEO disagrees (!), leading to the power struggles that are the subject of Chapter 2.

Consequence No. 3: Crisis-Driven Alignment Is Rarely Permanent

"I thought you'd be interested to know that we figured it out."

So spoke Mark, an executive who called us in May 2020, a few months after the COVID-19 pandemic hit.

Aware that we were writing a book about LTs, he wanted to help us by explaining how his LT had recently instituted practices that, he felt, had transformed it from a highly dysfunctional group into a highly effective team. Infighting had ceased, and he and his teammates had never been better aligned.

One thing they did was to cut the number of LT meetings. Whereas these had been held weekly, they were now held monthly. Meanwhile, the CEO and three LT members, including Mark, continued to meet weekly to make the many critical decisions the pandemic forced onto their plates. These decisions were then communicated by email to the rest of the LT.

"We are so much more effective this way," Mark told us, "and everybody on the LT is happy to attend fewer meetings because they are feeling overwhelmed."

We well understood why Mark's LT colleagues might feel overwhelmed. Many executives we spoke to felt this way in the early months of the pandemic. We could also understand why many were relieved that someone else was making difficult decisions in a period characterized by uncertainty.

But what Mark had not considered was that his LT's new-found alignment might not have been entirely due to the changes they had instituted and may have had something to do with the crisis itself.

As you may have experienced over the course of your own career, an LT's alignment invariably improves when a crisis hits.[15] This is because a crisis tends to fix everyone's attention on the one goal that overrides every other: survival—for example:

- If survival requires finding new customers quickly, your legal VP may put up less of a fight when sales brings in a customer contract that legal may have deemed too risky prior to the crisis.

- If survival means lowering costs, your CFO may find that getting colleagues to accept cuts in their departments is easier. As one CFO told us when the 2008 financial crisis hit, "At budget time, I had colleagues offering to make deeper cuts in their budgets than what I had asked for!"

But once a crisis subsides, conflicts provoked by strategic dualities re-emerge because they never disappeared; they were merely lying dormant. Each LT member returns to being a staunch defender of the strategic objectives that their unit traditionally defends.

Thus, it is to misunderstand the rules of the LT game to think that the spirit of collaboration and effortless alignment that prevails during a crisis will survive after the crisis subsides. This is something many LTs discovered two years into the COVID-19 pandemic when it ceased being a crisis and became the "new normal."

If crises afford a moment when team-building efforts are less necessary, this does not mean they can be paused indefinitely.

Actionable Insights

If strategic dualities mean that conflict is part of LT reality, it does not mean that conflict should go unmanaged. So, what is a CEO to do?

We have suggested that LT members must learn to recognize when a conflict is rooted in a strategic duality and so avoid misdiagnosing it as a purely interpersonal affair. To that end, in Table 1.1, we presented examples of real LT conflicts caused by strategic dualities. Now we turn to other practical measures CEOs can adopt: six of them.

Actionable Insight No. 1: Have LT Members Share Their Individual Objectives

When conflicts erupt between two LT members, it is common for each to think they are acting in the company's best interests and believe their colleague is incompetent, selfish, or irrational.

In our experience, LT members are less likely to believe this when they clearly see that their colleague's behavior is motivated by the latter's individual objectives as approved by the CEO. But for this to happen, LT members must be aware of the objectives of the other team members. CEOs often assume their LT members know each others' objectives, but that is not what we see on most LTs we observe unless they share them explicitly.

On LTs where individual objectives are shared, we observe that executives see conflicts coming long before they blow out of proportion and are therefore able to resolve them more easily.

When asked what measures have the most impact on an LT's effectiveness, this is one we point to. We return to it at the end of Chapter 4 to discuss how certain LTs have implemented it.

Actionable Insight No. 2: Hire and Train LT Members for Conflict

Because LT members are expected to act as spokespersons, those who are successful are comfortable challenging colleagues. Furthermore, they do not overreact when they are themselves challenged.

Our observation finds support in research done by others, notably that of Amy Colbert and her colleagues who examined "agreeableness" on LTs. Agreeableness is one of the Big Five personality traits, the dominant framework for personality assessment. People scoring high on agreeableness are seen as "perceptive, diplomatic, warm, and considerate." Those scoring low would be characterized as "likely to confront poor performers, tough, and willing to take unpopular positions."[16]

Colbert and her colleagues' work reveals that being high in agreeableness may be useful for nonexecutive teams but not so much for LTs.[17] They are quick to say that this did not mean that cordial relationships on LTs were unimportant, but they add: "In a team composed of nothing but leaders, there is likely to be little gained from being modest or overly agreeable. More important, given the importance that creating and setting organizational strategies (i.e., making decisions) has to the [leadership team], it is critical that the team avoid groupthink."

In line with these findings, you could hire executives who are at ease with conflict. An interview process that would assess this by measuring their level of agreeableness might be considered, although we must admit that we have yet to see an organization do this.

But to be clear, we are not saying that organizations should hire LT members who are pit bulls who steamroll their colleagues. We emphasize this to avoid anyone misinterpreting our message as did a participant in one of our executive MBA programs who called us to say, "Thank you so much for your class. I'd been taught that team play was about collaboration. But you taught us it was more about conflict and competition. So, I stopped trying to collaborate with this guy on my team who was [a real pain] and worked to get him fired."

We were appalled and spent the remainder of the call echoing the message in Adam Galinsky's book *Friend and Foe: When to Cooperate, When to Compete, and How to Succeed at Both*, which teaches that top performers are those who strike the right balance between competition and cooperation.[18] But as our anecdote illustrates, this is not always easy, as inferred by novelist F. Scott Fitzgerald's famous phrase: "The test of a first-rate intelligence is the ability to hold two opposed ideas in the mind at the same time, and still retain the ability to function."[19]

Thus, beyond selecting LT members who are at ease with conflict, you should also consider offering conflict training to first-time LT members. Such training should differ from the nonexecutive team training, which emphasizes collaboration but does not address the conflict management skills required to function effectively at the LT level.

The emphasis on collaboration in team training, to the exclusion of conflict management, may explain why many executives hold an unrealistic expectation: that their LT colleagues are principally collaborators there to help them achieve their objectives, and certainly not people who will challenge them and whom they must challenge. Unable to recognize the strategic dualities that spark conflicts with colleagues, these new LT members lash out at their peers as "poor team players" and misinterpret their behavior through the overly simplistic lens of the LT-as-*Game-of-Thrones* fable.

Eventually some will come to understand that life at the top is not a lawless war zone, but simply a new and rougher game with different rules than on nonexecutive teams. Think rugby rather than soccer. Those who fail to see this will not be successful and eventually must bow out of the game.

Actionable Insight No. 3: CEOs: Trust, with Your Eyes Open

In her 2018 book on psychological safety, Harvard professor Amy Edmondson quotes Marc Costa, then CEO at Eastman Chemical, as saying: "Your greatest fear as a CEO is that people aren't telling you the truth."

These words are echoed by a client, a former executive vice president at one of the world's top testing and inspection companies, who once told us, "The CEO is by far the person most exposed to manipulation in the organization."

Hearing these words, many CEOs tell us, "I don't have this problem. All my team members are honest." David Fubini heard very much the same from the CEOs he advised over his thirty-four-year career at McKinsey & Company.[20] In his book *Hidden Truths: What Leaders Need to Hear But Are Rarely Told*, he recounts how, upon telling CEOs that they should hardly expect "the whole unvarnished truth" from their teams, these CEOs invariably respond by first noting, "This is an incredibly important point and something you must say to other aspiring and soon-to-be CEOs!" They then go on to add, "But of course my situation was so different: I always got the real story."

Fubini believes this response shows that many CEOs "are in denial even as they're recognizing the validity of this hard truth." To be fair, it may also be that CEOs reject the inference that they are being duped or that their LT members are dishonest.

No matter why CEOs respond in this manner, our point is not that LT members lie to their boss and that CEOs should mistrust them. It is that CEOs should not expect their LT members, even the most honest, to tell them the entire truth. Just as lawyers do not bring up evidence that weakens their case in court, LT members see no point in sharing facts that weaken a case they present to their CEO.

For example, a strategy vice president who needs to convince their CEO to make an acquisition will probably not highlight that the acquisition target comes with twenty collective agreements that will make integration a challenge. Why do this if they have concluded that the acquisition will benefit the organization despite the risk? But as CEO, you are the one who ultimately assumes the risk. Thus, although you should have faith in your LT members, this faith cannot be blind. A former CEO once told us, "You should trust your team members, but you can't be naive. You can't manage from thirty thousand feet. If you accept all their reports without scratching beneath the surface once in a while, you're only asking for trouble."

To borrow a phrase from Belgian psychotherapist Esther Perel, CEOs should "trust with their eyes open."[21] There are many ways to do this. Because many of them dovetail with the measures presented in Chapters 2 and 6, we refer readers to the last sections of those chapters for further details.

Actionable Insight No. 4: Don't Tell Them to Leave Their Hat at the Door at First

Knowing that LT members have biases and incentives leading them to act as spokespersons for their unit, CEOs often tell their LT members to "leave their hat at the door" at the start of an LT meeting. This is another way CEOs have of telling their executives not to place their unit's objectives ahead of the company's.

Although logical, this rarely has any effect. In fact, it is often counterproductive because LT members who hear these words cannot imagine their CEO is speaking to them. They think: *How could giving priority to my unit objectives not be in the organization's interest? I set them with my CEO.*

Therefore, when CEOs say, "Leave your hat at the door," all assume the CEO is speaking to everyone but them. This merely confirms what many already believe: their CEO does not trust the other LT members to do what is right for the company. In this way, the phrase "leave your hat at the door" is not merely useless; it sows distrust.

So rather than say "leave your hat at the door" to counter the biases that CEOs know their LT members bring to the table, what should they do? The better strategy, although counterintuitive, is to insist explicitly that everyone keep their unit hat on at the *beginning* of a discussion. Only in this way can it be certain that all biases are on the table for all to see rather than driving them underground where they foster power games (the topic of the next chapter).

Only once all positions and biases have been put on the table should CEOs ask LT members to take off their unit or functional caps.

Actionable Insight No. 5: Assist LT Members in Getting to Yes
by Leveraging Common Ground

While conflicts on LTs should be accepted as normal, they can nonetheless go off the rails. When they do, CEOs need to step in to mediate.

When doing so, CEOs can take a page out of negotiation best-seller *Getting to Yes*.[22] Although it was meant to be a negotiation manual, we recommend it in our executive education programs as an unofficial LT textbook because it offers tactics well suited to LT conflicts. These tactics include leveraging the common ground that battling LT members may have lost sight of. That common ground can come in two forms, which we address:

- The organization's strategy

- Its culture

An explicit reminder of the **organization's strategy** can help two warring LT members resolve their differences. as illustrated by a dispute involving a logistics director and his counterpart in customer service we were asked to mediate.

At stake was the product distribution policy the logistics VP had drawn up requiring the company's delivery trucks to be at least 75 percent full before leaving the company plant. Until then, trucks regularly left the plant only 50 percent full. The policy's primary goal was to save on fuel costs by reducing the number of delivery trips per truck.

But soon after the CEO announced the policy, it provoked a delivery delay that put the company in breach of its contractual obligations with an important client. The client loudly complained to the company's customer service VP, who in turn wrote to plant staff telling them to disregard the logistics VP's distribution policy. When the logistics VP found out, he flew into a rage. We were asked to intervene shortly after.

What seemed at first to be an intractable dispute was settled when we asked both parties to jot down the company strategy on a flip chart and come up with a solution that best respected it. That strategy emphasized cost control in the face of debt levels, which had soared after a series of costly acquisitions. The strategy also included aggressive top-line goals because revenue was needed to service the debt. After this exercise, the customer service VP conceded that his colleague's distribution policy made sense given the strategic need to cut costs. This concession encouraged his logistics counterpart to admit that the distribution policy could be relaxed to not interfere with contracts generating much needed revenue. Later, the customer service VP sat down with clients to negotiate later deliveries in return for minor discounts. Thus, the conflict was resolved.

Of course, leveraging the company strategy does not always lead to such harmonious outcomes. But in our experience, it often helps, not only because it impels LT members to adopt a common perspective but also because it reminds both parties they are on the same team.

The effectiveness of this approach depends on LT members being familiar with their company's strategy. And although most people find it almost difficult to believe, very few are as reported in an article tellingly entitled *"No One Knows Your Strategy—Not Even Your Top Leaders."*[23] (To address this, see the four methods discussed at the end of Chapter 4.)

An **organizational culture** that promotes constructive conflict can also form the common ground that prevents LT member conflicts from derailing. Although developing the appropriate culture is no simple matter, we have seen CEOs who benefited greatly by starting in two ways:

- Instituting ground rules that capture the values they would like staff to emulate and then making sure LT members emulate them. We return to this in Chapter 4.

- Understanding how promoting the appropriate culture inside LT meetings can bear on the culture adopted by LT members, and others, outside the LT meetings. This topic is addressed in Chapter 6.

Actionable Insight No. 6: Beware of Stoking the Fires of Competition

If the strategic dualities we discussed at the beginning of this chapter inevitably lead to conflict and competition among LT members, CEOs who feel their LT members are competing too much are wise not to stoke competitive fires further. For example, CEOs should be particularly careful at budget time when, as seasoned executives know only too well, competition between LT members intensifies.

Nevertheless, some CEOs make the mistake of highlighting the competitive aspects of the process by, for example, saying to LT members, "Tell me why I should give you the budget you are asking for rather than giving the money to one of your colleagues." Presenting the budget exercise as a bidding war creates tensions between LT colleagues that linger well after the exercise is over and eventually reduces their willingness to collaborate.

A better way to proceed is one adopted by CEOs we met who required that LT members justify their budgetary demands by answering a very different question: "How will the budget you are asking for further the organization's strategy?"

By doing this, CEOs focus their LT members' attention on what unites them, not what divides them. A bonus is that it enables CEOs to find out the extent to which LT members understand the strategy and are aligned with it.

The Chapter in a Nutshell

Strategic Dualities: The Root Cause of Most LT Conflicts

- Organizations face **strategic dualities**—sets of interdependent yet *seemingly* contradictory **strategic objectives** (e.g., growth versus profitability, productivity versus innovation).

- Strategic dualities lead to LT conflict because LT members often act as **spokespersons** or advocates for different strategic objectives. Example: Sales executives who fight for growth may be at odds with CFOs defending profitability.

- These structural conflicts between LT members are helpful and necessary because they enable organizations to find the right balance between strategic objectives, but they are **misperceived as detrimental** because of the mistaken belief that "teammates shouldn't fight."

Consequences of the LT Members Being Spokespersons

1. *Consequence no. 1: LTs are designed for conflict.* When LT conflicts are treated as exceptional or, worse, evidence of dysfunctionality, they end up being suppressed rather than managed, based on the mistaken assumption that teammates should not fight. Managing such clashes well begins with recognizing when their source is a classic strategic duality.

2. *Consequence no. 2: Alignment is harder to achieve on LTs than on nonexecutive teams.* LT members will inevitably define organizational success differently. This distinguishes an LT from a nonexecutive team (e.g., a sports team), where the team's success, or end goal, is readily identified and agreed on.

3. *Consequence no. 3: LT alignment improves in a crisis, but that alignment rarely lasts.* Crisis-driven alignment is rarely a permanent state, and efforts to ensure LT alignment and effectiveness are needed once a crisis passes.

Summary of Actionable Insights

1. *Have LT members share their individual objectives.* LT members are less likely to see their colleagues as incompetent, selfish, or irrational when they see that their colleagues' behavior is motivated by unit objectives that the CEO has formally validated.

2. *Hire LT members comfortable with conflict.* You should also train them to handle the inevitable conflicts they will have with colleagues.

3. *CEOs should trust LT members— with their eyes open.* Even the most honest LT members will omit giving their CEO information when it runs counter to their unit's interests. CEOs need to dig for it.

4. *Don't tell LT members to "leave their hat at the door."* At least, not at the start of a discussion when it will be counterproductive. Make this request later in the discussion, notably after all initial positions and biases are on the table.

5. *Help LT members "get to yes" by helping them find common ground.* The strategic dualities LT members defend will be more easily reconciled if they are reminded of the common ground they stand on: the organization's strategy and its culture.

6. *Be careful of stoking the fires of competition.* LTs are primed for conflict and competition. Beware of inciting more conflict, especially at budget time.

$$\bigcirc \atop 2$$

POWER GAMES AT THE TOP

Quickly: without thinking more than a second or so, answer the following question: What type of emotion do you *immediately* feel when you hear "power and politics in organizations"? Is it:

- Positive?

- Neutral?

- Negative?

Check one of the above. We will return to your answer shortly.

The pervasiveness of power games and politics distinguishes LTs from teams below them. While this is widely acknowledged, you would hardly know it from reading popular leadership books.[1] Very few offer practical advice to executives on how to address the power issues they tell us they are confronted with.

In his book *Leadership BS: Fixing Workplaces and Careers One Truth at a Time*, Stanford professor Jeffrey Pfeffer offers an explanation for this. The leadership industry, he says, is so obsessively focused on "what leaders should do and how things ought to be—that it has largely ignored asking the fundamental question of what actually is true and going on and why."[2] He is not alone in noticing this.[3] Pfeffer offers another reason by quoting Harvard professor

Rosabeth Moss Kanter who says, "It is easier to talk about money—and much easier to talk about sex—than it is to talk about power."[4]

This malaise is reflected in the answers that leaders in our EMBA and executive education programs provide to the question you were asked at the start of this chapter. Many say they feel a negative emotion when they hear "power in organizations," which evoke images of ambitious executives abusing their power in their self-interest.

But some tell us they feel a positive emotion and add—often with a hint of bravado—that they feel quite at ease discussing power. But their declared comfort quickly dissipates when we ask if they would discuss the following question with colleagues at their next LT meeting: "Who are the most powerful people on our LT, and what are the implications for our effectiveness and decision making?" We have yet to find executives who would relish addressing this question. Indeed, power is, as some LT experts have put it, a prime example of a "moose on the table" that all see but no one dares to mention, making it quite challenging to improve LT functioning.[5]

This challenge is amplified by CEOs who claim publicly never to have played power games or who say that power games are played in LTs everywhere—except their own. Such "power-free" accounts of leadership perpetuate two myths: that we can eliminate power games and that only ambitious, self-interested executives engage in them. We address both myths in the first section of this chapter.

If you already accept that power games are inevitable, you may want to skip directly to the second section where we examine how power games harm your LT in ways too often ignored. In the third section, we explain why many wrongly assume that CEOs who deploy strategies to maintain their power are flawed leaders. Finally, we present actionable insights for CEOs to ethically manage the power dynamics on their teams.

Power Games Are like Death and Taxes: Why All Executives Must Play Them

The words *power* and *politics* are often used interchangeably, in part because both are frequently defined in relation to one another. For example, politics has been defined as "those observable, but often covert, actions by which people enhance their power to influence a decision."[6] It is these covert actions—for example, coalition building, behind-the-scenes lobbying, and personal attacks (hereafter simply "**power games**")—that many wish to see eliminated.

This is what Harvard professor Linda Hill and her colleague Kent Lineback report after speaking to leaders who expressed distaste for "ego-driven, adolescent games." These leaders wanted disputes settled "through data, analysis, and logic, by what's 'right'— not by who knows whom, who owes whom, or who plays golf with whom."[7]

Implicit in such reactions are the two remarkably resistant myths we referred to earlier: that we can get rid of power games and that only ambitious, self-interested executives play them. Both myths are harmful in ways we must recognize if we want to improve LT functioning.

Myth No. 1: Objective, Power-Free Decision Making Is Possible

To address this myth, it is useful to ask, What would decision making look like if it were determined by "what's right," as the leaders quoted above wished or, in other words, if it were purely objective?

The strategic decision-making literature often answers this question by listing several ingredients for objective decision making.[8] We zoom in on one of them: an objectively "right" decision requires **perfect or complete information**. A quick example demonstrates why this condition can never be achieved and thus why power will always be part of LT decision making.

Imagine you are a CEO faced with the decision to acquire a company to enter a new market. Two acquisition targets are on the table, ABC Inc. and XYZ Inc. **ABC Inc.** has annual revenues of $200 million and an expected annual growth rate of 5 percent over three years, and **XYZ Inc.** has annual revenues of $100 million but with double the expected growth rate during the same period: 10 percent. (See Table 2.1.)

The leader of your company's second largest business unit, BU2, favors acquiring ABC Inc., whose operations she would oversee. Her argument is that financial markets will reward you for making the larger acquisition, and the resulting stock price increase will provide latitude to make further investments. Her position is supported by the CFO. As CEO, you take a mental note of this. You also consider that absorbing ABC Inc. into BU2 would mean that BU2 becomes the largest business unit in the company.

The leader of what is currently the largest business unit, BU1, is adamant that XYZ Inc. is the better choice. His argument is that XYZ is a much safer business and will be easier to integrate because it would be absorbed into his own unit. And, he is quick to point out, he has had experience with such integrations, experience his dear colleague in BU2 sorely lacks.

TABLE 2.1. Acquisition Targets Information

Company	Annual Revenues	Expected Annual Growth Rate	Business Unit It Would Be Absorbed Into
ABC Inc.	$200 million	5%	BU2
XYZ Inc.	$100 million	10%	BU1

Now if you are like most executives, your brain has shifted into high gear. You are processing the little information provided and wondering which acquisition you would make if you were CEO.

Of course, you would want to ask several questions. One of the most critical is how robust are two of the assumptions presented to you, notably that ABC Inc. will grow at 5 percent and that XYZ Inc. will grow at 10 percent over the next three years. To assess these assumptions, you would need to gather large quantities of macroeconomic data (e.g., GDP growth, inflation). You would also need to anticipate your competitors' moves, estimate post- acquisition staff retention rates, and much more.

Fairly quickly you realize that no amount of research will transform either of these two assumptions about ABC's and XYZ's growth rates into objective facts. There are simply too many variables. Thus, the first condition for objective decision making—perfect or complete information—is impossible to meet.

This example illustrates that acquisition decisions, like all other strategic decisions, always have a certain level of subjectivity. This means they will be determined by executives who, when they run out of facts and rational arguments, need to use their power to steer matters in the direction they believe to be "right."

Yet some of our students ask whether we can remove power from this equation by, for example, having LT members make the decision by majority vote. If the vote is anonymous, they argue, it will prevent the powerful from influencing the ballot. Unfortunately, such a solution does not take power out of the equation because the decision to institute a vote is itself subject to power plays. In addition, backroom influence is also known to determine votes, even when they are anonymous.

Our example demonstrates what seasoned executives tell us to be obvious: although injecting a decision-making process with more information and data will bring us further down the path to an objectively "right" decision, it will

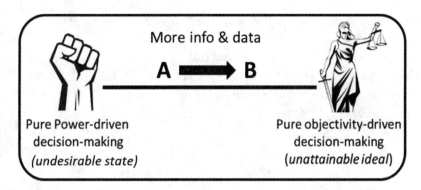

FIGURE 1.2. The Impact of More Information and Data on Decision Making

never get us to the end of that path. There will always be some subjectivity left in the decision-making process (see Figure 2.1).

From this proposition flows the corollary that remains, as unsavory as it is to some: no matter how much effort is expended, pure objectivity is out of reach, and thus power will always play a role in the outcome of a decision-making process. Thus, our message is simply the following:

- Power games are like death and taxes: they are a fact of LT life.

- Deploring or ignoring this, something many books on LT effectiveness do, prevents us from thinking about the steps to minimize and manage such games.

Myth No. 2: Only Ambitious, Self-Interested Executives Play Power Games

Many people do accept that power games are an inevitable part of LT life. But this does not prevent them from believing that such games are only played by unethical, self-interested executives—in other words, by people other than themselves.

This is the second myth we want to dispel. So long as it stands, we are encouraged to go on a witch hunt to root out unethical executives. When none are found, we conclude that our organization is free of power concerns. This is a mistake.

If you accept the proposition that power plays a role in every decision your LT makes, then no executive who wants to be successful can simply submit data and rational arguments and sit back hoping that this alone will sway colleagues. All executives—without exception—must "power up" if they want to have an impact.

Once we come to terms with the reality that *all* executives play power games, we can focus our energy where it really matters: distinguishing unethical power games that must be eradicated from those that we must simply accept as part and parcel of the LT game.

This is what we tackle next.

Power Games with Negative Impacts on LTs

In theory, LTs enable CEOs to leverage diverse perspectives for decision making. In practice, the ability of LT members to participate in decision making is curtailed by power games in many instances.

A full inventory of such games is beyond the scope of this book and so we focus on a few that are common and particularly harmful to LT functioning.

Unethical Power Games between LT Members: Conflict Scenarios

On October 1, six months into his new job with an industrial manufacturer (IM), Marcos sensed that things were not going well. Hired by IM's CEO, he was the company's first marketing VP. Having worked with IM for a few months, we knew his integration would not easy as many of his new LT colleagues believed marketing was as useful as tarot card reading.

Improving IM's profitability was Marcos's main objective but not the only one. IM was a heavy polluter, and the CEO had asked Marcos to launch a special recycling project to shore up the company's environmental bona fides. Dubbed "Recycling for a Sustainable Future," the aim of the project was to collect used product from clients and reuse the raw materials in new products.

If Marcos could rely on his counterpart in operations, Osana, to boost profitability, she was not a likely ally on the recycling project, which would eat up her staff's time and hurt productivity. Thus, when Marcos set up a cross-functional project team and called meetings to draw up a project plan, Osana was conspicuous by her absence.

Nevertheless, when the plan was completed, Marcos emailed her to get her feedback. No answer. Two days later, on October 1, he hesitated to reach out to her again. He did not want to pressure her unduly because his CEO had been clear when he had hired him: "Your challenge will be to gain acceptance from your new teammates, especially Osana. She is the future of this company."

Cruising the halls, hoping to run into Osana by chance, he instead ran into a project team member to whom he confided his difficulty in arranging a meeting with Osana. The team member looked surprise. "But there is a team meeting tomorrow at 1:00 p.m." he told Marcos. "Osana set it up. Hadn't you heard?"

No. Marcos had not. When he ran into Osana later that day, he asked why he had not been invited. "I don't know," she replied. "My secretary must have made a mistake. Sorry." But she did not look sorry. And when Marcos asked her to postpone the meeting because it conflicted with a client lunch he had to attend, a lunch Osana surely knew about, she replied, "Look, you've been pestering me about this damn project for weeks. and now you want to postpone the meeting I've set up because you have a lunch?" Marcos felt it wise to back down.

The next day, after his client lunch, Marcos returned to the office to attend the weekly LT meeting. His CEO's first question was about the recycling project. Before Marcos could say anything, Osana spoke up. She thanked Marcos for having developed a "great project plan" but went on to say that she and the project team had agreed that it made sense for her to take over the project's lead given her staff's responsibility in delivering it.

Oblivious to Osana's power play, the CEO responded: "Great idea." He then turned to Marcos: "What do you think?" Marcos knew he had been had. Object to Osana taking the project lead and he would appear petty. Complain on the spot, or later in the CEO's office, about her machinations and his boss would immediately know he had failed to develop a good relationship with Osana, to say nothing about how Osana would react when she found out. "Fine with me," he said without much conviction.

Over the next few months, Marcos's intuition that Osana would let the project fail proved prescient. The CEO nevertheless held Marcos partly responsible because it had been one of his objectives. He fared no better with his other objectives because his LT colleagues never fully embraced him after seeing that Osana held him in low regard. Why help Marcos and risk getting on Osana's bad side? A year later, Marcos was gone and IM had made no headway on any of the priorities Marcos had been hired to address.

While we could devote space to how CEOs can address behavior such as Osana's, we find most know what to do in such instances … if they are aware of the problem. But therein lies the rub: CEOs who lead from their office, rarely venturing out, as was the case with Marcos's CEO, may never find out about such maneuvering. None of the LT members involved have much incentive to let them know, especially the least powerful.

CEOs who want to find out when power games are interfering with the organization's interests and how their LT members are truly getting along need to do more than question their executives. The "Actionable Insights" section of this chapter shows what successful CEOs do.

Social Undermining: An Openly Used Power Tactic
That CEOs Ignore at Their Peril

We now turn to a far more common and insidious power tactic: social undermining. CEOs need to be mindful of it because it is one of the most widespread power games we observe. We present it using the case of Danielle, another executive we worked with.

Danielle, a vice president of a financial services firm, had a strong track record and a warm manner. Widely admired, she was a hard worker keen on developing her competencies. She had been taking a "power and influence" course at the local business school and had invited us for lunch to discuss it. At one point, she mentioned that the class had broached the topic of social undermining a phenomenon we were well acquainted with. It refers to behaviors "intended to hinder, over time, the ability to establish and maintain positive relationships, work-related success, and favorable reputation."[9] Such behaviors can be deployed to harm the reputation of superiors and colleagues alike.

> *Those who are particularly adept at undermining cover their tracks by appearing genuinely concerned for their colleagues.*

Case studies reveal how executives who practice social undermining use innuendos to plant seeds of doubt in the listener's mind regarding the competence of the colleague they wish to undermine—for example, saying that the colleague is having a hard time making decisions or is overworked and needs time off.

We notice that those who are particularly adept at undermining cover their tracks by appearing genuinely concerned for their colleagues (*"Isn't it a shame about Sandra? She looks so stressed out. I think they should pull her off that file. I'm afraid the pressure is too much for her!"*). They may also mention some of their target's shortcomings, real or imagined.[10]

Another common undermining tactic is spreading rumors or dropping hints that a colleague is considering implementing an unpopular decision such as laying off staff, knowing that this will spread discord within that colleague's unit.

As Danielle mentioned such tactics to us, we asked whether she had ever used any of them. Mortified, she replied: "Of course not!" And then she was further mortified when we replied, "What if we said that we had seen you use them?"

She looked genuinely puzzled. We then reminded her of the time she had spoken of her colleague, Tim, a brash, young executive who had the infuriating habit of speaking over her and other women in LT meetings and, in her opinion, never adding great value to the conversation. This did not prevent him from being treated like a superstar by the CEO. And so, Danielle had learned to keep her disdain of Tim to herself, at least in public. But when speaking of Tim to us or to selected colleagues, Danielle often speculated that the business contacts Tim bragged about were not as extensive as he claimed. She also mentioned a rumor that members of Tim's team thought he was a "blowhard" and were less than happy with his leadership style.[11]

Danielle's reaction to what she felt was an accusation was immediate. "Well, I did hear that rumor!" she said defensively. When we pointed out that spreading such negative rumors was precisely what social undermining was, this usually mild-mannered executive justified her action by saying: "Well, even if it is, Tim deserves it because he is a self-serving prick who doesn't give a [expletive] about this company!"

Is such behavior unusual? Not in our experience. Is it only the purview of "bad people" who will do anything to get to the top? Once again, no. In fact, rare is the executive who does *not* socially undermine colleagues, at least on occasion and often unconsciously. This is because LTs are fertile ground for social undermining due to factors mentioned in Chapter 1:

- LT members often act as spokespersons for a "cause" that they feel strongly, even passionately, about due to their training and incentives.

- Naive realism, which is the tendency to consider those who do not view the world as we do as irrational, incompetent, or biased.

Thus, it is easy to see why social undermining is widely practiced on LTs, even by executives considered to be "nice" people. If there is an enemy, it is us.

Social undermining as a power tactic would be relatively harmless if CEOs nipped it in the bud, but many do not. They listen to their LT members take swipes at colleagues without saying a word and with little thought to how this damages LT trust and cohesion. Indeed, as we have experienced on certain LTs, when executives realize that their CEO tolerates what is, in essence, nasty gossip, they are tempted to pre-emptively undermine colleagues they fear may undermine them. And so, a vicious cycle begins.

Having viewed instances where power games can lead to open conflict between LT members, let us turn to another way power harms LT dynamics in less overt ways: through silence.

Power-Induced Silence: The LT Disease par Excellence

"I should fire them all" is how Jean-François, CEO of a multinational engineering firm, greeted us as we were about attend one of his LT's meetings. He was speaking about his LT members. "I've put an acquisition on the agenda. I'll bet you that not one of them will have the guts to give me their opinion." As he spoke, he tapped a binder under his arm that, he told us, was a report from a top consultancy recommending the company make an acquisition, and he was about to present the details.

Just as Jean-François predicted, when came time to discuss the acquisition and decide whether to acquire the target company, an embarrassing silence followed. The CEO looked over at us knowingly as if to say, "See? I told you so!"

Although Jean-François correctly anticipated his LT members' silence, he was mistaken that a lack of courage lay behind it. When we later asked one LT member why he had not spoken up, he answered: "Why bother? Jean-François made it clear in his intro that he favored the deal. And what was I going to tell him that his consultants had not already told him after they'd spent weeks studying it?"

What this executive did not add was that Jean-François believed in being "authentic," which in his case meant letting his LT members know—at times quite bluntly—when he thought their ideas were foolish. In such circumstances, the decision LT members make to withhold their opinion has less to do with a lack of courage than a **rational cost-benefit analysis**.

To understand this is to understand that executives who offer their opinion on a matter that sits outside their area of immediate responsibility gain little direct benefit in doing so. There is no extra bonus at the end of the year. There may not even be a pat on the back. However, they will lose a great deal if their opinion is dismissed or, worse, ridiculed by their CEO.

The reason for LT members' silence stems from a factor that few CEOs we meet seem fully conscious of is the extent to which their LT members are constantly looking for signals regarding who is in the CEO's good graces and who is in the CEO's doghouse. As any executive will tell you, the perception that one is in the CEO's good books is an important source of power and is thus closely monitored.[12]

This explains why many executives drop hints that they have a special relationship with the boss by, for example, casually mentioning the drink or the special dinner they had with that person recently.[13] Conversely, an executive who is perceived to be in the CEO's doghouse becomes less effective because this signals they may not receive the boss's backing in a clash with a colleague.

The second reason for the silence of LT members in meetings lies in the **norm of reciprocity**. In its positive form, this norm leads people to respond to each other by returning benefits for benefits. In its negative form, it leads them to retaliate when someone does them harm.[14]

Thus, executives soon learn that if they want their CEO's approval for a project, it is best not to oppose one of their CEO's ideas beforehand unless, of course, they have very strong reasons to do so. Absent such reasons, it is self-defeating to disagree with the CEO because it weakens their hand when they present something.

When we explain this, some, mostly nonexecutives, respond: "Well, all this is childish! A CEO should never punish someone for opposing their ideas. CEOs should be grateful because such opposition serves the interests of the company." While that may be the case in an ideal world, in real life, CEOs are not always grateful to those who do not immediately endorse their ideas, and not necessarily because they are ego-driven narcissists. Rather, it may be because few CEOs propose ideas unless they believe it to be in the best interests of their company. Thus, when a member of their LT opposes them, CEOs are likely to interpret that opposition as unwarranted resistance.

Until CEOs become hyperrational, emotionless robots, LT members are right to be wary of a boss who tells them, "I welcome all opposition to my ideas." Why take the risk when the consequences can be rather unpleasant, as one might guess from the following quote attributed to famous film executive Samuel Goldwyn: "I don't want any yes-men around me. I want everyone to tell me the truth, even if it costs them their job."

The norm of reciprocity also explains why LT members are wise to think twice about opposing not only their CEO's ideas but those of their colleagues as well. Frustrate a colleague's plans and you may find that person less than enthusiastic about collaborating with you when you need it.

Thus, we commonly observe LT members staying silent when their colleagues present ideas they have told us they disagree with. One executive explained that he felt it is unwise to squander his political capital by raising objections to a colleague's plans during meetings. "On our team," he explained, "the golden rule is 'don't rain on my parade if you don't want me to rain on yours.'" He could have been speaking about a great many LTs we have observed.

Now, lest you believe that we accept, or even condone, behavior that prevents LT members from participating fully in LT discussions, let us assure you that is not the case. Our point is that the natural power dynamics on LTs discourage open discussion *unless CEOs make a concerted effort to create a safe environment for their LT members.* Simply telling them to be more courageous will not cut it.

Recommendations to create a safe environment come at the end of this and later chapters. But until such measures are implemented, the authentic and frank discussions that both CEOs and LT members say they crave will continue to be the exception rather than the rule.

Agenda Control: The Next-Level Power Game between LT Members

So far we have discussed how LT power dynamics can be an obstacle to full LT member participation when a topic is on the table. Now we turn to instances when power dynamics prevent a topic from ever making it to the table.

This phenomenon has been well studied by New York University sociologist Steven Lukes, who, building on political science insights, sees in it the "second dimension of power" (the first being influencing how decisions are made).[15]

Among the few management scholars who have explored this topic, some remark that an executive's power over the agenda "is perhaps more important than his or her potential to influence one type of strategic decision (e.g., resource allocation)."[16] and quote others who argue that preventing an issue from becoming the focus of decision may be one of the most effective uses of power by an LT member.

We see this firsthand when we are involved in setting the agenda for LT meetings or strategic offsites. The following example highlights why CEOs must pay close attention to agenda setting if they wish to retain control over their own LT. It involves an LT member we will call Fred, who was sales vice president of a North American manufacturing firm we were supporting when a dispute erupted with Celia, the firm's CFO. It centered on the pricing strategy Fred was implementing in Asia and involved selling product at below cost to gain market share.

The negative impact the Asian strategy was having on the firm's profitability had Celia, guardian of the bottom line, quite worried. She shared her concerns with Fred who, as a powerful member of the CEO's inner circle, felt quite comfortable telling Celia to "mind her own business."

Frustrated, Celia asked that the Asian pricing strategy be put on the agenda of the next LT meeting. In this way, she felt, it would be more difficult for Fred to dismiss her concerns in front of all his peers. Fred, no doubt thinking the same, went directly to the CEO to block the topic from making it to the agenda. "Am I in charge of pricing or is Celia?" he asked the CEO rhetorically. The CEO, wishing to respect Fred's autonomy and not having bothered to fully ascertain Celia's concerns, reassured him the topic would not be part of the agenda.

But in the meantime, Celia had reached out to other LT members to alert them to the "grave danger" Fred's Asian pricing strategy posed to the company. This tactic soon had other members of the team also expressing concern about the strategy to the CEO, who now felt obliged to go back on his word to Fred. He added the Asian pricing strategy to the next meeting's agenda.

When the meeting began, Fred opened with a short presentation explaining the why and how of his pricing strategy and then answered all questions patiently. A consensus soon emerged that the strategy was a sound one. But Fred was visibly angry when his colleagues suggested he monitor its impact on company margins and report back on it to the LT for the next six months. Celia was also disappointed. She had hoped the pricing strategy would be struck down. Nevertheless, she was happy her power play had made it possible for the pricing strategy to be discussed openly.

Although Fred and Celia left the meeting unhappy with the outcome, you may feel all's well that ends well for their organization. Unfortunately, not. Because of their power struggle, Fred and Celia's relationship deteriorated and caused problems for the organization in later months.

While Celia and Fred share some responsibility for this situation, it is critical to understand that conflicts such as theirs are bound to occur when CEOs let the LT agenda become a battleground or are unaware when the agenda is being used in that way.

Power Games That Threaten the CEO

We have examined power games with impacts on LT members. We now turn to those that threaten CEOs.

Although power struggles involving CEOs can have dramatic consequences, they are rarely discussed. One reason is that many assume CEOs are all powerful. Certainly, many CEOs have more power than their executives, but that is not always the case. One need only look at the CEOs of professional service firms who are often less powerful than the rainmaker partners sitting on their LTs.

Another reason we know little about power struggles with impacts on CEOs is that CEOs are loath to admit they occur because that might lead others to believe they do not control their LT, an unforgivable offense for a CEO. Furthermore, admitting to being engaged in a power struggle with an LT member might be interpreted as a weakness that could encourage other dissenters, thereby transforming the CEO's admission into a self-fulfilling prophecy.

> *CEOs commonly face three types of threats: the threat of a coup, the threat to their ability to steer the organization, and the threat of outright manipulation.*

All of this leads to two unfortunate consequences. The first is that it is hard to recognize when CEOs legitimately exert their power to respond to unjustified power plays from below. The second is that those hired to help LTs and who believe CEOs to be invulnerable can be manipulated by seasoned LT members who want to gain power over their CEO. In a classic tactic, LT members complain to a team consultant about their CEO's "autocratic tendencies" on the eve of an offsite meeting, leading the consultant to facilitate the session in a manner that ensures the CEO's voice is muted. The result is that the team's effectiveness is hampered because the consultant undermines the CEO's power and negates the latter's ability to break stalemates when they occur.

CEOs commonly face three types of threats: the threat of a coup, the threat to their ability to steer the organization, and the threat of outright manipulation. Our goal in highlighting these threats is to ensure these are kept in mind when you institute measures you hope will improve your LT's effectiveness. Such measures should never increase a CEO's vulnerability to these threats because the result will be the opposite of what you hoped for.

Threat No. 1: Coups—A CEO's Tenure Can Be Nasty, Brutish, and Short

The first threat that CEOs face is that of an outright coup. Although it is the board of directors that makes the decision to sack a CEO, LT members often play an active behind-the-scenes role. The 2018 downfall of former superstar CEO Carlos Ghosn offers a good illustration in which Japanese members of his Nissan LT collaborated with Japanese prosecutors to have him arrested.[17]

Such cases certainly make for intriguing reading. The way the press presents them leaves the impression that such coups are exceptional and happen only to megalomaniac CEOs or to ones who were naive enough to surround themselves by Macbeth-like, backstabbing LT members. But the reality is that all CEOs are at risk of being deposed, except—possibly—those who own major stakes in the companies they lead.

The pervasiveness of this threat, little understood by those who have not played the game at the top, is well summed up by Jeffrey Pfeffer: "As a consultant to a Swiss CEO told me, once you are CEO, most if not all the people reporting to you will think they are more qualified for the position than you are. Some of these rivals will be willing to wait for you to leave or retire, others will not."[18]

But CEOs should not be concerned only about LT members who feel more qualified than they are. They should also not lose sight of the many who simply dream of running their own show. These executives may feel their CEO is doing a reasonable job but nonetheless want to replace the boss to fulfill their dream. They may not throw their CEO under the proverbial bus themselves, but their desire to take the crown may mean they encourage those who will.

The incentive to overthrow the CEO is stoked by the prestige and perks associated with the CEO title, which "provide further incentives for senior executives to challenge the CEO and to participate in the power tournament in the firm's internal labor market."[19] This quote is from one of the rare studies addressing how LT power contests are an important cause of CEO dismissal. Its authors provide another motive LT members may seek to dislodge the boss: **brand management**. Indeed, when an organization's performance suffers, it harms executives' value on the labor market. Thus, even LT members who do not wish to wear the crown themselves "have incentives to monitor the CEO's leadership and join others in taking action against the CEO when they perceive him or her to be less than capable."[20]

For our part, we surmise that the increasingly short tenure of CEOs is further encouragement to depose the CEO since it now takes less effort to convince a board to pull the trigger.[21]

In short, the threat of a coup is a clear and present danger for all CEOs. Thus, it is no surprise that they may need to fight fire with fire and deploy their power to hold onto their seats. Once we recognize that this is unavoidable, their efforts to retain their seats should not be automatically condemned but judged according to the harm or good they do to the organization. This judgment must take into consideration what might have been if a CEO had not deployed their power to ward off pretenders to the throne. As the spectacular departure of Carlos Ghosn from Nissan and Renault can attest, a company usually suffers ill effects when its CEO is overthrown.[22]

Threat No. 2: When CEOs Lose the Ability to Set Organizational Direction

If the first thing CEOs must worry about is fending off coups, the second is fending off coalitions that prevent them from introducing measures necessary for their organization's success. We have had front-row seats to such struggles.

One such instance was when the CEO of a European multinational asked us to help modify the company's bonus formula. The goal was to incentivize line managers to develop sales at a time when a maturing market was slowing revenue growth. After working with leaders in the strategy unit and consulting with executives, a new bonus formula was established. Not wishing to wait until the next LT meeting to announce it, the CEO detailed it in an email to his LT members and ordered them to waste no time in implementing it. When we followed up a few weeks later, imagine our surprise when we discovered that more than half of LT members had failed to do so. Our surprise was all the greater because the CEO was known for a temper that cowed even the veterans on his team.

When we called these rebellious executives, some feigned to have simply forgotten, but they reassured us they would get to it immediately. Others expressed their absolute support for the new formula—but then recited a litany of obstacles that made implementation extremely challenging. Such stalling tactics are common and are intended to test a CEO's resolve to follow through with unpopular measures while deflecting accusations of insubordination.

A further illustration of the challenge CEOs face in setting direction and making changes due to internal opposition comes from Jeffrey Immelt, former CEO at GE. It took place in 2010, when Immelt was at the height of his power:

> I was sitting in a hotel restaurant in Ghana with two great young leaders on our Africa team. They were describing a big opportunity in the power industry, but it was complicated. I was in love with their passion, but I realized that even if I spent the next month helping them, we would not get the deal approved inside GE. And I ran the place![23]

Understanding how even powerful CEOs sometimes lack the power to achieve what they feel is in the best interests of their company sheds new light on why CEOs sometimes need to exhibit behaviors that appear on the surface to be egregious abuses of power. While they sometimes are, they might also be legitimate uses of power by CEOs faced with unjustified resistance from members of their own team.

The game at the top is a rougher one than the game at the levels below, and as a result, the actions of the CEOs who participate in them must be judged with that context in mind.

Threat No. 3: When CEOs Face Outright Manipulation

Imagine the following scenario: It is 2004. You are the CEO of an $8 billion publicly listed company whose flagship product was launched three years earlier. This product has quickly become your cash cow. In a few years, it will account for close to 40 percent of your company's total revenue.

But for now, you are listening to a small group of engineers, designers, and marketers who, encouraged by members of your LT, are making a presentation. Their goal is to convince you that your company should launch a new product that will revolutionize the industry, or so they claim. There is one catch: introducing this new product will cannibalize the revenue of your flagship product. It may even lead to its complete obsolescence.

The fact that those presenting to you are downplaying this risk annoys you. Your reaction is as clear as it is succinct: "That is the dumbest idea I've ever heard," you say. And just in case you have not been clear enough, you later swear over and over in private meetings and on public stages that your company will never develop such a product. Case closed—or so you think.

Some time later, you discover that research efforts are still being poured into the new product behind your back. Some of your LT members must be encouraging this or, at the very least, turning a blind eye to it. As CEO, what should you do?

To most people to whom we present this scenario, the answer is clear: fire the LT members responsible. Would you agree?

Before you give a definitive answer, consider the following paradox:

- If you do not fire the LT members, you send the signal that your orders as CEO are little more than suggestions. In our experience, this is rarely a recipe for success.[24]

- But if you do fire them, your company, Apple, would never have launched the iPhone, which is the new product in question.[25] And without the iPhone, Apple would never have become at one time the world's most valuable publicly traded company.

Does the fact that Steve Jobs's LT members were right about the iPhone mean they were right to override their CEO's express wishes? That is the impression one is left with after reading this wonderful story told by Adam Grant in his best-selling book, *Think Again: The Power of Knowing What You Don't Know*.[26] Grant uses it to illustrate a best practice in overcoming a person's resistance to new ideas—in this case, Jobs's resistance to building a smartphone. However, it is also a great illustration of the principle that it is better to ask the CEO for forgiveness than permission that many successful LT members tell us they live by. If you are familiar with this principle (and may even be applying it in your own career), it is a testament to how unremarkable many find it when executives conspire to thwart their CEO's express wishes.

It should then come as no surprise that CEOs, even those as powerful and feared as Apple's Steve Jobs, may need to deploy their power in ways others may feel are excessive, simply to maintain their ability to steer the organization.

Lest we forget, CEOs are the ones who will be held accountable by their board if the secret plans of their LT members go off the rails.

Actionable Insights

In the previous section, we discussed various LT power games we have observed to distinguish between the unethical ones that must be eradicated and those that we must simply accept as part and parcel of the LT game. In this section, we present nine actionable insights to help you minimize the negative impact of power games on your LT some of which are what Battilana and Casciaro would call "structural safeguards" that promote power sharing and accountability.[27]

Actionable Insight No. 1: Refer to the Organization's Strategy and Its Priorities Often

Certain conditions exacerbate power struggles among LT members. One is when they disagree about the organization's strategy and priorities, or the latter are unclear. The reasons are easy to understand: absent clear organizational priorities, LT members will advance the priorities that are clearest to them—their own—assuming these to be in the organization's interest. Otherwise, why would their CEO have agreed to them?

Therefore, suggestions to improve your LT's functioning by, for example, developing trust or psychological safety are premature if your LT members are not aligned behind your organization's strategy. No matter how much trust LT members develop or how safe they feel, their power struggles will persist as long as they are pulling your organization in different directions.

Knowing this, one would think CEOs would be diligent in assessing their LT members' alignment. But as we discuss in further detail in this book, most CEOs are unaware that their LT members are misaligned and are surprised when our assessment shows the extent to which they are.

For that reason, beyond doing such an assessment, the first measure we suggest CEOs take to reduce LT power games is to ensure that they refer to their organization's strategy as often as possible and expect LT members to do the same. This reaffirms the common ground on which all LT members stand and helps identify those who are misaligned more easily.[28]

Specific measures that will enable you to do so are set out at the end of Chapter 4 when we discuss vertical and horizontal alignment measures.

Actionable Insight No. 2: Crowd Out Power as Much as Possible Using Data and Information

As discussed earlier, the more we make decision making fact based, the less room we allow power dynamics to influence decisions. Although most CEOs do not need to be reminded of this, we find it remarkable how many let their LT members propose strategies and plans that are supported by insufficient data.

Thus, for example, we see marketing VPs launch marketing campaigns and human resources VPs propose costly leadership programs without strong business cases. Although these campaigns and programs face little overt opposition when first presented at LT meetings because of the power-induced silence we have discussed, CEOs are only setting the scene for intense LT member power struggles when the time comes to implement them.

There are, of course, limits to how many data you can gather. This has prompted Amazon's Jeff Bezos to enact the principle that decisions should be made with 70 percent of the information you wish you had. "If you wait for 90 percent, in most cases, you're probably being slow," he wrote in his 2016 letter to shareholders.[29] Nonetheless, his comment testifies to a decision-making culture in which data are key. Infusing your decision making with data will not only minimize the impact of power but will also reduce bias. It may be one of the most fundamental elements of what Kahneman, Sibony, and Sunstein call "decision hygiene," a set of routines implemented to reduce errors in decision making.[30]

Actionable Insight No. 3: Make Monitoring Activities Part of Your Routine

Beyond expecting better data from their LT members, CEOs must become expert information gatherers themselves so they can inject data into the decision-making process, but also to catch wind of the power games that LT members may be playing at their expense and that of the organization.

Much like the parents of a teenager who know their son or daughter will be tempted to misbehave when they go out on a Saturday night, CEOs must "trust with their eyes open," as discussed in Chapter 1. CEOs must take proactive measures because LT members will not volunteer much of the information CEOs need.[31]

One of many measures you can adopt may be familiar: management by walking around (MBWA). First described in the business best seller *In Search of Excellence*, it sees leaders devoting time to wandering around the organization, listening to the problems and ideas of their staff.[32] This allows them to get facts unfiltered by their LT members.

Thus, for example, Howard Schultz is said to have visited at least twenty-five Starbucks stores per week back when he was the company's CEO. As for Walt Disney, he apparently wandered his company's studios and even went so far as to wear a disguise to tour the park, discovering on one occasion that an amusement ride that should have taken seven minutes, had ended after only four and a half.[33] That is certainly not something one of his LT members would have volunteered or even known about.

As one CEO who did not wish to be quoted for obvious reasons told us: "I manage the level below me, but I ask questions to the levels below them. In that way I make sure I am getting the full story." This leader would have agreed with Lou Gerstner, the CEO famous for turning IBM around in the 1990s, who said: "People do what you *inspect*—not what you *expect*."[34]

When MBWA is described, it can appear to be an informal and haphazard practice. However, we have observed that CEOs who do it successfully ingrain it into their routine. They make it a habit and have a clear idea of what information they are looking for when they leave their office.

Because CEOs must have their ear to the ground to encourage LT members to be straightforward with them, another information-gathering method many use resembles the one used by President Franklin D. Roosevelt, summarized as follows by a biographer:

> The essence of Roosevelt's technique for information-gathering was competition. "He would call you in," one of his aides once told me, "and he'd ask you

to get the story on some complicated business, and you'd come back after a few days of hard labor and present this juicy morsel you'd uncovered under a stone somewhere, and then you'd find out he knew all along about it, along with something you didn't know. Where he got this information from he wouldn't mention, usually, but after he had done this to you once or twice you got damn careful about your information

Although LT members often denounce this practice as wasting their time and outside observers may see it as an abuse of CEO power, those who are familiar with the power dynamics on LTs understand that these are measures CEOs often need to take to maintain their ability to guide the organization.

One last measure worth mentioning is meeting with clients. This, of course, helps CEOs better understand client needs and support sales, but it is also useful because LT members regularly invoke the special needs of their clients as a pretext to resist initiatives sanctioned by the CEO. In such circumstances, CEOs will always be at a power disadvantage unless they have their own appreciation of client needs.

All of these activities are "monitoring activities," to use the words of management guru Henry Mintzberg, who goes on to say that as a consequence of these activities, the CEO "becomes the nerve center of the [organization]—its best-informed member, at least if he or she is doing their job well."[35]

Actionable Insight No. 4: Nip Social Undermining in the Bud

Social undermining is one of the most widespread and insidious power games we observe, and CEOs must nip it in the bud. When they hear an LT member taking a personal swipe at a colleague, they must clearly show that such behavior is not part of the team culture they wish to build.

How to do this depends on the CEO's style and that of the LT members involved. One example we can offer is of a CEO who, when she was promoted to the top role, put an end to the social undermining that had flourished under her predecessor. She did this by showing her impatience whenever an LT member attempted to socially undermine a colleague with whom they were in conflict. Disregarding the personal attack, she would cut to the chase: "What's the business issue between the two of you?" Embedded in her question is a conflict management best practice: get clashing LT members to focus their attention on the problem, not the person. In using it, she was also sending the message that she had little patience for such power tactics.

Actionable Insight No. 5: Create a Safe Environment inside Meetings

Minimizing the negative effects of power to create a safe environment for LT members to express themselves cannot be achieved overnight. If you, as CEO, want fuller participation from all your LT members, we propose you begin with two measures: speaking last and using subgroups.

Speaking last might have served Jean-François, the CEO we mentioned earlier who had attributed his LT members' silence to a lack of courage. Given LT dynamics, he should have taken precautions not to reveal his opinion before asking his members for theirs. For example, he could have had someone else present the acquisition he wanted to discuss to ensure his body language and words did not betray his preference. And, of course, he should have presented his own opinion after others had presented theirs.

While this may appear obvious, when we suggested it to a CEO who needed help getting his LT members to speak up during meetings, he objected: "But if I speak last, we'll waste too much time. The discussion goes quicker when they know how I feel." We then pointed out the obvious: if speed was his major concern, then, by all means, he should state his opinion first. However, if he wanted a true discussion and meaningful insight on how others truly felt about what was being proposed, it was **wise to go last**.

Of course, there is a danger in letting your LT members express themselves first. If two or three immediately voice strong opposition to a proposal you want enacted, you will find it extremely difficult to turn the tide around afterward. This threat explains why CEOs sometimes speak first to avoid losing the battle before they even open their mouths.

However, you can counter this threat by implementing a second tactic, which is as effective as it is simple: have LT members **address an issue in subgroups** before tackling it in plenary. Not only do subgroups prevent a vocal minority from imposing its viewpoint straight out of the blocks, it also offers other advantages:

- LT members will be more open about their opinions in subgroups because they offer a measure of anonymity. This means they face less risk of retaliation from a colleague whose strategy or idea they may criticize.

- Using subgroups reduces the risk that a large coalition of LT members can form to force the CEO to go in any one direction, as may happen in plenary. This is because it is unlikely all subgroups will come to the same conclusion.

- Introverts are more at ease and have more space to express their opinions in subgroups.

- Subgroups ward off groupthink.

When we suggest to CEOs that they use subgroups during regular meetings to help create a safer environment, some balk at it, once again invoking how little time they have.

While they are right that subgroups can add time to an agenda topic, the question remains: Do they want to go quickly, or do they want to have a discussion that minimizes power dynamics and enables them to benefit from the diversity of their team? In some cases, speed may be of the essence. In all others, slowing down to benefit from all viewpoints may be wiser.

The two process measures we have mentioned—CEOs offering their opinion last and the use of subgroups—are designed to create a safe space for LT members *within* the LT meeting room. But what about *outside* of meetings? This is what we look at next.

Actionable Insight No. 6: Create a Safe Environment Outside of Meetings

CEOs must also take steps to create a safe environment for LT members outside of meetings where the weaker members of their team may be overpowered by stronger colleagues. In such cases, creating a safe environment may mean that the CEO must "protect" the less powerful party when, for example, he or she asks for help in mediating a dispute with a stronger colleague.

Some CEOs hesitate to get involved. Possibly inspired by the famous 1999 *Harvard Business Review* article, "Who's Got the Monkey?" which teaches leaders to avoid taking on their subordinates' problems, many CEOs choose not to intervene when their team members quarrel.[36] Much like parents who tell warring siblings to work things out in the hope they will learn to manage conflicts autonomously, many CEOs believe good leadership dictates they stay on the sidelines rather than arbitrate disputes among members of their team.

A laissez-faire approach is certainly appropriate at times, but not always, as when the weaker party is defending a strategic imperative that is critical to the business. A good illustration might be the well-publicized failures of the Boeing 737 Max, which led to two accidents claiming close to three hundred lives in 2018–2019. The direct cause of the accidents was the new software developed to prevent the plane from stalling during a climb. However, one could argue that an indirect cause of the accident can be found in the battle that engineering lost to the more powerful sales function.[37]

The need for CEOs to put their finger on the scale to level the playing field between competing LT members is particularly important at budget time and any other situation where the allocation of scarce resources is involved. As some have noted, if the CEO fails to recognize these situations and does not intervene, the team is likely to become demoralized.[38]

Beyond the issue of team morale, we would add that organizational harm can be the result because resources are not optimally allocated.

Actionable Insight No. 7: Ward Off Coups and Unjustified Opposition

Because CEOs may fall victim to LT members who wish to oust them or oppose measures they wish to implement, it is only normal that CEOs would seek to ward off such threats. But ironically, some efforts CEOs make to foster collaboration between LT members actually encourage the formation of coalitions that prevent CEOs from setting the company direction.

This paradox is well illustrated by the example of Rudi Gassner, former CEO of BMG International, a subsidiary of what was, at the time, the second-largest media conglomerate in the world. In a Harvard Business case, Gassner explains how he had first encouraged the three European members of his global LT to meet in advance of their full LT meetings so that they could address issues that concerned only Europe. However, he came to realize they often did more than that: "They even discuss the [full leadership team] agenda before the meetings, and they sometimes come over with what I call a 'prefabricated opinion.' So now sometimes I have to work to break this group up a little bit."[39]

The case does not tell us what measures Gassner used to "break this group up," but whatever they were, they do not appear to have been successful as the case goes on to chronicle Gassner's failure to get his LT members to reset their budget targets midyear, a failure partly due to European members of his team coalescing to oppose him.

This is not to say that CEOs are powerless to ward off illegitimate or unjustified opposition from below. They do so every time they enact change management strategies to deflect resistance on specific projects.

More generally, they can employ **monitoring techniques** such as the ones highlighted previously in this section because these enable them to see threats as they materialize. The successful CEOs we observe are master monitors who become the nerve center of their organization, to use Mintzberg's words.

Actionable Insight No. 8: Centralize or Decentralize But Do So with Care

We have seen many CEOs **centralize** and **decentralize** their organizations to solidify their hold on to power. Of course, restructuring for the sole purpose of maintaining power is not something we recommend.

The primary motive for centralizing functions, for example, should be to produce tangible synergies or improve cross-unit collaboration. This was the case of a company we worked for in which the CEO created a central marketing function to lower costs, thus removing the marketing responsibility from her business unit heads. A secondary benefit of this restructuring was to curb the power of business unit leaders by providing the CEO with a window into their sales pipeline to ensure they were targeting the clients dictated by the company's strategy. Until then, these leaders had been less than enthusiastic to do so.

On the issue of centralization, interesting research has been done suggesting that CEOs wishing to centralize front-end functions (e.g., marketing, R&D, sales) will be more successful if their portfolio of products is less diversified, whereas product range is a less important consideration when the goal is to centralize back-end functions such as finance, law, HR, IT, strategy, PR, or communications.[40] We recommend that you briefly review this research if you are considering centralizing a function because in our experience, restructuring efforts are so disruptive that CEOs should treat them as a last resort.

Actionable Insight No. 9: Make Judicious Use of Hub-and-Spoke Mode

We briefly mention that CEOs who make judicious use of what we call the **Hub-and-Spoke** mode of functioning also minimize the threats they may face from below. However, the motivations driving this strategy extend far beyond power considerations, and so we address them in Chapter 3.

The Chapter in a Nutshell

*Why Power Games Are like Death and Taxes
and Why All Executives Must Play Them*

- Power and politics are a fact of LT life. All executives must deploy power if they wish to be successful. Those who wish to improve an LT's effectiveness but ignore this reality are destined to fail.

- Coming to terms with the reality that *all* executives play power games enables us to focus our energy where it really matters: distinguishing unethical power games from those that we must simply accept as part and parcel of the LT game.

Power Games with Negative Impacts on LTs

- CEOs usually know what to do when confronted by egregious and unethical uses of power—if they find out about them. (We discussed the importance of monitoring activities in Chapter 1.)

- Social undermining is a widely used and insidious power tactic. CEOs need to nip it in the bud.

- Power-induced silence is a fundamental LT disease. It does not result from a lack of courage on the part of LT members, but from a rational cost-benefit analysis. CEOs need to understand the logic behind it if they want to turn LT meetings into forums for genuine discussion rather than the monotonous presentation fests these meetings typically are.

- Agenda control by LT members is the ultimate power tactic. CEOs must take more control of the agenda-setting process to prevent organizational harm arising from agenda-related conflicts.

Power Games That Threaten CEOs

- CEOs face a trio of threats: the threat of a coup, the threat to their ability to steer the organization, and the threat of outright manipulation.

- Those offering advice on how to improve LT effectiveness would do well to remember that CEOs are not all-powerful. LT improvement measures whose side effect is to prevent CEOs from setting organizational direction, or curtails their ability to resolve strategic disputes, should be avoided.

Summary of Actionable Insights

1. Refer often to the organization's strategy and its priorities to assess alignment and create the common ground that is necessary for collaboration.

2. Crowd out power as much as possible by supplying data and information.

3. Make monitoring activities part of your routine to become aware of the power dynamics on your LT so you can address them.

4. Nip social undermining in the bud.

5. Create a safe environment *inside* meetings by speaking last and addressing issues in subgroups before doing so in plenary.

6. Create a safe environment *outside* meetings by assessing power differentials between LT members and supporting weaker LT members when the need arises.

7. Take measures to ward off coups and unjustified opposition through the judicious use of change management strategies and monitoring.

8. Centralization or decentralization strategies can solidify a CEO's hold on power but should always be implemented as a last resort and never enacted solely to address power concerns.

9. Leverage the Hub-and-Spoke mode. (See Chapter 3.)

OF HUBS, SPOKES, AND SILO BUSTING

> Our LT is not a team. We live in silos and never discuss anything together.
> Our CEO has one-on-one discussions with us outside of meetings and these
> one-on-ones often continue *during* meetings. It's frustrating.

So spoke Sei Young, the VP of operations of a client company. What she described is commonly called a leader-centric or **Hub-and-Spoke** model of LT functioning (Figure 3.1), defined as follows:

> The CEO (or general manager) sits at the center of a wheel surrounded by
> business unit leaders, each of whom confers and communicates only with the
> CEO, not with one another. The CEO manages each spoke of the wheel separately, and each business unit relies heavily on the leader.[1]

When we asked Sei Young why she thought her CEO operated in this way, she shot back: "He manages individuals because he is afraid the team will take over. It's incredible!"

Perhaps it is not so incredible considering how many executives have shared similar complaints about their CEO with us. "What can we do?" they ask. This chapter answers that question.

To do so requires determining if Hub-and-Spoke functioning, often associated with working in **silos**, is truly a problem. Not always, as we shall see in the first section of this chapter.

Problems begin when LTs get *stuck* in Hub-and-Spoke mode because it robs

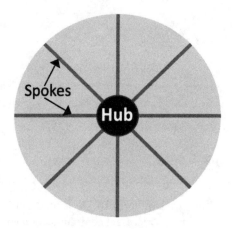

FIGURE 3.1. Hub-and-Spoke Model

them of the benefits of teamwork. The second section examines why LTs get stuck and reveals the chief culprits. The answer may surprise you.

If LTs must avoid getting stuck in Hub-and-Spoke mode, they must nevertheless spend time there, which begs two questions: When should they? When is it optimal to switch to Team mode? This is what we examine in the third section using the case of Pan-European Financials as it navigated the 2008 financial crisis.

We wrap up the chapter with some silo-busting actionable insights. There we describe the bridging role—perhaps the most important and overlooked role in leadership development today—CEOs must play.

Three LT Operating Modes

Theories, Models, and What Actually Happens in the Field

The Hub-and-Spoke model is often presented as emerging in a simpler era when "heroic leaders" sat atop their organization and made decisions single-handedly. Today, this is considered suboptimal by many who argue that modern business requires a more collective decision-making approach.[2]

The argument that the Hub-and-Spoke model is unsuitable now is strongest when the model is presented in its most simplistic form: LT members operating in silos and communicating with each other only outside of LT meetings through the CEO, who alone makes all decisions. This caricature of the model

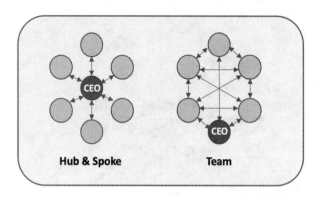

FIGURE 3.2. The Two Dominant LT Decision-Making
Models. Note: Arrows represent communication channels.

is often trotted out when promoting its competitor: the ring-team, or **Team,
model,** which

> brings unit leaders together in the CEO's key circle. Decisions are made *col-
> lectively* [emphasis added] by the senior team about how to allocate resources
> and make trade-offs between the present and the future.[3]

Because the Hub-and-Spoke and Team models (Figure 3.2) have dominated
organizational decision-making research, Lucy Arendt and her colleagues asked
a simple question no one else had bothered with: Had any organizations adopted either model in practice?[4] They found little evidence that *either* model
has been widely adopted.

With respect to the Hub-and-Spoke model, they surmised it was because
few CEOs had the power to adopt it unless they were owner-managers or "ce-
lebrity" CEOs (Bernard Arnault, Elon Musk, and Steve Jobs immediately come
to mind).[5]

As for the Team model, they write, "To the extent that it implies collective
decision-making, [this] model likely applies to a relatively small percentage
of firms."[6] They are certainly not alone in thinking this as collective decision
making is rarer than many assume, as we discuss in Chapter 4.[7]

But if most LTs adopt neither model for decision making, what *does* their
decision-making process look like?

Arendt and her colleagues answer by highlighting the work of researchers
such as Michael Roberto, who paints the following picture of organizational
decision making, one that of you may recognize:

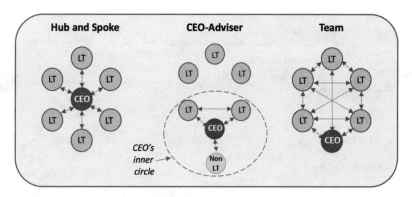

FIGURE 3.3. The CEO-Adviser Model Sits between the Hub-and-Spoke and Team Models

The [top management team] did not make important decisions as a group. Instead, in most firms, different sets of individuals worked with the chief executive to make each strategic choice. A small core group of senior managers (including the chief executive) tended to work together intensively on all decisions. However, the rest of the key decision makers varied depending on the issues involved. Often, they included other individuals who reported directly to the chief executive, as well as key individuals from lower levels.

Their conclusion is that a third model deserves consideration: the **CEO-Adviser mode**, which sits between its Hub-and-Spoke and Team siblings because of its following characteristics (Figure 3.3):

- CEOs retain ultimate authority for decision making, but for reasons including information overload, they enlist advisers who gather information, interpret it, and then provide recommendations.[8]

- Advisers may be LT members, selected for their expertise on the issue at hand, and often include members of the CEO's inner circle.

- But advisers may also be non-LT members ("Non-LT" in Figure 3.3) when LT members lack the necessary expertise or are unable to set aside their functional or unit biases.[9] Non-LT member advisers may be lower down in the organization or even outside it (e.g., a board member).

How LTs Operate in the Real World

Question: Which of the three models best reflects your own LT's functioning or that of an LT you are involved with?

- Hub-and-Spoke

- Team

- CEO-Adviser

- A mix of the above

- None of the above

We asked a group of executives this question at the break of an LT offsite we were facilitating. Without hesitation, one replied, "The **CEO-Adviser model**," pointing to the fact their CEO was, at that very moment, off in another room, huddled with members of her inner circle "and, no doubt," he added ruefully, "making important decisions she will spring on us later today." But a colleague immediately intervened to say that, no, their LT model was clearly **Hub-and-Spoke**, citing a decision their CEO had made on her own earlier that month after consulting individual LT members. After a few minutes of this back and forth, one of them said: "At least there is one thing we can agree on: our LT's model is definitely *not* the Team model!"

Yet when we spoke to the CEO later, she explained that her LT's model was obviously the **Team** model, citing as proof the many topics she had put on the team table for decision at the very offsite we were helping her facilitate.

How could three executives, sitting on the same LT, perceive its functioning so differently? Are these three models somehow inadequate and the answer lies in finding a fourth?

Occam's razor points us to a simpler explanation: the problem lies not so much in the three models but in the assumption that lies behind them: that LTs have one, and only one, way of operating.[10] This assumption is reinforced by the term *model*, which makes LT functioning seem static. But nothing could be further from the truth. As we witness every time we interact with LTs, they are constantly shifting from what is more accurately described as one "mode" (rather than "model") to another, depending on where they are in their decision-making process.

Take the scenario of a CEO who is considering an acquisition to grow the company's top line:

Step 1: The CEO may begin in **Hub-and-Spoke** mode, consulting LT members one-on-one to gauge their appetite for an acquisition and whether a deal is worth pursuing.

Step 2: Sensing most are onboard with the idea, they shift to **CEO-Adviser** mode, asking one or two of their LT members to identify acquisition targets and enlisting a merger and acquisitions expert consultant to assist them. At this stage, they exclude other LT members because they lack the requisite experience and the work must remain confidential. The fewer people involved, the better.

Step 3: Once a suitable acquisition target has been identified, they briefly return to **Hub-and-Spoke** mode by engaging once more in one-on-one discussions with those LT members who will be most affected by the acquisition, to address concerns they might have.

Step 4: Finally, they transition to **Team** mode, bringing all LT members together to announce the deal, ensure no stone has been left unturned, and bring closure to the exercise.

This simple scenario highlights how, from a CEO's point of view, the question is not, "Which *model* should I choose?" but, rather, "When should I use each *mode*?"

This last question cannot be answered if you assume that LTs operate in a fixed manner or, as some team-building consultants propose, that LTs should always function in Team mode. CEOs who disagree are accused of lacking the courage or leadership ability to transform their LT into a "real team."

In our experience, most CEOs would welcome the opportunity to spend more time in Team mode because, as many tell us, it is lonely at the top. But that is easier said than done. Many factors make it difficult to switch into Team mode, leaving LT members operating in silos, disconnected from peers.

Who is responsible for this situation? Being able to answer this question is essential; otherwise, your silo-busting attempts have little chance of succeeding.

Who Is Responsible for LTs Getting Stuck in Hub-and-Spoke Mode and Silo Thickening?

THE AUTONOMY ILLUSION AND THREE STRATEGIES EXECUTIVES USE TO REINFORCE THEIR SILOS

No study has ever proven that organizational leaders are, as a rule, uncommonly evil. But you would never guess this from watching popular television series or Hollywood movies. From Gordon "Greed Is Good" Gekko (played by Michael Douglas in the movie *Wall Street*) to Miranda Priestly (played by Meryl Streep in the movie *The Devil Wears Prada*), the unethical, power-hungry leader is a character cliché.

Thus, it is easy for executives to blame their CEO when their LT is stuck in Hub-and-Spoke mode, with its associated power grabs and divide-and-conquer tactics. They are therefore dumbfounded to hear that much of the responsibility lies with them, spurred on by a phenomenon many of you will be familiar with: the **autonomy illusion**. Here is what we mean.

When hired, LT members are handed responsibility for an area—a unit or function—and then given objectives they are held accountable for and whose achievement bears on their year-end bonus. This deal is so common that few question its fairness. But this fairness is suspect the moment LT members face task **interdependence,** when they must work together as a team rather than independently to achieve their individual objectives.[11]

The Autonomy Illusion: Being held 100 percent accountable for objectives with less than 100 percent autonomy to achieve them

Under these circumstances, LT members lack full autonomy to make decisions in their assigned area. They need to negotiate with one another to achieve their objectives. Despite this, they are deemed 100 percent accountable for them. Therein lies the *autonomy illusion*, a term we coined to describe when executives have 100 percent accountability for objectives without the matching autonomy to achieve them. Executives who do not accept the illusion rarely succeed.

Beyond acceptance, how do executives operate with this illusion? We see them adopt three strategies, all of which seek to increase their autonomy:

- The rookie strategy

- The task versus true objective strategy

- The leverage-the-CEO strategy

CEOs need to be on the lookout because these strategies thicken silo walls.

We call the first strategy executives use to deal with the autonomy illusion the *rookie strategy* because it is mostly used by newly promoted LT members. It is the least sophisticated strategy and is deployed when LT members negotiate their yearly objectives, asking their CEO questions such as, "*So, do I have free rein to do what's needed to attain my objectives?*" or "*Do I have your full*

TABLE 3.1. Examples of the Task versus True Objective Strategy

Who	Task Masquerading as an Objective	True Objective
Sales	Visit 10 new clients per month	Generate sales of $1M per quarter
IT	Release a new version of our system software	Increase internal user satisfaction of our system software by 10%
Finance	Develop a plan to reduce days sales outstanding (DSO) from 79 days to under 50 days	Reduce DSO from 79 to under 50 days

support to achieve my objectives?" These are not so much questions as thinly disguised attempts to obtain the impossible from their CEO: full autonomy to do whatever they need to achieve their objectives, no matter how that might affect their LT colleagues.

The second strategy, more sophisticated, is the *task versus true objective strategy.* Used by craftier LT members, it consists of convincing their CEO to hold them accountable solely for tasks they can achieve without the collaboration of colleagues rather than for true objectives. Because this strategy enables them to work alone in their silo, they now have autonomy that matches up with their accountability.

Table 3.1 provides a few actual cases we have seen after reviewing LT member objectives in dozens of organizations:

- The sales VP who negotiated to be held accountable for "visit[ing] ten new clients per month" instead of a true objective such as "generating sales of $1M of widgets per quarter," which would have obliged him to align with his counterpart in operations to ensure adequate widget supplies

- The IT executive who got her CEO to accept "releas[ing] a new version of our system software" rather than a true objective such as "increase internal user satisfaction of our system software by 10 percent," which would have required her to reach out to her peers to ensure the software matched their needs

- The CFO who convinced his CEO to hold him responsible for the task of "develop[ing] a plan to reduce days sales outstanding (DSO) from 79 days to under 50 days" rather than the true objective of "reducing days sales outstanding (DSO) from 79 to under 50 days."

Getting one's CEO to accept that "developing a plan or process" is a true objective, rather than a step toward meeting a true objective, may be the most widespread use of the task versus true objective strategy. When CEOs allow LT members to get away with this strategy, it contributes to silo building because it allows LT members to work in their corner without collaborating with LT colleagues.

The third strategy LT members use to mitigate the effects of the autonomy illusion is the most sophisticated. We call it the *leverage-the-CEO strategy* because LT members use it to impose their plans on their colleagues by leveraging the CEO's power rather than by negotiating directly with them.

We illustrate how the leverage-the-CEO strategy contributes to silo building with the following case.

Hub-and-Spoke Case Study: The Leverage-the-CEO Strategy

Maria was a health and safety (H&S) executive we met shortly after she was hired to reduce long-term injuries (**LTI**) at an industrial firm. Her new CEO had no H&S experience, something he admitted when he called Maria to offer her the job. "We've needed an H&S expert for a while because our safety track record sucks," he told her bluntly.

When Maria expressed concerns that her new colleagues might resist the safety measures she needed to institute to achieve the LTI target the CEO gave her, he reassured her by saying: "You have my full support."

Satisfied with this response, Maria immediately got to work. Visiting the company's facilities, she interviewed her new LT colleagues, all of whom seemed genuinely delighted with her arrival. Given her run-ins with operations in her previous job, she was pleased when the head of operations told her: "I'm glad you're here. LTI costs are killing me." Having studied his financials, she could see he was right. She was certain she could help him.

We caught up with Maria soon after she had finished her assessment. She was preparing a first draft of her H&S plan, a plan the CEO wanted her to present at the upcoming offsite we were facilitating.

We looked over the plan briefly. It contained strict controls based on H&S best practices that would certainly curb LTIs. But the controls would slow critical processes and reduce operational productivity. Her operations colleague would be none too pleased.

"Who will you show your new plan to before the offsite?" we asked. "Oh, just my boss, I guess," she answered. "I really don't have time to do more than that. There is so much to do!"

When we suggested it would be wise to present her plan to a few of her colleagues, she balked, telling us, "I thought about it, but no. It was hard enough getting a first meeting with them. They're very busy. And besides, they're not safety experts. I would never tell our CFO how to manage cash flow, or our HR VP how to develop talent. So, I don't want to ask them their opinions on safety and then pretend they're fantastic. That's not my style. Plus, my CEO said he liked my plan, and he's their boss too, right?"

This was not so much a question as a signal the conversation was over.

No doubt, you will not be surprised that Maria's decision to bypass her colleagues and bank solely on her CEO's support in Hub-and-Spoke mode meant she got little help from her colleagues when the time came to implement her plan.

What reasons led her to bypass colleagues in this way? They are the same reasons that motivate executives in all organizations to follow a similar path.

Reason No. 1: The Double-Sided Time Squeeze

Validating any plan is time-consuming. An executive like Maria who has spent weeks developing her plan feels pressure to implement it immediately from a CEO who wanted it yesterday.

When executives have more than a handful of LT colleagues—let's say eight or more—it can take weeks to run a plan by all of them, especially if they are not co-located. You need to schedule meetings with every colleague, expose your plan to each one, answer their questions, and then work out how to modify your plan to address all their concerns. This is no mean feat!

But even if Maria had time to meet all her colleagues, many of *them* may not want to. They face a choice: meet with Maria, an activity with potentially few benefits, or do the work for which they are accountable. When you are a time-starved executive, the choice is easy.

Reason No. 2: Asking for Feedback Gives Rise to an Expectation You Will Incorporate It

A further disincentive for LT members to validate their plans with colleagues is the expectations this may create. Whenever executive A presents a plan to colleague B for feedback, B often expects their suggestions will be implemented. Is this a rational expectation? Probably not. Nevertheless, it is what we observe, especially when B is more powerful than A.

Had Maria decided to present her plan to her operations counterpart, he would undoubtedly have wanted her to amend it. He might even have suggested that Maria drop the plan altogether, creating a major conflict. It is easier for Maria to bypass him and ask her CEO for approval so she could then leverage the CEO's power to impose her plan on her operations counterpart.

REASON NO. 3: THE COMPOUNDING EFFECT OF THE
LEVERAGE-THE-CEO STRATEGY

Once one LT member successfully uses the leverage-the-CEO strategy—in other words, once their CEO approves their plans without obliging them to consult first with their LT colleagues—it encourages every LT member to adopt the same strategy.

Thus, Hub-and-Spoke functioning is reinforced, as are the silos behind which LT members work, isolated from their colleagues except when they cross paths by chance or in LT meetings.

Growth: The Cement That Thickens Silos

Executives tell us that over time, silos grew thicker in every organization they worked in. It made their organizations more bureaucratic and less fun to work in. They wonder: Is it inevitable?

Yes, but the good news is that you can slow the process if you understand why silos thicken over time. It is not only because executives use the three strategies just described. It also has to do with growth, one of the main centrifugal forces identified by renowned LT scholar Donald Hambrick that isolates LT teammates from one another.[12]

Understanding how growth contributes to "oversilofication" is useful and points to how you can lessen this effect:

- Growth often means LT members cease to work in close physical proximity. Their desire to be co-located with their own growing teams has them move to another floor or even another building, away from LT colleagues. As a result, informal meetings between LT members are less likely to occur and formal, in-person meetings are more difficult to schedule, especially if growth means dispersion of LT members across time zones.

- As their staff grows, LT members need to spend more time inside their silo to manage subordinates. They spend less time thinking about the organization as a whole and the interdependencies with LT colleagues. Attending LT meetings and coordinating with colleagues soon become unwanted distractions that interfere with managing their own team, which each soon views as their "real job." LT members find it more efficient to find out what their colleagues are doing indirectly through one-on-ones with the CEO who sits at the hub of a now much looser LT network. When CEOs are not careful, they become the sole person responsible for bridging the gaps between their LT members.

> *Growth sparks a vicious cycle: The more LT members spend time with their staff who share a common mind-set, the more difficult it is to interact with LT colleagues whose mind is different.*

- As social network theory predicts,[13] growth sparks a vicious cycle as LT members spend more time with their staff, people who typically share a common mind-set.[14] They find it increasingly difficult to interact with LT colleagues whose mind-set is different and they are less likely to want to engage with them, even when the opportunity presents itself.

- The less LT members engage with one another, the greater the gap between them grows, further eroding their desire to communicate. When they are obliged to do so, the language and shared assumptions each LT member has developed with his or her own team, or "tribe," make it harder to understand and reach compromises with their colleagues. It is far easier to avoid colleagues altogether and negotiate with them indirectly through the CEO in Hub-and-Spoke mode.

The "Formula": Why LT Meetings Often Fail to Break Teams Out of Hub-and-Spoke Mode

We just examined how growth thickens silo walls and reinforces Hub-and-Spoke functioning. Prior to that, we examined three strategies LT members deploy that have the same effect because they enable executives to achieve their objectives without leaving their silos.

One way to counter this oversilofication is for CEOs to insist that LT members emerge from their silos to present their plans for discussion in Team mode at LT meetings. In theory, this should break the LT out of Hub-and-Spoke mode. In practice, it may not because of the formula executives adopt when they present their plans in meetings.

This formula, whose steps we describe next, is designed to make it difficult for anyone other than the CEO to comment on the plan being presented. Thus, instead of a team discussion, what occurs is, for all practical purposes, a public one-on-one between the LT member presenting the plan and the CEO. Hub-and-Spoke mode is thus transported into the meeting room.

To be clear, what we are calling "the formula" is not a recipe that LT members consciously follow. It is a pattern of behavior that we see so often across LTs that one might think it is something executives are taught in business school. It has three steps.

Step 1: Get your plan preapproved by the CEO. When you are an LT member with a draft plan, ask for a one-on-one meeting with your CEO to get preliminary validation. Like a true spokesperson or advocate, make sure you present only the information that supports your plan and reassure your CEO that you consulted your colleagues. Whether you did this seriously or not is immaterial because few CEOs bother to check.

This is another example of the leverage-the-CEO strategy we illustrated with health and safety executive Maria earlier. But your CEO does not approve it yet and wants you to get it validated by your colleagues in an LT meeting so on to step 2.

Step 2: Prepare your "case," but don't reveal the details. Prepare a presentation that, once more, includes only evidence that supports your plan, and then send it out to your colleagues. Make sure your presentation is very detailed. This will discourage your colleagues from reading it beforehand. But just to be sure, send it the day before the meeting to give them as little time as possible to read it or time to complain to the CEO about it. After all, would a lawyer give opposing counsel time to prepare before going to court?

Step 3: Say you want a discussion ... but then do everything you can to prevent it. At the meeting, begin your presentation by saying your objective is "to get feedback." This sends the message you are open-minded and you welcome your colleagues' opinions. But then use one, or all three, of the following tactics to make sure your colleagues stay silent:

- Spend up to 95 to 100 percent of your allotted time presenting, leaving little, if any, time for comments.

- Leverage the power dynamics discussed in Chapter 2 by dropping subtle hints that the CEO has seen your plan and approves of it. In this way, your colleagues understand that opposing the plan means opposing both you and the boss. How to do this? One classic approach we often see is LT members speaking only to their CEO throughout their presentation and saying such

things as, "I'll go over this section of my presentation quickly because this is
the material you and I covered together last week."

- Another widely used tactic we observe is executives who explain, in excruciat-
  ing detail, how they developed their plan (e.g., whom they consulted, how challenging the work was, and how they followed "best practices"). This sends the
  message that they have thought of everything and that any further feedback is
  superfluous. They avoid detailing what is in the actual plan, however, or how
  it might affect their colleagues. This could lead to the plan being scuttled. That
  would not do because the goal of the formula is to get a positive verdict from
  the CEO that can then be used to override resistance from colleagues.

Are we suggesting that all LT members behave this way? Of course not. We are
merely pointing to tactics we see executives use to prevent LT meetings from
becoming a true forum for discussion. In other words, these tactics prevent LTs
from escaping Hub-and-Spoke mode and entering Team mode.

Switching in and out of Hub-and-Spoke Mode: The Pan-European Finance Case

We just explored how growth and strategies LT members use thicken the silos
around them, leaving them stuck in Hub-and-Spoke mode. As a result, the LT
does not benefit from Team mode and the collective exchanges that lead to
better decision making and stronger alignment.

But that is not to say that an LT would be better off if it spent all its time
in Team mode (i.e., in meetings). This is hardly anyone's idea of effectiveness.
LT effectiveness is about being in the right mode at the right time and for the
right reasons.

Knowing how to achieve this is what we explore with the following case.
It presents a textbook use of the three LT operating modes depicted in Figure
3.3.: Team, Hub-and-Spoke, and CEO-Adviser mode.

As you read through the case, we encourage you to jot down the criteria
that Robert, the CEO in question, uses to switch from one mode to another.
Ask yourself: are these the criteria I would have used?

After the case, we summarize these criteria so you can compare them with
your own list and apply them to avoid the oversilofication of your own LT.

Introducing Pan-European Finance and the Gathering Storm

The morning of March 30, 2008 is one that Robert, CEO of Pan-European Finance (PEF), remembers well. He was sitting in the kitchen of his Mayfair home, a thirty-minute drive from PEF's London headquarters. He had just finished reading the morning paper and catching up on the latest developments of the unfolding financial crisis in the United States.

His morning read confirmed something he had sensed for weeks: the storm brewing in America might eventually hit Europe very hard. He pulled out his smartphone and wrote to his assistant: "Pls book meeting room (6–8 people) for meeting at regular Marriott April 8–9. Details to follow."

To provide context for what would transpire at the Marriott meeting a week later, in April 2008, we must look back two years earlier.

In 2006, subprime borrowers in the United States started defaulting on their loans, and the housing bubble burst as the Federal Reserve raised interest rates.[15] By March 2007, the housing crisis was reaching the corners of the finance industry, but as the year ended, PEF and many others remained unscathed. Nevertheless, Robert began thinking America was headed for a recession that could then spread to his markets in Europe given how dependent the world had become on US consumers as a source of demand.[16]

By the end of 2007, Robert decided PEF needed to plan for a recession in Europe, and the sooner the better. But he could hardly expect his executives to help him prepare such a plan if they were not aligned behind a shared vision of what the future held. He decided to put the topic on the agenda at his LT's end-of-year offsite in Venice in December.

Venice Offsite, December 2007: Developing a Shared Vision in Team Mode

Persuading his LT members that the US subprime crisis posed a threat to PEF's lending business in Europe was a tall order in December 2007. European's future was still looking rosy: the year had been exceptionally good, and the pipeline for the next twelve months was full. The Lehman Brothers collapse was still almost a year away.[17]

Robert had twenty people to convince: ten UK-based functional heads and ten managing directors (MDs) spread out over a dozen countries including Germany and France.

Presenting his case in Team mode before his twenty LT members was risky. He knew from experience that all it would take was a handful of vocal MDs downplaying the possibility of a crisis and it would then be practically impossible to get his team to work on a plan to address it. Nevertheless, it was a calculated risk. He was coming in well prepared. Leaving nothing to chance, he had chatted one-on-one with his ten functional heads prior to their arrival in Venice and knew he could count on most of them for support. Furthermore, he felt he had little choice but to put things onto the team table. The plan he wanted the team to draw up would alter their 2008 forecast and budget, which he needed to submit to PEF's corporate headquarters by December 31. It was now or never.

Robert laid out the facts, explaining why he felt PEF's European markets would soon be affected by the problems in the United States and why the team needed to plan for this eventuality. As he expected, he faced pushback from a few of his MDs. However, his grasp of the macroeconomic data and the timely backing of key members of his LT, including his CFO, Deepak, one of the most powerful members of the team, prevented any serious opposition from emerging.

An hour later, he perceived that enough people shared his sense of urgency that he could set them to work on a plan to prepare for the storm he had convinced them was on the horizon. By the end of the offsite, Robert had the plan he wanted.

Marriott Meeting, April 2008: Reimagining the Organization in CEO-Adviser Mode

Sitting in his Mayfair kitchen three and half months after Venice, on March 30, 2008, economic factors ranging from falling industrial production to declining car sales supported the pessimistic scenario Robert had painted for his team in Venice. Although the news was bad, Robert was nevertheless energized. Here was an opportunity to make the far-reaching changes at PEF he had wanted to make for months. As he explained:

> In December 2007, in Venice, I told the team a storm was coming and the plan we came up with was largely about boarding up the windows and hoarding supplies. But I wanted to do more than just protect the house. I wanted to redo its foundations so we could emerge stronger than our competitors once the storm passed.

Reconvening all twenty members of his LT in Team mode to "redo the foundations" never crossed his mind. He had to act quickly. More important, he wanted only the right expertise around the table. Although he would not have used the term, the moment called for the CEO-Adviser mode, not Team mode. "I wanted people who understood all the key levers of the business—processes, IT, tax aspects, etc.," Robert recalled, "but I also wanted people who had a pan-European perspective, not just a single country vision." This meant excluding most of his ten MDs.

There was a further reason to exclude the MDs and opt for the CEO-adviser mode:

> We needed to start with a blank slate. No sacred cows. This would be impossible with the MDs because no matter what we came up with, it would pose problems for one of them. So we would always have someone explaining how such-and-such a solution could never work in their market.

Robert's CFO, Deepak, agreed: "When you're brainstorming and an idea pops into your head, you want to put it on the table without worrying what others are going to think about it. That's not going to happen if you're constantly wondering if that idea will make things more challenging for the person sitting across from you."

A last reason to exclude the MDs was confidentiality. Robert knew the changes he had in mind might entail layoffs. If one of the MDs wanted to block the process, all he would have to do was leak this information and the process would inevitably stall once the unions got wind of it.

Thus, after sending his assistant the email saying, "pls book meeting room (6–8 people) for offsite at regular Marriott April 8–9. Details to follow," he phoned six of the ten functional members of his team. This group was small enough to achieve consensus quickly but large enough to give Robert the client and operational knowledge he needed given that two of the six had been MDs in the past.

When Robert and these six executives met on April 8, 2008, for their "redo the foundations" meeting, one issue they identified was the complexity of certain loan approvals processes and the resulting drag on profitability. These processes introduced costly variability and had been instituted to mitigate risks associated with smaller, single-country clients. It soon became apparent that transforming PEF lay in weeding out these clients and redefining the "ideal client." Once this was done, they could simplify processes and cut costs.

Over the next two days, they worked to define their ideal client along three dimensions: profitability, growth potential and ease of service. At 4:30 p.m. on day 2 of the offsite, Robert was satisfied they had found the right formula. He could see his six LT members were spent, but he did not let them go home just yet. He needed to make sure all of them felt "100 percent comfortable" with what they had come up with. If they were not, they could not present a united front. Such disunity would then be exploited by any one of the MDs who wanted to stall the process for the wrong reasons.

Robert was wise not to rush off. He discovered that a few concerns remained. But soon these were worked out. As they left the Marriott, Robert now felt confident they could move on to the next step.

The May 2008 London Meetings: Back to Hub-and-Spoke Mode

Having defined criteria to identify "ideal" clients at the April Marriott meeting in CEO-Adviser mode, the next step was clear: determine which specific PEF clients fit the criteria, then weed out the rest. But that could not be done without the ten MDs who held the client data. For this exercise, Robert decided once more against Team mode. Hub-and-Spoke mode would be wiser, and so he invited all ten MDs to come to London, each on separate days. He did so for several reasons.

First, the next official team offsite was weeks away and the chances of finding a date suitable to all before then were nil. Second, as Robert noted, proceeding in Team mode would have turned the event into a "massive complaint fest" with each MD piling their individual concerns one on top of the other. Robert recognized that his MDs might have legitimate concerns about applying the ideal client criteria in their market and wanted to address each person's concerns fully. If he tried to do so in Team mode, the others in the room would be left twiddling their thumbs. It might also provide some with an opportunity to form coalitions to derail the process entirely.

The decision to have the MDs travel to London rather than have Robert meet with each MD on their home turf was also deliberate. Having Robert travel to ten different cities would have meant a lot of wasted time but, more important, as Deepak, his CFO, explained:

> Having them come to London sent the message that the exercise was not optional, that it was serious. Furthermore, we didn't want them to be distracted, which they would have been had they been at home. The work had to be done quickly. The crisis was on the doorstep but some of them were still in denial. We had to keep them in London at least until they had made a preliminary assessment of which clients to keep.

A few weeks later, the process was over. PEF had pared down its customer port-folio by 75 percent, removing smaller, single-country clients who, despite their number, had represented only 20 percent of revenue. This enabled the company to drastically reduce its cost base and serve its remaining clients more efficiently. Thus, while its competitors struggled through 2008, PEF had a record year.

The PEF story (see the simplified depiction in Figure 3.4) shows that not all LT tasks are best dealt with in Team mode. Depending on circumstances, it may be better to adopt Hub-and-Spoke mode, or CEO-Adviser mode, because involving all LT members in Team mode can be costly and poses risks that CEOs are unwise to assume.

If you have been taking notes regarding the criteria Robert used to select different LT operating modes in different contexts, you can compare them with the criteria we set out in the Actionable Insights section that follows.

Actionable Insights

The main points raised up to now in this chapter are simple:

- An LT cannot, and should not, spend all its time in Team mode. Said differently, LT members cannot have their finger in every pie or spend all their time in meetings. One need not be a disciple of Adam Smith's division of labor principle to see why this would be ineffective, let alone impractical.

- If LT members are not constantly in Team mode, it necessarily follows they will spend time in other modes that, to simplify, we have labeled Hub-and-Spoke and CEO-Adviser modes.

If one accepts these simple points, then CEOs must answer three questions:

1. What criteria determine the appropriate mode for a given context?

2. How do you prevent your LT from getting stuck in Hub-and-Spoke mode and robbing your organization of the LT's collective power?

3. What should you do and what skills must you master as CEO to increase your LT's effectiveness when you are in Hub-and-Spoke mode?

We provide answers to these questions next.

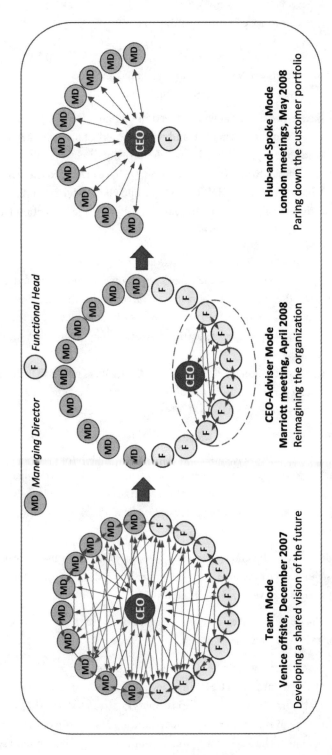

MD Managing Director   F Functional Head

Team Mode
Venice offsite, December 2007
Developing a shared vision of the future

CEO–Adviser Mode
Marriott meeting, April 2008
Reimagining the organization

Hub-and-Spoke Mode
London meetings, May 2008
Paring down the customer portfolio

FIGURE 3.4. Depiction of PEF's CEO's Use of the Three Modes

Actionable Insight No. 1: Knowing When to Use Which LT Mode: Value, Time, and Power

CEOs routinely face a fundamental question: When should I leave my LT members to work in their own area, and when should I take them away from their area to address organizational issues they are not directly responsible for?

To make it simpler to answer that question, we have leveraged three models from the LT literature (Team, Hub-and-Spoke, and CEO-Adviser) and used the PEF case study as an illustration. That case highlights three important factors to consider: value, time, and power.

FACTOR No. 1: VALUE—DIRECT AND INDIRECT

CEOs can obtain two types of value when they involve LT members in decision making outside their area of responsibility: direct and indirect. *Direct* value comes when an LT member has expertise that is directly relevant to the topic. Involving someone who has no expertise destroys value because they steal airtime from those who do.

Using Team mode often means including LT members who add little direct value. This is an error that Robert sidestepped when he made the following decisions for his April 2008 Marriott offsite:

- Exclude his ten MDs because it would be nearly impossible for them to approach weeding out unprofitable customers with an open mind. "You don't ask turkeys to vote on whether to hold Thanksgiving," Robert told us. Excluding the ten MDs was facilitated by the fact that it was unlikely they would find out about the meeting because they did not work at PEF headquarters.

- Exclude four of his functional leaders because "they didn't have the strategic mind-set the exercise required, nor did they bring knowledge of where the opportunities lay or what our clients needed."

- Include the six functional executives who had the knowledge he needed for the task to be accomplished.

This was a textbook application of CEO-Adviser mode.

Indirect value comes when CEOs involve an LT member because that person will be critical in implementing decisions emerging from the decision-making process. Such involvement increases understanding and buy-in of the decision to be implemented, the keys to alignment. But involving LT members solely for indirect value purposes is a catch-22: it makes implementation easier, but

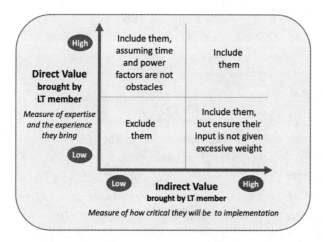

FIGURE 3.5. Using Value to Determine Which LT Members to Involve

it destroys direct value when they have no expertise to contribute, as noted above. Robert weighed this downside when he decided to use Team mode at the December 2007 Venice offsite to develop a plan to address the upcoming storm. The quality of the plan to be developed was, at that time, less important than ensuring understanding and buy-in from all LT members as to the necessity of the plan.

Figure 3.5 summarizes the points made above.

This brings us to the second factor to consider when selecting the most appropriate mode of LT functioning.

FACTOR NO. 2: THE TIME BURDEN

An LT member who is asked to address an issue outside his or her primary area of responsibility—whether in Team or CEO-Adviser mode—has less time to address issues within their area. This is a time-related consideration that strong CEOs never fail to keep in mind.

A second time-related consideration CEOs may overlook is how much of their own time will be swallowed up by Team mode. CEOs often underestimate how much preparation is required if it is to surrender anything of substance.

A last time-related issue is the challenge of gathering an LT in Team mode on short notice, outside of regularly scheduled LT meetings. Because CEOs cannot always wait for these meetings before moving ahead on issues, LTs are obliged to address them in Hub-and-Spoke mode as did PEF's CEO when he convened his ten MDs:

Transforming an organization is all about momentum. After the Marriott off-site, if I had waited until the next formal LT meeting to ask the MDs to weed out their undesirable clients, it would have sent the message it wasn't urgent. I had to call them in for one-on-one meetings or the transformation would have stalled.

While Hub-and-Spoke was the best option available to Robert in his context, many CEOs overcome the short-notice challenge by increasing the frequency of LT meetings when turmoil in their industry requires more frequent alignment. Thus, when the COVID-19 pandemic hit, some of the LTs we had worked with began meeting biweekly, whereas they had previously met monthly. Adjusting meeting frequency because of turbulence in the environment is surprisingly not something many CEOs think about but would do well to consider.

Factor No. 3: Power

As discussed in Chapter 2, CEOs are not all powerful. When they want to introduce change, LT members may form coalitions to resist it. Assuming the resistance is unjustified, CEOs must counter this threat.

To do so, it is often best to first introduce the change in Hub-and-Spoke rather than Team mode for the obvious reason that coalitions form more easily when LT members are gathered. Team mode makes it easier for resisters to identify colleagues susceptible of joining them in opposing the CEO.[18]

Despite the risk of coalition formation, Robert chose Team mode in December 2007 in Venice to plan for a European recession many did not believe would materialize. He was willing to take that risk because he had built his own coalition of supporters beforehand.

However, he did not choose Team mode when it came time to get his MDs to cut their client portfolios. That mode would have been more efficient as this would have permitted Robert to explain the criteria for weeding out nonideal clients only once. On the other hand, the risk his MDs would have coalesced to stall the process would have been greater. For this and the other reasons noted, he invited each MD to meet with him individually in London.

Actionable Insight No. 2: How to Prevent LT Members from Hiding behind the Walls of Their Silo

In this chapter, we have explored three strategies LT members employ to counter the autonomy illusion. These strategies contribute to their LTs getting stuck in Hub-and-Spoke mode. CEOs need to counter these strategies. When LT members use the *rookie strategy* by asking their CEO questions such as, "So, do I have free rein to do what's needed to attain my objectives?," many CEOs respond with something evasive such as, "You have my full support." This is hardly helpful.   CEOs need to coach LT members so that they understand the reality of the LT game and the negotiations with LT colleagues that the game entails. Getting more junior LT members to understand the reality of LT life depicted in Chapter 1 is a good start.

Countering the *task versus true objective strategy* also requires some straight talk from CEOs. Thus, at the beginning of the year, when executives negotiate to be held accountable for tasks (e.g., "Develop a plan to do x") rather than true objectives, CEOs must make sure they are more ambitious. They can do so in Hub-and-Spoke mode (i.e., one-on-one), or they can leverage Team mode. We have seen CEOs do the latter by gathering their LT for objective sharing sessions that see LT members providing each other feedback on their individual objectives. In this way, LT members whose objectives are not true ones receive this feedback from colleagues as well as the CEO.

Finally, we have LT members who use the *leverage-the-CEO strategy*. They avoid running their plans by their LT colleagues by getting their CEO's approval and using that approval like an executive order to get their colleagues to collaborate.

To counter this, CEOs must insist that their LT members socialize their plans with colleagues, especially the colleagues who will be most affected by those plans. CEOs need to check that this socializing has been done and withhold their own support until they have assurances that it has. This is not complicated, yet many CEOs fail to do it. When they fail to do so, they should not be surprised that conflict on their LTs ramps up.

Actionable Insight No. 3: Beware of Relying on Collective Incentives to Bust Silos

When we ask the executives in our programs how they would break down silos, the first solution they often propose is bonuses based on collective performance. Their assumption is that LT members retreat into their silos because their bonuses emphasize individual objectives. In theory, this works. In practice, not so much.

While collective bonus schemes may help, we have yet to see an organization where they chipped away significantly at silos. This is partly because LT members know that their performance in their own area remains the major determinant of rewards and sanctions.[19] Indeed, we can think of no executive who ever got promoted to CEO unless they had knocked it out of the ballpark in their own area first.

But perhaps the more important reason that collective or team-based bonus solutions are not as effective as many think is because LT members generally do not see a clear distinction between what is good for their unit and what is good for the organization. As we saw in Chapter 1, LT members tend to confound their unit's interest and the organization's. They strongly believe that doing what is best for their unit also means doing what's best for their organization.

> *LT members generally do not see a clear distinction between what is good for their unit and what is good for the organization.*

This is not to say that we would advise organizations not to institute collective bonus schemes, which can serve many useful purposes. But you must not think they are the panacea many assume them to be.

Actionable Insight No. 4: CEOs Must Master Three Bridging Roles

It is hardly news that LT members must spend much of their time toiling away with their own teams within silos, disconnected from their peers. However, leave them disconnected in this way for too long and the result is inevitably misalignment and destructive conflict.

Obliging LT members to reconnect in Team mode with meetings and offsites is one solution. But executives cannot spend all their time huddling together. Thus, in between meetings and offsites, it is up to the CEO to bridge the gaps between them.

Despite how obvious this is, it is surprising that so little leadership literature focuses on the CEO's three bridging roles: conflict pre-emptor, mediator, and disseminator.[20]

BRIDGING ROLE NO. 1: CONFLICT PRE-EMPTOR

When LT members devise their plans within their silos, they may not realize that those plans may clash with those of their colleagues. Because CEOs sit at the hub of the network formed by their LT members, they need to anticipate these clashes and so pre-empt them.

Given that LT members are not often forthcoming with their CEOs about all they are doing, for reasons we explored in Chapters 1 and 2, this provides another good reason for CEOs to engage in the monitoring activities we described at the end of Chapter 2. After all, CEOs can pre-empt conflicts between two LT members only if they have in-depth knowledge of what each of them is planning to do.

BRIDGING ROLE NO. 2: MEDIATOR

CEOs are not always able to pre-empt conflicts between LT colleagues. When conflicts do erupt and the executives involved cannot resolve the conflict themselves, CEOs must step in to mediate. Here again, the monitoring activities we discussed at the end of Chapter 2 come in handy because power dynamics may prevent clashing LT members from sharing the existence of their conflict with their CEO. Weaker LT members avoid doing so for fear of retribution from their more powerful colleague, while the latter may be concerned they will not come out on top if the CEO gets involved.

Once CEOs get wind of a conflict between members of their team, many are reticent to play the mediator role. They prefer to remain on the sidelines, possibly inspired by the famous 1999 *Harvard Business Review* article "Who's Got the Monkey?,"[21] which warned leaders against taking on their subordinates' problems.

Such a laissez-faire approach may be appropriate in some instances, but not always, as the CEO of a financial services company discovered when he let a quarrel between his two most senior C-suite members fester for months. Each was leading a major project, and their competition for resources led them to raid other departments, eventually putting a strain on operations. When the dispute was brought to the CEO's attention, he declined to intercede and said, "They will eventually hit a wall and realize they need to compromise." Unfortunately for this CEO, they never did, and this cost him his job when one of the projects went off the rails.

Deciding when to intervene is more art than science. However, when two of a CEO's key LT members are fighting, especially over scarce resources, we are not alone in warning CEOs they should not imagine things will magically get better.[22] They rarely do because the longer a dispute lasts, the more personal it will become.

Perhaps another reason some CEOs do not intervene as rapidly as they should is that they lack confidence in their mediation competency. A strong mediator masters many skills, including that of cultural translator: helping parties understand each other's perspective and so facilitate compromise.[23] But such skills do not come naturally to everyone. CEOs with no formal mediation

training might consider seeking coaching in this area as we expect the importance of mediator skills to become even more acute as LTs grow.[24]

BRIDGING ROLE NO. 3: DISSEMINATOR

The third bridging role CEOs must learn to master—the disseminator role—
is one that sees leaders pass privileged information directly to their subordinates when the latter lack easy contact with one another, a common occurrence
when LT members are working within their silos.

The following examples represent two instances in which this disseminator
role was critical:

- *Best-practice dissemination.* When the CEO of a European company was informed by an LT member heading an eastern European business unit that she
  was undertaking an exercise to reduce workplace accidents, he was able to
  inform her that one of her LT colleagues in western Europe had successfully
  completed a similar exercise a few years earlier. The CEO thus heartily encouraged them to collaborate, something the western European LT member
  had little incentive to do without an invitation from above given the pressure
  to deliver results in his own business. When an organization does not have
  someone in charge of knowledge management, and even when they do, CEOs
  who master this best practice disseminator role can add tremendous value to
  their organization.

- *Client intelligence dissemination.* In large organizations, and some smaller
  ones, it is common for an LT member to possess information about a client
  that would be critical for a colleague to have. It also happens that two colleagues are unaware that both are pursuing the same client.

  We saw this happen in another European multinational whose country leader
  in Germany was preparing to meet a client from a global key account in Munich.
  When she informed us of this, we assumed she knew that her LT colleague from
  France had met representatives of the very same client organization the week before
  to discuss the very same services. She did not. In organizations such as this one,
  which did not possess customer relationship management (CRM) software, the
  CEO's client intelligence dissemination role is critical, just as it is for companies
  that do have CRM software but whose sales force fails to use it.

Of course, CEOs who take on full responsibility for bridging the gap between
disconnected LT members must be careful. Indeed, if they assume full responsibility for bridging, their LT members will be quite content to remain behind

their silos. The bridging responsibility must be shared, and CEOs must make this clear by clarifying that it is part of the responsibility that comes with being named to the LT.

The exact scope of that responsibility is the topic of Chapter 4.

The Chapter in a Nutshell

Three LT Operating Modes

- The management literature presents three LT operating models: Hub-and-Spoke, Team, and CEO-Adviser.

- The term *model* creates the impression that LT functioning is static, and that CEOs must provide a once-and-for-all answer to the question, "Which LT operating *model* should I choose?"

- In practice, LT functioning is far from static. It is more useful to view the three models as modes that LTs move in and out of. Therefore, the better question for CEOs is: "When should I use each *mode?*"

Who Is Responsible for LTs Getting Stuck in Hub-and-Spoke Mode and Silo Thickening?

- The autonomy illusion: LT members are 100 percent accountable for their unit objectives but do not possess 100 percent autonomy to achieve them. To do so, they must negotiate with their LT colleagues.

- To enable them to function despite the autonomy illusion, executives employ three strategies that get their LT stuck in Hub-and-Spoke mode: the rookie strategy, the task versus true objective strategy, and the leverage-the-CEO strategy

- When CEOs let their LT members get away with these strategies, the walls of their silos thicken.

- Recognizing these strategies is the first step to countering them.

Switching In and Out of Hub-and-Spoke Mode: The Pan-European Finance Case

- PEF CEO Robert orchestrated a very difficult organizational transformation during the challenging and uncertain period of the 2008 financial crisis.

- His approach offers a prime example of how to leverage the three LT operating modes over a period of months to bring about needed change despite LT member resistance.

Summary of Actionable Insights

1. Know when to use each of the three modes. Your criteria are value, time, and power.

2. Prevent LT members from hiding behind their silo walls by countering each of the three strategies they use:

   - *Rookie strategy:* Coach them to understand the reality of the LT game.

   - *Task versus true objective strategy:* Make sure executives are sufficiently ambitious using hub-and-spoke or team mode.

   - *Leverage the CEO strategy:* Insist that LT members socialize their plans with colleagues and verify they do it.

3. Beware of relying too heavily on collective bonus schemes. They are not the panacea many think they are.

4. Master the three bridging roles: preemptor, mediator, and disseminator. All three require that you become a master monitor.

PART II

SYSTEMATICALLY IMPROVING
YOUR LEADERSHIP TEAM'S
EFFECTIVENESS

WHO REALLY SITS ON YOUR LEADERSHIP TEAM, AND WHAT IS ITS ROLE?

Quick exercise: On the lines below, jot down the first name of all the LT members of your organization. Include the CEO or leader. Include your own name if you are an LT member.

_____ _____ _____ _____

_____ _____ _____ _____

_____ _____ _____ _____

_____ _____ _____ _____

_____ _____ _____ _____

Questions:

Did you hesitate, even for a moment, to include any one of the names you listed above? (Circle one.)

- YES

- NO

Is there a name you initially considered putting on the list but eventually omitted? (Circle one.)

- YES

- NO

In your opinion, what are the odds that each person you listed would provide the very same list as you did? Express your answer as a percentage.

——— percent

We will return to your answers shortly.

Over twenty years ago, we were awarded a first LT coaching mandate. The kickoff was a team offsite. Two weeks before the event, we asked the CEO if he could provide his LT members' emails so we could send them details about the session. He said no. When we asked why, he answered, "Because I haven't decided who to invite yet." We were, to say the least, surprised.

The next day, he sent us ten email addresses. They belonged to the executives who attended his weekly LT meetings. And so, we thought nothing more of it until we began working with a second CEO a few months later. She also wanted us to facilitate an offsite with her LT. When we asked how many would attend, she answered: "I don't know yet. I'll get back to you."

When a similar scenario was replayed shortly after with a third CEO, we were genuinely puzzled. How could three experienced CEOs hesitate when asked to name the members of their LT?

We soon discovered others had had comparable experiences. In a study involving the executives of 120 big and small businesses around the world, team scholars Wageman and Hackman asked a similar question to the one we posed at the start of this chapter: How many people sit on your LT?[1] The results were unexpected. In only 11 of the 120 cases did all LT members agree on the size of their own team.[2] That is a mere 9 percent.

What is ironic is that in the remaining 109 teams—the ones where there was no consensus among members regarding their own team's size—most executives nevertheless strongly agreed with the statement, "Team membership is quite clear—everybody knows exactly who is and who is not on this team."[3]

In hindsight, these results are not as surprising as they appear.[4] This is because you might interpret the question, "Who are the members of my organization's LT?" quite differently—for example:

- You might take it to mean, "Who attends the regular meeting of the firm's senior managers?"

- You could also interpret it to mean, "Who are the *real* decision makers in this organization?"

- If you are legally inclined, you might think you are being asked, "Which executives have legal authority to act on behalf of the company?"

Each of these questions can point to a different group of people.

Now you may be thinking, *All this is well and fine, but why should I care?*

To be honest, many of you might not need to. We explore the question of who sits on your LT only because we need to be clear about this before addressing what this group of executives should be doing together, that is, its role.

But you might not care about your LT's role, and justifiably so. You should care about it only if your LT is misaligned, is unable to put tough topics on the table, or suffers from a lack of collaboration because all three of these issues persist when executives misunderstand their role as LT members.

If none of these issues plague your LT—in other words, if your LT works fine—then we invite you to move on to Chapter 5. Otherwise read on because we cover the following in the four sections of this chapter:

- The mystery of who sits on an LT and why it matters.

- The LT's first critical role: strategic decision making. You will read about three misconceptions and the specific dysfunctionalities they cause in many organizations, and probably your own.

- The LT's second critical role: alignment. We highlight the distinction between vertical and horizontal alignment that when overlooked, contributes to excessive silofication.

- Actionable insights to help your LT play its decision-making and alignment roles much more effectively.

The Mystery Behind Who Sits on Your LT and What They Are Meant to Do

"Leadership team" and equivalent expressions (e.g., top management team, executive team) can be interpreted differently. Lest you believe this is merely a theoretical issue, it is not, as demonstrated by the exchange we had a few years ago with the CEO of an industrial company's subsidiary when it was created.

Its CEO told us she wanted help in setting up her LT in time to define the plan for her organization's expansion. What profiles would she need? What would be her team's optimal size? These were questions she wanted us to help her with before she met with her board four months later.

As a first step, she explained, her HR director, Eric, would reach out to us. The next day, he did. After exchanging niceties, he asked us with a hint of embarrassment, "So, if I've understood correctly, you've been hired to help us set up our leadership team."

"Yes, that's right," we replied.

"Well, I'm confused," Eric said, "because ... well ... we already have one."

We were momentarily as confused as he was, so we simply asked, "Who sits on it?" He proceeded to list the names of the CEO's eight direct reports, including his own. He added: "We meet every Wednesday at 2:00 p.m. for two hours."

After the call, we contacted the CEO. She confirmed that her eight direct reports did meet every Wednesday at 2:00 p.m.; however, she did not consider this to be her LT. Furthermore, she expressed surprise that her HR director and the others did! She pointed to her organization's website where, under the tab "Executive Team," only two names appeared: her own and that of her VP of corporate affairs.

Be that as it may, she understood that if her direct reports *thought* they were LT members it would make it more challenging for her to formally set up the LT she wanted. If she did not include all eight of her direct reports, those she excluded would complain they had been "demoted." And while she was not afraid of this, she had to consider what impact this could have on the organization. For example, if she excluded her HR director, could this demotivate him and his HR team who were playing a crucial role in recruiting the talent the organization desperately needed? Would others in the organization stop giving HR initiatives their full support when they found out that HR was not a sufficiently important function to warrant being represented on the LT?

She was right to have this last concern because LT membership confers status and power that enable executives to get things done. This is, no doubt, why her direct reports were keen to have others perceive their Wednesday 2:00 p.m. meeting as an LT meeting, and not simply a coordination meeting, which is what the CEO considered it.

As this example illustrates, how an organization's LT is defined and who are its members are not mundane issues. We therefore set out the different approaches to defining a leadership team and why we encourage you to adopt only one of them.

How Do You Determine Who Sits on Your LT?

When it comes to determining which executives sit on an organization's LT, LT writers and advisers fall into one of four groups (spoiler alert: we fall into group 4).

- Group 1: Those who provide no explicit definition of "leadership team"[5] or who use criteria that are sufficiently **ambiguous** that two people might interpret them differently—for example, "The top management team of a company consists of the senior and highest executives who are responsible for directing the company."[6]

- Group 2: Those who define LTs "**objectively.**" They use criteria that leave little room for interpretation, such as "the five highest paid executives in an organization" or "all executives with a title higher than or equal to VP."[7] Although this approach is an improvement on the first, it often excludes influential players such as a CEO's chief of staff who, in some organizations we work with, is the most powerful person next to the CEO. It may also exclude executives who are not identified as LT members on the company's website but attend every LT meeting and thus wield great influence.

- Group 3: Those who define an LT "**subjectively.**" This entails asking someone—typically the CEO—who they believe to be LT members.[8] We call this the **"real LT"** approach because that is often how CEOs refer to the executives they name. This enables them to distinguish them from those who meet regularly or those officially identified as LT members on their website.

The issues with the "real LT" approach are twofold. The first is that CEOs do not always want to share who the members of their "real LT" are, much like parents hesitate to name their favorite children. When CEOs do share, they often do not want you repeating the names to anyone, including to the executives involved. As a result, they are unsure if they belong to the "real LT." It then goes without saying that this group never meets formally, or even informally, unless by chance. Because "real LT" members never actually do anything together officially, it may be no coincidence that some using the subjective approach to defining LTs conclude that LTs are not true teams.

The second issue is that "real LTs" are not stable. By this, we mean that when a CEO did share with us the names of their "real LT," the names changed when they shared them again later. This change seemed to be connected to the issue that was top of mind for them at the time. Thus, for example, if a CEO was worried about staff shortages, their human resources VP inevitably made the list. If the worry was declining sales, the human resources VP often did not.

This may explain why some conclude that an organization has many LTs.

However, this conclusion has more to do with the approach used to define an LT than any on-the-ground reality.

- Group 4: Because of the problems associated with the above three approaches and the confusion surrounding the term *leadership team* more generally, we employ a fourth approach to identify an LT's members.[9] We label it the "meeting" approach simply because it defines an organization's LT as *the group of executives that meets formally with the CEO on a regular basis.*

> LT defined: The group of executives that meets formally with the CEO on a regular basis.

We use this last approach first because it is objective and simple to apply: an executive who regularly attends LT meetings is considered an LT member, whether he or she officially has that status or not. Second, when a CEO reaches out to us to improve the effectiveness of their LT, this is the group of executives they want help with, regardless of who their website identifies as the LT and who these CEOs might call their "real LT." We thus take for granted that "real LTs," if they truly exist, work just fine.

Having established what "leadership team" we are talking about we can now turn to the question: What role should it play?

Indeed, one cannot determine if an LT is effective, let alone increase its effectiveness, if we do not know what it should be doing. Those who have little contact with LTs imagine this is a straightforward task. That is not always the case, as we shall see.

If You Can Define Your LT's Role Precisely, You Are in the Minority

Most CEOs agree that a team needs a clear role, which is what distinguishes it from a mere group. Nevertheless, when we ask CEOs to specify their LT's role, they find it challenging. Here again, the experience of Wageman and Hackman mirrors our own. They write:

> Our data show that many chief executives either leave team purposes unspecified or loosely define them, as, for example, "Providing the leadership to accomplish the strategy."[10]

When we have asked CEOs what their LT does, we have heard, "My LT is there to improve company performance" or "My LT's role is the company mission."

But as Jon Katzenbach, author of the best-selling book *Teams at the Top* has noted, such statements rarely provide adequate focus or accountability for a real team effort.[11]

In the next two sections we address two critical roles your LT needs to master: supporting strategic decision making and maintaining alignment.

The LT's Strategic Decision-Making Role and Three Misconceptions about It You Need to Debunk

There is no shortage of LT roles proposed by theorists. We have identified dozens, from problem solving and optimizing resource allocation, to supporting CEO succession. One reason for such a lengthy list is that those writing about LTs do not always distinguish the roles LTs *could* play in an ideal world from the roles LTs *must* play in practice. Our interest is solely the latter. This is where you need to start if you want to fix your LT.

The one role that elicits the widest consensus is strategic decision making. That this should be an LT's role has been widely assumed by researchers for some time.[12] Nevertheless, few bother to define what it means concretely. As a result, three misconceptions about LT decision making are common:

1   All LT members must participate in all strategic decision making.

2.   LT members must be held accountable for strategic decisions.

3.   LT meetings are where strategic decisions get taken.

These are the source of many LT dysfunctionalities, and debunking them may be one of the quickest ways to improve your LT's effectiveness. Next, we give you ammunition to do just that.

Misconception No. 1: All LT Members Must Participate in All Strategic Decisions

When people say that an LT's role is strategic decision making, very few add: "*All* LT members must participate in *all* strategic decisions." Nevertheless, this misconception is promoted implicitly by LT members, CEOs, and team theorists alike.

LT members do so because they wish to be perceived as decision makers, which implies they are resource controllers, which solidifies their power and status, two things many look for when they seek LT membership.[13] Thus, LT members have every interest in perpetuating the misconception that they participate in all strategic decisions.

They do this notably by expressing righteous indignation whenever they walk into an LT meeting and discover that a decision has been made without them. In doing so, they send the message that it was their *right* to be involved. Later, when speaking to subordinates, they will feign to have been aware of the decision all along to maintain the appearance of being a "decider."

CEOs also make efforts to maintain the illusion that decision making is an all-LT affair. They do so, for example, whenever they give advanced warning to LT members that an important decision will be announced to all staff. In this way, LT members can maintain the pretense that they were involved. Another example is when CEOs insist on saying "*We* decided" or otherwise refer to a decision as a "team decision."

To be clear, we are not condemning or condoning these CEO practices, merely noting how they sustain the misconception that strategic decision making is an all-LT affair.

Finally, *team theorists* perpetuate the misconception that LT members should participate in all decisions when they recommend that an LT's size not exceed the optimal size for decision making.[14] In the literature, two arguments emerge to justify why CEOs should involve their LT members in strategic decision making: it improves decision quality, and it supports decision implementation. We present these arguments to help CEOs make it clear to their LT members when they may be included in a strategic decision-making process and when they may be excluded, and so dispel the misconception that LT membership confers a right to participate in every strategic decision.

Before we move on, it is worth clarifying that a strategic decision may originate with the CEO, but it can also originate with an LT member. Indeed, a decision is not strategic because of the person who initiates it[15] but because of its relevance to organizational success or competitiveness.

ARGUMENT 1: DECISION QUALITY IS IMPROVED BY INVOLVING SOME LT MEMBERS BUT RARELY ALL OF THEM

It is commonly accepted that decision-making responsibility should not reside with CEOs alone because they do not possess all the expertise required to make quality decisions in complex environments.[16] Many assume this means strategic decision-making responsibility must shift from the CEO to the entire LT. This is a faulty leap in logic.

While it is clear CEOs should rarely make decisions alone, it does not follow that they should involve all LT members as a rule. In fact, involving all LT members in every strategic decision has a negative impact on decision quality for three reasons.

- The first reason is that not all LT members have relevant expertise to contribute to every decision. Involving those with little or no relevant expertise decreases decision quality because they take up airtime from those who do. Furthermore, we notice that the social pressure to include the nonexperts' input, no matter how poor, further dilutes decision quality. Excluding LT members who bring little expertise to the table frees up time to involve experts outside the LT, whether they are lower down in their organization or outside the organization, such as board members whose advice may be just as prized as that of insiders.[17]

- The second reason why involving all LT members in every decision is an error is the LT member biases discussed in Chapter 1. When LT members cannot put their biases aside, CEOs are justified in excluding them from a decision-making process. We presented an example of this in the Pan-European Financial case study in Chapter 3. Another example comes from an LT discussion we witnessed a few years ago. The purpose of the discussion was to decide the best date to launch a staff consultation process. One LT member—Francis—was opposed to the consultation because he did not want his own team consulted, fearing some of their feedback would reflect poorly on his leadership. As Francis's colleagues proposed dates, he raised objections to each one. It soon became obvious he wanted to stall the process. The CEO decided to take the discussion offline, and the launch date was later decided without Francis in the room.

- The final reason is that "the more the better" is not an adage that applies to decision making. Adding players increases the potential for conflict and makes consensus more difficult to achieve.[18] This can harm a team's confidence in its own effectiveness and, as we have observed numerous times, staff's confidence in their organization's leadership decreases when rumors of the conflict filter down.

ARGUMENT 2: PARTICIPATION IN DECISION MAKING SUPPORTS THE ALIGNMENT OF DECISION IMPLEMENTERS

If the previous discussion on decision quality explains why all LT members should not assume they have a right to be involved in every strategic decision, remember that decision quality is not the only goal CEOs seek when involving LT members. Alignment, a central theme in the field of strategic management and in this book, is another.[19]

The reasoning is simple: the best decision does little good if the LT members who must implement it are not aligned behind it—in other words, if they do not have a thorough understanding of the rationale behind the decision they must implement and/or they lack the conviction that the decision is a good one and thus are not **committed** to implementing it.[20]

Involving implementers contributes to understanding and commitment[21] if their involvement is genuinely sought and the process is deemed fair.[22] When these conditions are met, the oft-repeated adage "Alone you go faster, together we go further," applies.

But does this alignment then justify that all LT members participate in all decisions? No, because not all LT members will be deeply involved in implementing every strategic decision. For example, a health and safety VP will rarely have a central role in implementing a decision to target a given client segment. Thus, a CEO would be right to exclude that person from the process.

CEOs are also justified in excluding an LT member who has more urgent issues to attend to inside their area of responsibility. For example, it would be foolish for a CEO to include the legal VP in deciding on a new ad campaign if that took him or her away from defending the company against a major lawsuit.

To summarize, an LT's role includes strategic decision making. This implies that CEOs should involve LT members in making strategic decisions because it promotes decision quality and alignment. However, this should not be interpreted to mean that all LT members have a right to participate in every strategic decision.

When LT members believe they have such a right, as many do, it leads to the following dysfunctionalities:

- CEOs face pressure to involve LT members who have little expertise to contribute. As a result, the decision that emerges is suboptimal or delayed, and often both.

- When LT members believe they should have been included in a decision-making process but were not, they may react angrily, obliging CEOs to spend precious time soothing bruised egos.

- More precious time is wasted when disgruntled executives demand that their CEOs clarify their decision-making process. In our experience, these executives are not truly seeking clarity but an unrealistic guarantee they will not be excluded again.

Misconception No. 2: LT Members Are Accountable for All Strategic Decisions

The second misconception stemming from an LT's strategic decision-making role is that LT members should be held accountable for all strategic decisions. However, if involving all members in all strategic decisions makes little sense, as we have noted, it makes even less sense to hold them accountable for all such decisions. Doing so would be to hold them accountable for decisions they had no voice in making, and even ones they were opposed to. That would hardly be fair, which is what executives tell us.

In this, they receive support from Elliott Jaques. Best known for being among the first to introduce the concept of organizational culture, Jaques criticizes those who believe in LT accountability because, in practice, it equates to denying a CEO's hierarchical right to have the final word.[23] Indeed, if one accepts that CEOs have the final word—or, said differently, that an LT is not a democracy with majority rule—then, logically, accountability stays with the CEO.[24]

> ### Team Accountability versus Team Solidarity
>
> We have yet to meet a CEO who does not believe they are solely accountable for their organization's strategic decisions. Yet they muddy the waters when they insist these decisions are "team decisions." Many LT members interpret this to mean their CEO is shifting accountability to the team, which encourages them to fight for the right to be involved in every decision.
>
> CEOs should thus be careful. When they insist a decision is a "team decision," their goal is not to shift accountability to the team but to send the message that LT members must show team solidarity. In other words, LT members must support decisions outside the LT meeting room, whether they agree with them or not. It does not mean the CEO will make them suffer consequences if that decision turns out to be misguided.
>
> When LT solidarity is absent, staff receive mixed signals, which results in destructive organizational politics and staff frustration. It also sends the message that teamwork is not valued. When LTs present a united front, the result is better goal alignment across the organization.

And this is certainly what many CEOs themselves believe.[25] As one told us: "You can talk about team accountability all you want. But if anyone in this organization screws up, the only person the board is going to call onto the carpet is me" (see the "Team Accountability versus Team Solidarity" box).[26]

But this does not mean CEOs do not want team solidarity, which is quite different from team accountability.

Misconception No. 3: LT Meetings Are Where Strategic Decisions Are Taken

The last misconception associated with the LT's strategic decision-making role is that strategic decisions get taken in LT meetings. Notice we say *get taken*, and not *made*, a distinction introduced in previous work done with INSEAD professor Charles Galunic.[27] Here is what we mean:

- Decision *making* refers to the process leading up to a decision.

- Decision *taking* refers to the moment the choice is finalized, or what some have called "a specific commitment to action (usually a commitment of resources)."[28]

While this distinction may give language purists fits, it helps new LT members understand what they should, and should not, expect when they join an LT.

One thing team members should not expect is for every strategic decisions to be taken before their eyes in LT meetings.[29] Although it happens from time to time (e.g., in times of crisis or when a decision is simply being ratified (see the "The Illusion of Inclusion and the Wedding Question" box), decision taking in LT meetings is not as common as some believe for reasons tied to the process of strategic decision making:

- This process is far from the linear, rational affair involving a handful of ac-tors, as depicted in case studies. Anyone who has been involved in a decision to restructure a business, launch a new product, or even acquire enterprise system software understands this only too well.

- The process is more a "groping, cyclical" one that involves multiple actors, both inside and outside the LT, and typically unfolds over weeks, months, or even longer.[30]

To expect that a decision will emerge from such a lengthy, messy process pre-cisely on the day an LT meeting is scheduled is at best naive. It is just as naive to expect a CEO to delay making a critical decision for days or weeks to ensure it is taken during an LT meeting. This explains why so many strategic decisions get taken prior to LT meetings.

The Pan-European Finance case in Chapter 3 provides an example of a decision taken well before an LT meeting. As you may recall, the case involved the decision PEF made to focus on a narrow range of profitable clients. The process leading up to this decision spanned months, from 2007 to 2008. In the end, the final decision was taken three weeks before the next scheduled LT meeting, because, as Robert, the CEO, told us, "Anybody who thinks we should have waited three weeks to finalize that decision needs to learn a little something about momentum. We had no time to waste, and, besides, waiting would have killed the initiative."

Furthermore, even if a decision can be taken during an LT meeting, that does not mean it should be. CEOs often will not announce a decision seconds after LT members have had a heated debate, just as a judge does not render judgment in court the moment lawyers have finished closing arguments. Otherwise, it would send the message that their mind was already made up.

Finally, as many readers may have experienced, a CEO who

The Illusion of Inclusion and the Wedding Question

The illusion of inclusion refers to the pretense of asking LT members for feedback on an idea, strategy, or plan but with little intention of taking their feedback into account. LT members often accuse CEOs of such manipulation when a topic on the LT agenda is labeled "For decision" but they suspect the decision has already been taken.

While some CEOs do engage in such manipulation, we tell our executives not to jump to conclusions. It may be a "wedding question" scenario in which the CEO is all but certain about a decision yet wants to be sure nothing has been overlooked. In such cases, CEOs are much like wedding officiants who ask, "Does anyone show just cause why this couple cannot lawfully be joined together in matrimony?" The question is sincere, but it is best not to raise your hand if you merely want to point out that one of the soon-to-be spouses could have done better. You would only speak up if you have something truly material to add.

Such wedding questions make sure nothing has been overlooked and contribute to alignment by offering an opportunity to all LT members to become aware of the decision and to ask clarification questions. This, in turn, helps them explain the decision to staff when they cascade it.

takes a decision on the spot runs the risk of relaunching the debate or setting off those who feel they "lost" the argument, neither of which bodes well for the rest of the meeting. Wise CEOs we have observed often defer announcing a difficult decision to let everyone cool down and reach out to the "losers" in Hub-and-Spoke mode afterward to help them understand the rationale behind the decision.

Nevertheless, because some people persist in believing all strategic decisions should be taken during LT meetings, CEOs need to debunk this misconception because it encourages LT members to turn every meeting topic into a "for decision" item, even when a decision is not ripe for taking.

And while we certainly condemn LT agendas packed thoughtlessly with "for information" items, the expectation that complex strategic decisions can be taken by a dozen executives within the typical twenty- to thirty-minute time frame does more harm than good because it leads to these unfortunate results:

- *A ramping up of conflict.* The pressure to take a decision within a narrow time slot motivates the topic owner to suppress discussion, notably though use of "the formula" described in Chapter 3. If, by chance, there is a discussion, time pressure means that other LT members focus on delivering their points rather than listening to colleagues. Predictably, conflict is ramped up.

- *A negative impact on team potency.* Team potency is a measure of the positive beliefs a team has about its effectiveness[31] and has an impact on team performance.[32] LT potency is harmed each time a topic that is not ripe for decision taking is nonetheless put on the agenda "for decision." Unable to finalize the decision in the allotted time, the LT runs overtime, which prevents remaining agenda items from being addressed. The failure and frustration that result reduce the team's confidence they can address future issues as a team.

For those looking for strategies to avoid these outcomes, we direct you to Chapter 6.

Recap: LT's Role in Decision Making and Resulting
Accountability for LT Members

In this section, we discussed LT's role in strategic decision making and identified three misconceptions associated with this role that CEOs need to debunk to avoid common dysfunctionalities. We recap the ground covered here.

A Strategic Decision Is Not Always
Initiated by the CEO

It can also be initiated by LT members acting within their area of responsibility.

PARTICIPATION IN LT DECISION MAKING: THREE PRINCIPLES

An LT's role in strategic decision making does not mean that all team members must be involved in every decision. It does mean that anyone initiating a strategic decision must involve at least some LT colleagues. To determine which ones and to what extent, three principles must be considered:

- *Decision quality.* LT members who have relevant expertise to contribute should be involved. Those without expertise should be excluded unless there are reasons other than decision quality to involve them.

- *Alignment.* Anyone critical to implementing the decision should be involved because it will help them understand the decision and be committed to it, even if they lack expertise. The more central an LT member is to the implementation of a decision, the greater that person's involvement should be.

- *Team solidarity.* This third reason to involve LT members stems from these members' responsibility to cascade decisions. Involvement strengthens their grasp of the decision rationale, although such involvement need not be very intense.

LT members whose involvement in decision making is dictated by these three principles might nevertheless be excluded if, for instance,

- There is no time to involve them (as in a crisis period).

- They have insurmountable biases, as illustrated in the examples we gave earlier; or

- The CEO judges they have more pressing matters to attend to within their own area.

The decision to exclude an LT member from a decision-making process is the CEO's alone.

DECISION MAKING VERSUS DECISION TAKING

Decision *making* refers to the process leading up to a decision. Decision *taking* refers to the moment a choice is finalized.

While many LT members can be involved in making a decision, the entire LT rarely takes one. *Decisions are taken by those who are ultimately accountable for the decision*: the LT member under whose purview the decision falls and, ultimately, the CEO.

It is unrealistic to expect all strategic decisions to be taken during LT meetings. Knowing this, savvy LT members who wish to influence a decision must never wait for it to be posted on an LT meeting's agenda. They should constantly network with colleagues to find out what decisions are in the making.

ACCOUNTABILITY FOR STRATEGIC DECISIONS
An entire LT cannot be accountable for a strategic decision. But some CEOs create confusion about this when they insist that a decision was a "team decision." Accountability ultimately resides with the CEO who, in turn, holds accountable the LT member under whose purview it falls. That accountability implies involving their LT colleagues in accordance with the three principles of decision quality, alignment, and solidarity. Much of the lack of collaboration on LTs stems from CEOs who turn a blind eye when LT members fail to seek their colleagues' input.

CASCADING AND TEAM SOLIDARITY
LT members are responsible for cascading decisions and supporting them, even ones they were not involved in making or ones they disagree with. This is the principle of team solidarity that is so important to the LT's decision-making role.

This concludes our discussion of strategic decision making, the first of two critical LT roles. We now move to the second: maintaining alignment.

The Second Major LT Role: Maintaining Organizational Alignment

Less attention is given in the literature to the LT's role in maintaining alignment, which may explain why so few LTs we encounter do this well, as witnessed by the many CEOs who come to us with misalignment problems.

To understand how LTs should manage alignment, CEOs who have an LT can learn lessons from CEOs who did not have this team but decided to create one. We tell the tale of one such CEO, Patricia, and so introduce the two types of alignment all CEOs need to worry about: vertical and horizontal.

How LTs Contribute to the Vertical Alignment of LT Members and Those Below

Patricia first shared with us why she decided to create her LT during a conference we attended as guest speakers. Time pressure, she explained, had been the main consideration.

She was the CEO of a door and window manufacturer (which we refer to as D&W), a company that had experienced a tremendous growth spurt after winning a large contract, making it the preferred supplier of a local construction contractor.

The additional work, however, meant that Patricia had less time to communicate with staff to ensure their actions aligned with her vision and strategy. Such alignment of staff with the organization's vision and strategic priorities is commonly referred to as *vertical alignment*.[33]

Mistakes were piling up. For example, one newly hired manager negotiated the purchase of a huge supply of low-quality raw materials that would last them for months, thinking the cost saving would please Patricia. He could not have been more wrong. Patricia's philosophy was never to scrimp on the materials that went into D&W products or to tie up working capital in inventory.

In the past, Patricia had made sure staff were vertically aligned by holding regular, one-on-one meetings characteristic of the Hub-and-Spoke mode discussed in Chapter 3. She also made a point of walking by the office espresso machine frequently to chat with staff informally. But as her staff grew, it became more difficult to reach out to everyone in this manner.

Patricia's initial solution was to call ad hoc meetings whenever she had important information to share. In this way, she said, "I avoided having to repeat myself a hundred times." But she soon realized that she had something to share every week and trying to schedule a time where all were free was proving to be a headache. She thus instituted what she called an "information dump" with her senior managers every Monday at 9:00 a.m. These weekly meetings would eventually become her official LT meetings.

The evolution Patricia described to us is depicted in Figure 4.1 (albeit in a very simplified form) and illustrates why many CEOs set up an LT when they find it increasingly difficult to vertically align staff using Hub-and-Spoke mode.

In phase 1, the organization is small. Although staff meetings are called when there is important news, most vertical alignment is achieved in Hub-and-Spoke mode, in one-on-one meetings between the CEO and direct reports (DRs), some of them scheduled, many of them serendipitous. In this phase, accountability for vertical alignment falls entirely on the CEO's shoulders.

In phase 2, the organization has grown, but vertical alignment continues to be done using the one-on-one meetings characteristic of Hub-and-Spoke mode.

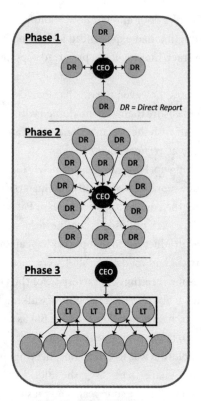

FIGURE 4.1. Why Growth Makes an LT Indispensable for Vertical Alignment

This now puts the CEO under intense time pressure because of the number of people who must be vertically aligned.

In phase 3, to relieve this pressure, the CEO sets up regular, formal meetings. Only a select few senior leaders are invited because the organization has become too large for all staff to attend. At times, this group is immediately designated as the "leadership team," but not always because some CEOs are concerned that those invited might let their status as LT members go to their head or that it might create a hierarchy that runs counter to the company's "family" culture.

Nevertheless, these meetings are the genesis of the LT and offer CEOs a new forum in which to promote vertical alignment in Team mode. The responsibility for vertical alignment is now a shared one between the CEO and the newly appointed LT members who are expected to cascade messages to their staff. Of course, LT members do not always take their cascading responsibility seriously, notably because CEOs do not bother to check if they do. This problem also plagues organizations that have had an LT for years.

Team mode does not replace Hub-and-Spoke mode entirely because CEOs continue to vertically align executives and staff when they meet with them one-on-one. In other words, Team mode and Hub-and-Spoke mode are complementary modes for vertical alignment.

Horizontal Alignment between LT Members: Avoiding
Coordination Bottlenecks and Conflict

Another reason Patricia wanted to create an LT was to stem the flow of direct reports lining up outside her office to complain about colleagues who were interfering with their work or not collaborating with them to achieve their objectives. Patricia joked that her title had become CMO (chief mediation officer) rather than CEO.

The source of Patricia's problem was mathematical. As Figure 4.2 illustrates, linear staff growth leads to an exponential increase in the number of duos who can clash and of the conflicts a CEO must mediate. In Figure 4.2, if n is the number of people reporting to a CEO, the number of duos who can potentially clash is $n (n - 1)/2$. A CEO with just two direct reports has only one duo who can potentially clash. With four direct reports, the number of duos who can clash climbs to six. With five direct reports, clashing duos jump to ten. A CEO with ten direct reports must live with forty-five potentially clashing duos!

When an organization is small, CEOs prevent such clashes by coordinating

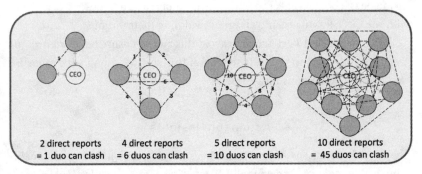

2 direct reports = 1 duo can clash	4 direct reports = 6 duos can clash	5 direct reports = 10 duos can clash	10 direct reports = 45 duos can clash

FIGURE 4.2. Why Growth Makes Horizontal Alignment Challenging for CEOs

activities from their position at the center (or hub) of the organization. Such coordination across people, functions, or units is called *horizontal alignment*, which ensures that how LT members achieve their individual objectives does not interfere with the efforts of LT colleagues to achieve their own. Horizontal alignment produces decision coherence and maximizes synergies.[34]

However, when organizations achieve a certain size, the burden of horizontal alignment in Hub-and-Spoke mode becomes too heavy for a CEO to bear alone because they can no longer do the three things required for horizontal alignment:

1. Keep up to speed on all direct reports' activities.

2. Anticipate how all those activities will affect one another.

3. Settle disputes they could not anticipate.

Patricia, our CEO, recognized that her inability to do all three tasks made her a bottleneck, which is not uncommon when a group operates exclusively in Hub-and-Spoke mode and depends on its leader to bridge the gap between siloed members.[35]

Thus, horizontal alignment became the second reason for Patricia to institute a regular Monday morning meeting with her senior leaders. During this meeting, her goal was to have them leave their silos to explain what they were doing, using the classic go-around-the-table method common in many LT meetings.

In an ideal world, this go-around-the-table exercise surfaces coordination problems between LT members that they then resolve and, in this way, share responsibility with the CEO for horizontal alignment. However, in practice, many LTs have lost sight of why they instituted the go-around-the-table agenda item. Instead of serving horizontal alignment, LT members use it as an opportunity to boast about recent accomplishments or pursue a one-on-one discussion with the CEO, leaving their colleagues twiddling their thumbs.

What measures LTs can take to avoid this and so ensure horizontal alignment are addressed in the next section of this chapter, along with other LT role-related effectiveness measures.

Actionable Insights

The two LT roles discussed in this chapter, strategic decision making and maintaining alignment, are the ones all LTs must master for organizational performance. Following are some practical measures you can take to ensure your LT members fulfill them well.

Actionable Insight No. 1: Make Your LT Members' Responsibilities Explicit

CEOs often make it clear to their executives what they will be held accountable for in their capacity as function or unit leaders: it is their so-called individual objectives. However, very few CEOs ever tell their LT members what they are accountable for in their role *as LT members*.

This is one reason executives retreat into their silo and focus exclusively on their individual objectives. To remedy this, the first step is obvious: clarify your executives' accountability as LT members.

But how?

Some advocate that CEOs go offsite with their executives to define their LT's role, but this rarely produces anything more than vague LT mission statements that are soon forgotten.

We recommend that you begin by debunking the three misconceptions about decision making we discussed earlier. More specifically, make it clear to LT members, as we did in the second section of this chapter, why they

- Will not be involved in every strategic decision.

- Are accountable only for strategic decisions they initiate, and this accountability includes involving LT colleagues to promote decision quality, alignment, and team solidarity.

- Should not expect all strategic decisions to be taken during LT meetings.

Next, take your LT through a facilitated ground-rules exercise covering norms addressing decision making and how alignment will be maintained. Formal team norms are the hallmark of effective LTs and are intended to create conditions that minimize power games and offer psychological safety, allowing LT members to focus on the substance of their most critical decisions.[36] Such an exercise can be conducted in less than two hours. We cannot overemphasize the impact this can have. As Wageman et al. note, "Of all the factors that we assess in our research, the one that makes the biggest difference in how well a senior LT performs is the clarity of behavioral norms that guide members' interactions."[37]

Because good decision making requires constructive conflict and productive collaboration capabilities, norms that support these capabilities need to be specifically added to the list. If you are at a loss regarding which ones your LT should adopt, you can find inspiration from the *Harvard Business Review* classic, "How Management Teams Can Have a Good Fight."[38] To keep your ground rules top of mind, follow the example of the CEO of a large pharmacy chain who prints his LT's ground rules at the bottom of every LT meeting agenda and encourages team members to refer to them whenever they feel they are not being respected.

Third, make it clear to LT members that they have a responsibility to maintain the two types of alignment:

• Vertical alignment, ensuring their objectives and actions and those of their teams are aligned with organizational priorities

• Horizontal alignment, ensuring their objectives and actions are coordinated with those of their LT colleagues

All three of these measures improve the chances that LT members will act on their LT responsibilities by making them explicit, but they offer no guarantee. Tangible measures ensuring those responsibilities are taken seriously must be added to the mix, as we show next.

Actionable Insight No. 2: Assess and Reward the Right LT Behaviors

If you want executives to take their decision-making and alignment responsibilities as LT members seriously, you may need to devise financial incentives to offset the forces that make them focus primarily on their unit or function interests.

Some CEOs believe this can be achieved by tying a portion of LT members' pay to organization-wide or collective objectives. In our experience, however, this is rarely enough. CEOs must also reward or sanction[39] LT members based on specific behaviors such as the following five:

• Involving LT colleagues in decisions they initiate according to the 3 principles described in this chapter (decision quality, alignment, and team solidarity).

• Anticipating alignment issues with LT colleagues and making every effort to work them out rather than immediately calling on their CEO to mediate.

• Coming prepared to LT meetings and participating in all topics, not only those they bring to the table.

- Cascading priorities, decisions, and information to the levels below.

- Respecting any ground rules or norms that the LT has developed.

In addition to rewarding these behaviors, we have seen two CEOs use another method to motivate executives to pay more attention to their LT responsibilities. They gave them an ultimatum: take your LT member responsibilities seriously or the LT will be disbanded and replaced by a smaller team composed of the three or four most senior executives.

We were present at the LT meeting where one of the two CEOs in question presented this ultimatum to his team. Then he listened to the members' grievances regarding the inefficiency of their LT meetings and pledged to improve them in exchange for their commitment to fully assume their role as LT members.

A year later, both CEOs reported that their LTs' effectiveness had increased dramatically. Silos were down, collaboration was up, and the team engaged in discussions that were truly strategic. The LT members we interviewed corroborated their CEO's assessment.

In short, if you want LT members to take their decision-making and alignment responsibilities seriously, these must first be translated into specific tasks or behaviors that you must monitor. If LT members perform those tasks and exhibit the correct LT behaviors, they should be rewarded. If they do not, there must be consequences, including disbanding your LT.

Actionable Insight No. 3: Measures That Promote
Vertical Alignment of LT Members

To be vertically aligned, your LT members must at a minimum be able to list your organization's strategic priorities. As discussed in an earlier chapter, the odds are ridiculously low that they can and so CEOs need to take measures so that LT members never lose sight of these priorities.

Beyond involving LT members in your strategic planning process—an obvious measure, but one that may happen only once a year (if that)—here are a few simple things to do:

ASK LT MEMBERS TO JUSTIFY BUDGET DEMANDS BY INVOKING ORGANIZATIONAL PRIORITIES

When LT members submit their yearly budget proposals, have them set out, in writing, how their demands support the organization's strategic priorities.

This practice is a low-cost but powerful tool that allows CEOs to assess if an LT member is vertically aligned and that reinforces that alignment.

QUIZ YOUR LT MEMBERS ON YOUR ORGANIZATIONAL PRIORITIES
A client of ours does this every six months using an online questionnaire whose results are brought to an LT meeting. The results are confidential because the goal is not to expose who is misaligned but to get everyone back on the same page.

HOLD REGULAR OBJECTIVE-SHARING SESSIONS.
The first opportunity to validate vertical alignment is when you sit down at the beginning of the year with LT members to set their individual objectives. However, the fact an LT member is vertically aligned in the first quarter of the year does not mean he or she will remain so throughout the year. This is because strategies are works in progress whose interpretation evolves as circumstances change. Inevitably LT members become misaligned over time.[40]

Such misalignment is not something the typical midyear performance review will correct. In fact, these reviews may reinforce misalignment if the assumption is that the objectives set at the beginning of the year must be maintained until year end, as is often the case.

In recognition of this, many organizations have implemented more flexible objective-setting systems that enable LT member to adapt their objectives over the course of the year. One example is the OKR (objectives and key results) system. We mention it because we have seen it used to great effect in several organizations.

The OKR framework was developed by Andy Grove, Intel's highly successful former CEO, and later popularized by John Doer who implemented it at Google. It obliges LT members to review and then share their objectives at regular intervals (e.g., every quarter, every month, or even every week). Knowing that their objectives will be shared publicly puts pressure on them to be certain they are vertically aligned and to ask questions if they are unsure they are. The OKR system is not the only flexible objective-setting framework but for those interested in learning more about it, we identify a few resources.[41]

As logical as the sharing of objectives might appear, many executives resist it, often because, as we have discovered time and again, many are poor at setting objectives. This should not prevent CEOs from instituting objective sharing. Quite the contrary.

*OBLIGE LT MEMBERS TO LINK MEETING AGENDA
ITEMS TO STRATEGIC PRIORITIES.*

We often hear executives complain that their LT meetings are "too operational" and not "strategic" enough. Obliging those proposing an LT meeting agenda item to justify their request by explaining how their item advances a specific organizational priority helps to keep discussions at the strategic level and keeps those priorities top of mind. One LT we saw implement this practice soon realized how much time the team was wasting addressing nonstrategic issues. Details on how to implement this practice are in Chapter 6.

*Actionable Insight No. 4: Measures that Promote
Vertical Alignment below the LT*

The next three activities ensure that the teams below the LT are vertically aligned as well. Such measures are necessary because there is strong evidence that middle managers have an even more tenuous grasp on their organization's priorities than do LT members.[42]

Here are solutions we have seen implemented successfully:

MAKE CASCADING THE LAST ITEM OF EVERY LT MEETING

Although CEOs expect their LT members to cascade information, very few do anything to encourage it. One CEO did so by setting aside ten minutes at the end of every meeting to go through a three-step process:

- First, she flashed the agenda on-screen.

- Then she asked all LT members to take five minutes to reflect on the agenda items they needed to cascade to their teams and to jot down, in bulleted form, what they would say about each.

- Then she went around the table and asked each one to share, in no more than thirty seconds, what each member planned to cascade to their teams. Only the CEO could comment on what her LT members proposed to cascade. This avoided reopening debates.

Although this process has shortcomings, this CEO felt they were more than offset by its benefits:

- LT members are more inclined to cascade information when they have rehearsed what they will say.

- By listening to what colleagues cascade, LT members may add elements to their own list. It also gives them ideas regarding how to present the items they wish to cascade.

- It enables CEOs to gauge LT member alignment and understanding of the topics discussed during the meeting.

Given how important alignment is, many CEOs may not want to put too much faith in their LT members cascading messages downward and may want to do some cascading of their own.[43] We highlight three time-efficient methods CEOs can use to do just that: town hall meetings, coffee breaks, and extended LT meetings.. These can easily be combined with the critical monitoring activities we described at the end of Chapter 2:

Town Hall Meetings

A town hall meeting is hosted by one or more senior executives to which employees are convened, typically in a large conference hall. They can be used as a vertical alignment tool. One leader who has done this is Darren Entwistle, CEO at the Canadian telecom company that in 2015 became the global leader in total shareholder value creation among incumbent telecom companies worldwide, returning 351 percent to shareholders between 2000 and 2015.

During these town hall meetings, called "ignite" sessions, Entwistle would share Telus's values, six strategic imperatives, and its overall strategy, explaining why it was the right strategy for the company.[44] He would then turn the microphone to staff to get feedback from them, a reminder that vertical alignment is not a one-way street.

Coffee Breaks

If you do not like town hall meetings, the coffee breaks facilitated by Daniel, site head for the flagship plant of a Swiss-based pharmaceutical multinational, might be more your style.

Every month, Daniel sent out an invitation to employees in three or four departments for an informal coffee, fruit, and pastry meeting. These sessions were part of an organization-wide communications plan developed with his LT. Up to ten people could sign up on a first-come, first-served basis. The explicit objective of these coffee breaks was for Daniel to get to know his staff and to discover what issues they faced. However, the meetings also contributed to vertical alignment because whenever an issue was raised, it often gave Daniel the opportunity to explain the strategic context in which the issue was embedded and remind those present of the organization's strategic priorities.

Extended Leadership Team Meetings

This is another practice out of Daniel's playbook that we have seen CEOs in other organizations use as well: a handful of leaders just below the LT level are invited to attend an LT meeting once a quarter. These extended meetings support vertical alignment in numerous ways. First, they enabled Daniel to discover how well those below his LT understood the direction he wanted the organization to take. Furthermore, he said, "These meetings were an opportunity for them to hear messages directly from me. I could provide the broader context of the decisions we had taken, something that it was perhaps harder for others to do."

Of course, nothing prevents a leader from implementing all of these practices, as well as management by walking around discussed in Chapter 2. The need to combine practices may be wise when something in your company's environment (e.g., a pandemic) leads staff to wonder if strategic priorities have changed or after an acquisition that may make competing visions of the organization surface.

Actionable Insight No. 5: Measures That Promote
Horizontal Alignment and Break Down Silos

We now turn to four measures to promote horizontal alignment:

DEVELOP LT MEMBERS' CONSTRUCTIVE CONFLICT COMPETENCIES

This is a suggestion we made in Chapter 2 to address power games. We return to it here because such training also contributes to horizontal alignment by helping LT members master conflict resolution skills, which makes them better equipped to address the issues that divide them.

There are many types of conflict resolution training programs. We highly recommend that you select courses integrating the win-win negotiations material from Fisher and Ury's book *Getting to Yes* for all the reasons discussed in Chapter 2, but also because, in our experience, it is easy to convince executives to enroll in a negotiation program because what they learn can be useful in many other contexts.[45]

HOLD REGULAR OKR-TYPE OBJECTIVE-SHARING SESSIONS

This is one of the recommendations that we made earlier to promote vertical alignment. We bring this one back as well because OKR-type systems also serve horizontal alignment by obliging LT members to share their objectives on a regular basis, which inevitably surfaces coordination issues. For example, in one organization we worked with, an OKR session brought to the surface that the chief marketing officer was targeting a client segment that all business unit heads had dropped and provoked a much-needed discussion on the strategic importance of that segment.

To ensure horizontal issues emerge, we have found that it is helpful for LT members to highlight, by name, colleagues whose support they will need to achieve their objectives. In this way, there is no ambiguity regarding where alignment is required. As a bonus, it keeps LT members engaged as they wait for their names to come up.

CEOs with large LTs (more than ten members) are the first to tell us that they often learn what their LT members are truly up to when they institute such objective-sharing sessions.

Get LT Members to Socialize Their Initiatives

We first heard of this practice from Yves, the CEO of a complex health care organization with 10,000 employees, 550 doctors, and over 100 service centers. Whenever one of his LT members wanted to add one of their cross-functional initiatives to the LT meeting agenda, he would ask them: "Have you socialized your initiative?"[46] By this he meant whether they had run it by the LT members and other stakeholders the initiative would most affect in order to test its acceptability. If not, he declined to add it to the agenda until they had.

He instituted this practice because experience had taught him that meeting discussions went off the rails whenever he allowed an "unsocialized" initiative to be presented. In such cases, the one or two LT members most affected by the initiative often reacted angrily, offended they had not been briefed earlier. A heated debate would ensue between these executives and the LT member presenting the initiative. This left the rest of the LT on the sidelines, reaching for their phones to check messages and thinking what a waste of time LT meetings were. Obliging his LT members to emerge from their silos to socialize their initiatives before bringing them to LT meetings avoided all this drama and inefficiency.

CEOs whose LT members are not co-located must be especially vigilant and oblige LT members to socialize their initiatives and align horizontally with colleagues prior to meetings because distance thickens silo walls. Based on some of the research on remote working, CEOs whose LT members often work from home will need even more frequent reminders about socializing their initiatives with colleagues. [47]

Actionable Insight No. 6: Do Not Imagine That Creating a Second,
Smaller LT Will Solve Your Problems

When asked to improve the dynamics of a large LT (ten or more members), many team consultants recommend that CEOs pare down the team, usually to five to seven members. We have yet to find an organization where this has proven effective. The first reason is because of the assumption that an LT is there to make collective decisions which is a misconception about LT decision making we addressed earlier.

Second, when the problem on a large LT is silos and poor collaboration among members, creating a second, smaller LT does not make the silos and collaboration issues between the executives who have been dropped magically disappear. In many cases, it makes them worse because they see each other less often.

Third, it is optimistic to believe that CEOs can simply disband a large LT and start from scratch with a smaller one. In theory they can, of course. But in practice, disbanding a large LT leaves CEOs with bigger problems, notably the need to restructure reporting relationships because an LT's structure often mirrors the organizational chart. Add to that the threat that the "demoted" executives may resign.

Thus, in practice, CEOs who create a second, smaller LT will also be keeping the larger LT in a Russian doll structure. They must now manage two LTs, and in every instance of this we have seen, the new, smaller one inherits much of the dysfunctionality of the larger one. Those who sit on both teams—usually the most important executives in the organization—now waste their time in twice as many meetings as before.

So if you have a large dysfunctional LT, start by trying to fix this group. You may discover that the need for a smaller LT then disappears.

If, after fixing the larger team, you nonetheless still think creating a second, smaller LT makes sense, ensure you have a clear idea what its role will be and how it will differ from that of the larger LT. Organizations we have seen set up such smaller teams, which some called LT subcommittees, did so for two reasons:

- *Creating a forum where specific coordination issues could be debated in more depth.* In one organization, the subcommittee members were business unit leaders and members of the sales team who met biweekly to plan visits with clients and coordinate the preparation of request-for-proposal bids. In another organization, the subcommittee members were the ones with operational responsibilities who met to coordinate such matters as sharing staff across operational units.

- *Ensuring the effectiveness of the larger LT* was another reason one client organization created an LT subcommittee. The CEO and his three top deputies met every week to review the full LT meeting's agenda to ensure all agenda items had been socialized by the topic owners and to assess if there were any vertical or horizontal alignment issues that needed to be added to the agenda.

The Chapter in a Nutshell

The mystery behind who sits on your LT and what they are meant to do

- As surprising as it may seem, executives in most organizations rarely agree about the size of their own organization's LT because they do not share a common definition of "leadership team."

- Many definitions of LT have important drawbacks. Our definition is "the group of executives that meets formally with the CEO on a regular basis."

- Only once you have defined who sits on your LT can you determine what role they should play together. If your LT is perfectly functional, you need not worry about defining or refining its role. If it is dysfunctional, you should because many LT dysfunctionalities can be traced back to executives having a fuzzy idea of their LT's role and their own responsibilities as LT members.

The LT's Strategic Decision-Making Role and Three Misconceptions You Need to Debunk

There is consensus that an LT's role includes strategic decision making, but there are three misconceptions regarding this role. Debunking them helps clarify LT member responsibilities.

- *Misconception no. 1: All LT members must participate in all strategic decisions*

  - When LT members believe they have a right to participate in all decisions it contributes to LT dysfunctionality.

  - Decision quality improves when some LT members are involved ... but rarely all.

  - Decision implementation improves with LT member participation that is proportionate to their implementation involvement.

- *Misconception no. 2: LT members are accountable for all strategic decisions*

  - Holding LT members accountable for all strategic decisions makes little sense in theory and is rejected by executives in practice.

  - LT members should be held accountable for decisions they initiate and those falling under their purview. This implies having them involve their LT colleagues to the extent dictated by principles related to decision quality, implementation implication, and team solidarity.

  - Team solidarity should not be confused with team accountability.

- *Misconception no. 3: LT meetings are where strategic decisions are taken*

  - We need to distinguish between strategic decision making and decision taking.

  - An entire LT rarely takes a decision.

  - The fact that a strategic decision has been taken before an LT meeting is a practical necessity, not a sign of dysfunctionality.

The Second Major LT Role: Maintaining Organizational Alignment

The LT's role in strategic decision making entails the promotion of two types of alignment:

- Vertical alignment, when LT member decisions and actions, and those of their teams, support the organization's strategy.

- Horizontal alignment among LT members, when actions and decisions across all functions and units complement and support, rather than interfere with, one another.

- Why and how your LT supports both types of alignment is well illustrated by CEOs when they create an LT. The lessons from this experience can serve CEOs who inherit one.

Summary of Actionable Insights

1. Make your LT's role and related LT member responsibilities explicit

- Start by debunking the three misconceptions regarding the LT's decision-making role.

- Define ground rules or norms that are tailored to your team. Include norms that specifically address constructive conflict and productive collaboration.

2. Assess and reward the right LT behaviors in line with their decision-making and alignment responsibilities

- Tie performance pay to the specific LT member behaviors you want.

- Make LT membership conditional on fulfilling LT responsibilities.

3. Implement measures that promote vertical alignment of LT members

- Ask LT members to justify budget demands by invoking organizational priorities.

- Hold regular objective-sharing sessions.

- Oblige LT members to link meeting agenda items to strategic priorities.

- Make cascading the last item of every LT meeting.

4. Implement measures that promote the vertical alignment of staff below the LT

- Town hall meetings

- Coffee break meetings.

- "Extended LT" meetings.

5. Implement measures that promote horizontal alignment and break down silos

- Develop LT members' constructive conflict competencies

- Hold regular OKR-type objective-sharing sessions

- Oblige LT members to "socialize" their initiatives with colleagues before meetings.

6. Create a second, smaller LT only as a last resort:

- Creating a second, smaller LT often leaves CEOs with bigger problems than they began with.

- Subcommittees of your larger LT may make sense if they have a clear role, such as addressing coordination issues in more detail or helping to make the larger LT more effective.

- If you do set up a smaller LT, be clear about its role, and make sure it is different from that of the larger LT if you decide to keep the latter.

5

GETTING YOUR LEADERSHIP TEAM'S SIZE

AND COMPOSITION RIGHT

Question: Should CEOs have complete freedom to choose who sits on their LT?

Most people we ask answer: "Of course!" Furthermore, many LT authors implicitly assume CEOs have such freedom when they advise them to have no more than a specified number of LT members, imagining CEOs have complete latitude to implement this advice.

While CEOs do have some latitude to shape their LT, they have far less than many assume. This is especially true when they first take up their position.[1] To illustrate, this was the response of the newly named CEO of a US group's subsidiary when we suggested that he combine the supply chain and procurement positions on the LT he had just inherited because of the destructive conflict between the two position holders, "I'd thought of that but, you know, I just joined [company] and this is how all their subsidiaries' LTs are structured. With budgets due in three weeks, I have more important battles to fight with HQ than this one."

But new CEOs are not the only ones to face constraints. So do seasoned LT leaders, as exemplified by the veteran CEO of a $3 billion global company who recounted how one of their executive vice presidents had successfully resisted the implementation of company-wide HR policies for years. "I'd fire the guy," our CEO said, "but if I did he would take half his team and many of our top clients with him. So that's not an option."

CEOs not only face constraints in removing LT members; they also face pressure to add members. For example, when we asked the country head of a multinational group why she had promoted a health and safety director to her LT despite his subpar tolerance for uncertainty, she replied, "I didn't promote him. Group policy obliges every country head to have an H&S director on their LT."

Such pressure to add LT members is far from unusual because there is no shortage of people telling CEOs that catastrophe awaits unless they add a chief data officer, a chief happiness officer, or any other of the new chief "something" officer positions that seem to pop up every year (we refer to these as **CXO** positions).

Because of this pressure, you might expect this chapter to answer the question: "What is the ideal LT size?" or "What is the optimal LT composition?" It will not, for two reasons. First, there are no strong, evidence-backed answers to these questions. There are only opinions, and our goal is to stick to answers and ideas supported by evidence from the field. The second reason is equally important: we want to address questions that CEOs ask us in practice, and these two questions are not among them for reasons we will explain.

The questions they do ask are: "Should I add a CXO to my LT?" and "Is my LT too big and, if so, what can I do about it?" These are therefore the questions this chapter will answer.

It does so first by looking at the evolution of several critical LT roles, which reveals how certain LT positions are far from the natural or timeless necessities many imagine them to be and provides important lessons for CEOs wanting to add new CXOs today.

Second, we review the pros and cons of small versus large LTs to help you assess the benefits and downsides of adding a new position.

Third, we conclude, as always, with actionable insights to help you address the issues raised in this chapter.

What the Evolution of LT Roles Can Teach You about Your LT Today

When LTs first appeared is a subject of debate. Some point to the late 1880s, others to the 1920s. But one thing is clear: the modern-day LT, with its mix of operating executives alongside an ever-growing number of functional or CXO positions, is a relatively recent phenomenon.

Of those positions, the chief operations (or operating) officer (COO) and the chief financial officer (CFO) are so familiar that many are surprised to find out that most corporations had neither just a few decades ago. Since they became fixtures, so many new CXO positions have been created that organizations are running short of CXO acronyms with, for example, the traditional "CEO" also being used by chief engineering officers and chief ethics officers.[2]

The explosion of new CXO positions has led some business commentators to write that "C is for silly" and denouncing the phenomenon as "corporate Kindergarten playtime title-making."[3] One might understand why upon hearing that a firm has named a chief happiness officer,[4] a chief joy officer, or a chief purpose officer.[5]

These new positions are being pushed by what has been aptly named the "fast fashion industry of CXOs,"[6] populated by experts, professional networks, and media that busily promote and sustain CXO roles, some with the intent of securing audiences and customers.[7] Indeed, those exhorting CEOs to hire a chief digital officer (CDO), for example, are also implicitly offering to help them select their new CDO, while simultaneously ingratiating themselves to CDOs to whom they also extend support.

This is not to say that all new CXO positions add little value. Many have legitimately sprung up in response to technological, economic, and social changes.

We explore a few positions whose evolution offers insights to CEOs deciding to add these and other CXO positions to their LT.

Chief Operating Officer (COO)

Both the COO and CFO roles appeared in earnest in the 1960s, although it can be argued that the COO was the first CXO role to take center stage.[8] Management guru Peter Drucker may have had a hand in this when he argued that the duties of a modern CEO were simply too much for one person to handle, and thus supported the appointment of COOs in his 1954 book, *The Practice of Management.*[9] A common feature of CEOs who have hired COOs appears to be their lack of experience in operational activities and in managing the firm.[10]

Since its heyday in the 1960s and 1970s, the COO position has lost some luster. While almost half of Fortune 500 and S&P 500 corporations had a COO in 2000, only about a third had one fourteen years later.[11] Partly to blame is the rise of information technologies that allowed CEOs to handle many operational tasks directly and supported the rise of other functions centered on operational activities, for example, the chief technology officer (CTO).

The decline in COOs has spurred a great deal of research regarding whether COOs bring value. The jury is still out, no doubt in part because two people holding this title may be playing quite different roles.[12] A 2006 *Harvard Business Review* article describes no fewer than seven different types of COOs.[13] Nevertheless, when we have been invited by executives to discuss the benefits of adding a COO to their team, all of them assumed that others around the table shared their vision of what a COO did.

What to watch for: People who assume that all COOs play the same role. COOs rarely do. Thus, before discussing whether to add a COO to your LT, make sure all those participating in the discussion spell out what tasks they believe the new COO would manage. To ensure the best alignment, go a step further and have them detail what issues or problems they believe the new COO would address.

Chief Financial Officer (CFO)

The first major US corporation to adopt the CFO title is reputed to have been Dan River Mills in 1966[14] and the CFO's emergence is attributed to the increasing complexity of financial markets and evolutions in accounting rules.[15] Today, most large companies have a CFO, and many smaller companies have someone playing a CFO-like role.

CFOs have grown more powerful in recent years, notably due to the 2008 financial crisis, which obliged firms to pay more attention to costs, as well as advances in data gathering and computing power, which have enabled CFOs to monitor the behavior of their LT colleagues more closely.[16]

Thus, the issue for CEOs with respect to CFOs, unlike other CXO positions, is not, "Should I have one?" but rather, "Are they using their power appropriately?" CEOs are unlikely to get much help in answering this question from their other LT members who know enough not to directly criticize the person who can reject their budget demands.

This does not mean LT members are unwilling to share their opinion of their CFO colleague with outsiders, as we experienced when conducting interviews prior to an LT retreat. At that time, a few executives begged us to tell their CEO that her new CFO was, as one said, "a vindictive little despot."

What to watch for: Few CEOs can do without a CFO, but given the growing power of CFOs, you need to pay attention to how they are wielding that power. To find out, relying solely on feedback from your CFO's colleagues is unwise as they have a strong disincentive to give you a straight answer.

Chief Strategy Officer (CSO)

CSOs emerged in the 1970s and 1980s due to the professionalization and centralization of strategic planning. The position has since fallen from grace, which some attribute to the bureaucratic processes they instituted.[17]

Of course, some CEOs still want a CSO but it can be one of the most disruptive nominations they can make because a CSO's scope generally cuts across that of most of their colleagues' scope, provoking power battles of an intensity most CEOs do not always fully appreciate.

Furthermore, we have rarely seen a CSO whose scope was well defined. We are not alone. One survey found that 65 percent of CSOs themselves do not think their priorities are very clear and "they need to make up the role as they go along."[18] That is certainly not a recipe for success.

Finally, CSOs are often named to address a temporary need, such as overhauling a company's strategy. While this is a laudable goal, once they complete this initial mandate, their search for a new mission leads to another round of turf wars with LT colleagues, just as one might anticipate.

What to watch for: Alternatives to naming a CSO. Given the foreseeable power issues that naming a CSO provokes, think carefully before doing so. If the need your CSO will be filling is a temporary one (e.g., devising a new strategy), consider other solutions, as discussed in the Actionable Insights section later in this chapter.

Chief Talent Officer (CTO)

The existence of the CTO is a prime example of what has been described as the "karyokinesis," or deconstruction, of the chief human resources officer (CHRO) position into a variety of roles.[19]

CTOs appeared in the early 2000s, shortly after the publication of a *McKinsey Quarterly* piece entitled "The War for Talent," in what may be one of the most successful campaigns to create a new C-suite position.[20]

In "How McKinsey & Co. Created 'The War for Talent' in 1998 to Propagate a 'Myth of Brilliance,'" James Suzman attributes the success of this campaign to the suggestion made to corporate leaders "that the difference between good and bad companies was not the processes they followed or how efficient they were, but the clever people steering those businesses. Senior executives just like them."[21]

While companies operating in tight labor markets may have been justified in bringing a CTO onboard, many fell for the hype and hired one without a compelling business case. In one such company, we noticed that the addition of a CTO came at quite a cost. First, the CTO's budget demands created foreseeable frictions with LT colleagues, which did little to improve their team's already faltering dynamics. Second, the CTO's arrival provoked a turf war with the CHRO, and both worked to undermine each other in the hope that their two roles would be merged.

What to watch for: Whether it be a CTO or any another CXO position, make sure there is a compelling business case specific to your company to add it to your LT.

Chief Information Technology Officer (CITO)

The CITO position emerged in the 1990s in response to what some have called "the lack of business savvy" of IT staff, leading to a search for a senior executive who understood new technologies but also how these applied to business strategy.[22]

In theory, finding someone who can bridge the worlds of technology and strategy appears easy. In practice, it is not, as illustrated by the conversation we had with a CEO struggling to replace the CITO he had just fired.

"What are you looking for?" we asked him.

"I need someone who can look into the future and predict what technologies we will need five years from now," he began. "They also must be good with people: they need to speak English, not IT. I don't want a know-it-all who makes others feel stupid when they ask for help. And because we have so many legacy systems to replace, they need to be tough enough to deal with peers who resist change."

When we related this to a colleague, she chuckled: "Sounds like they are looking for a cross between da Vinci, Mother Teresa, and Stalin. I wish them good luck!"

What to watch for: Your expectations about what any one person who steps onto a new LT role can do. Do not expect to find a person for all seasons. You may need to prioritize the problems and issues you want this person to address and hire someone who can tackle the top one or two.

Chief Marketing Officer (CMO)

The rise of the CMO in the 1990s is explained by various factors, including corporations that wanted to become more customer focused and the growing sophistication of marketing techniques via big data.

While many CEOs initially jumped onto the CMO bandwagon, many have since climbed down. In one survey, four-fifths of CEOs said they were dissatisfied with their CMO and, consequently, CMOs have had the highest turnover of LT members.[23]

In firms where the CMO was shown the door, many succumbed to what we call the payback period paradox, which highlights the disconnect between the time in which CMOs are expected to deliver results (and thus provide a return on their salaries) and that required to perform the work they were hired to do.

In all cases we observed, the CMOs had been asked to determine what client segments sales staff should go after and which ones to abandon. While these CMOs imagined they had months to gather and analyze client data before coming back with tangible recommendations, they soon felt tremendous pressure to deliver client leads that sales could capitalize on immediately.

> *The Payback Period Paradox: A disconnect between the time CMOs are expected to deliver results and that required to perform the work they were hired to do.*

Predictably, in one company, much of that pressure came from the CMO's LT colleagues who were responsible for delivering sales in the company's four business units. One of them kept repeating to anyone who would listen: "[Our CMO] is spending thousands of dollars to find out what our customers want. My sales guys already know. Give me the money to hire more salespeople and I will deliver sales, not just talk about them."

While one can guess that such complaints were not entirely in good faith, they nonetheless prodded the CEO to ask the CMO more pointedly when he could expect results. Given this pressure, the CMO chose to leave a little over a year later. Had she not, it was clear she would have been shown the door.

What to watch for: A specific timeline defining how quickly you expect a person hired to fill a CMO or another CXO position to deliver results. Anticipate which colleagues your new CXO will clash with so you can pre-empt the conflict. Set the CXO up for success, not predictable failure.

Chief Digital Officer (CDO)

If CMOs offer an example of a CXO position whose star has faded, the CDO may well be another. The position appeared circa 2003 but did not gain traction until 2010 among S&P 1500 companies.[24] A few years later, from 2013 to 2014, the number of people in CDO roles had doubled, and at the time, some expected the number to double again in the short term as many CEOs wished to signal they were taking digitization seriously.[25] In the mid-2010s, we recall speaking to a CEO who pondered hiring a CDO because she did not understand how leveraging digitization would improve her company's performance and felt that having an expert would help her figure it out.

By 2016, the creation of CDO positions had peaked.[26] Two years later, articles with titles such as *"So You Think You Need a Chief Digital Officer?"* were questioning whether a CDO was wise and pointing to the many companies that were replacing or eliminating their CDO after a twelve- to eighteen-month experiment.[27] Its authors gave this explanation:

> Digital is a complex, moving target that touches every part of your business. Digital is no longer about mobile and web, but includes emerging technologies like AI, blockchain, mixed reality, robotics and the Internet of Things (IoT), and demands a new set of skills and thinking. All of this makes it even harder to converge on a single role to address the challenge.

What to watch for: Pressure to add a position to your LT before having defined specifically why your organization might need one. Ironically, advocates of new CXO positions will use a CEO's hesitation to their advantage by arguing: "If you don't understand why you need a CXO, this *proves* that you need one." Or they might argue that you need a new CXO position to signal the importance that the issue they will address. Before creating a new CXO position, ask yourself, "Is the issue my new CXO will address truly strategic for our firm?" If you are certain the answer is yes, ask if responsibility for this issue should be concentrated in one person or if you need to implement measures so the issue becomes a strategic priority across your LT.

Chief Diversity and Inclusion Officer (CDIO)

There is much literature supporting the view that good decision making requires a diversity of perspectives, "which is associated with greater variance in ideas, creativity and innovation."[28] Support for diversity also comes from research on how individual biases and other brain mechanisms impede good decision making, such as that of Nobel laureate Daniel Kahneman.[29]

Beyond these functional arguments lies a moral one for widening the number of actors involved in decision making as a lack of inclusion can be interpreted as a sign of organizational inequality.[30] However, criteria to define what type of diversity should be pursued—for example, gender, race, ethnicity, age—remain elusive.

Despite this, we strongly support many tenets of the diversity movement, but ultimately, it is up to the CEO to decide if diversity becomes a priority. If so, the question is then whether creating a CDIO position is the best solution to advance it.

What to watch for: Thinking that hiring a full-time CDIO is the best way to address the critical issue of increasing diversity. It may not be. The decision depends on a host of factors, including the current size of your LT, which we address in the following section, as well as others we address in the "Actionable Insights" section.

How Big or Small Should Your LT Be?

Is There an Optimal LT Size?

Some team theorists and consultants will tell you there is an optimal LT size. The number may differ, but it often hovers around seven or eight. Michael A. West from Lancaster University, for example, writes, "Team size will be as small as possible to get the task completed and no more than six to eight members."[31] Wageman et al. say much the same in their 2008 book explaining that the "best senior leadership teams ... are small, typically made up of no more than eight members."[32]

There are a few things to note about such claims. The first is that the argument for a smaller team often rests, implicitly or explicitly, on the assumption that it facilitates the LT's decision-making role. And while it is undeniable that a smaller LT makes decision making *simpler,* a definite advantage in circumstances such as a crisis, that does not mean a smaller team makes decision making *better.*

Second, those arguing for a smaller LT overlook the importance of the LT's critical second role: alignment. While having a larger LT may create coordination and communication problems, CEOs we have seen manage these problems well benefit from increased organizational alignment.[33]

It is perhaps for this reason that the case for a smaller LT is not supported by evidence from the field. This is something that Wageman et al. are the first to admit, albeit in a footnote, when they explain that the assertion that an LT should number no more than eight is supported by research on nonexecutive teams but not research on LTs. The research on LTs, they confess, is equivocal.[34]

They are quite right. Although many studies have sought to establish a link between LT size and organizational performance, none has been able to prove that LTs of any size lead to better organizational performance. In other words, that an LT should have no more than eight members is less fact than opinion. Unsurprisingly, not all share it.

Jack Welch and the Case for a Larger LT

One person who did not share this opinion is Jack Welch, former chairman and CEO of the General Electric Company (GE). Although Welch's legacy has been debated since his death in 2020, his take on LT size is worth examining because of his status as one of the most influential corporate leaders of his generation due to his formidable personality and track record.

When Welch joined GE in 1981, the company was worth $14 billion. When he stepped down twenty years later in 2001, it was worth close to $400 billion, and for a time, it was the most valuable company in the world. In 1999, *Fortune* named Welch the manager of the century.[35]

Commenting on Welch's influence on governance at the top of organizations, *Financial Times* columnist Andrew Hill writes:

> When military men first started talking about this "span of control" in the 1920s, they argued, based on centuries of battlefield experience, that a team of six was the maximum manageable size. GE's president at the time reckoned he should have no more than four or five direct reports. Since then, consultants have wasted a lot of time—and clients' money—calculating the ideal span of control. Mr. Welch blew through this in the 1980s by increasing the controlling span of some managers to as many as 18 direct reports.[36]

Welch explained why in the 2005 best-selling book *Winning*, written with his wife, Suzie Welch:

> An overburdened, overstretched executive is the best executive because he or she doesn't have the time to meddle, to deal in trivia, to bother people. Remember the theory that a manager should have no more than 6 or 7 direct reports? ... The right number is closer to 10 or 15. This way you have no choice but to let people flex their muscles, let them grow and mature. With 10 or 15 reports, a leader can focus only on the big important issues, not on minutiae.[37]

Welch followed his own advice: the number of his direct reports and LT members ran well into the double digits.

The Reality: LTs Have Been Growing Larger

While it is hard to gauge the precise impact of Welch's views on LT size and that of others arguing a similar line, LT size has been growing in large US firms since Welch became GE's CEO.

Research by INSEAD professor Maria Guadalupe and colleagues found that from the mid-1980s to the mid-2000s, the size of the executive team in such firms doubled from five to ten.[38] It is important to note that their widely cited study equated the number of LT members with that of a CEO's direct reports, which warrants some caution. Although we know of no similar studies for smaller-sized firms or for firms in Europe, they appear to have followed a similar trend.

The trend toward ever larger LTs is attributed to functional centralization in response to global competition because the increase in LT size was mostly due to the addition of functional managers rather than general managers, who typically have profit and loss responsibility.[39]

Interestingly, CEOs added more administrative, or back-end, functions (e.g., finance, HR, IT) than product, or front-end, functions (e.g., marketing, R&D, sales, manufacturing). It is surmised this is because delivering the synergies that make centralization worthwhile requires that central functions aggregate and synthesize information across business units, and this is simpler to do for back-end than front-end functions.

Direct Reports and LT Size

The number of a CEO's direct reports may not always be equal to the number of people sitting on that CEO's LT.

However, those two numbers are rarely far apart when you define LT in the practical manner we have in Chapter 4. And when CEOs add a direct report, that person usually gets added to the LT unless, of course, that person has been hired in an administrative position such as executive assistant.

One reason for this is that information on back-end functions is less product specific. For example, a back-end function such as finance can more readily harmonize financial data (e.g., revenue and margins) across business units selling different products than a front-end function such as marketing can harmonize marketing-related information (e.g., click-through rates or the number of sales leads).[40]

If creating synergies is one reason behind functional centralization, it is not the only one. Power is another, with CEO Lou Gerstner's example being cited for his centralization of functions at IBM in the 1990s to offset the "inordinate power" of one division and thus facilitate corporate-wide coordination.[41]

Such leveraging of LT membership for power motives is nothing new. Bestowing privileges in this manner has been used by leaders for years, as attested by the example of Napoleon who distributed about thirty-six hundred titles—some of them purely honorary—to consolidate his power.[42]

Actionable Insights

Whether one approves or not, new CXO positions are being added to LTs everywhere. The result is ever larger LTs.

This makes the debate over an LT's "ideal" size largely theoretical. By the time the CEOs we meet become concerned about their team's size, its membership has typically climbed north of twelve, and they may be feeling pressure to add yet another position.

At that stage, telling them that their LT should have no more than eight members does them little good because a CEO with, say, fifteen LT members will not stop to think: "Hmmm, if the experts say I can only have eight LT positions, which seven shall I cut?"

Although many authors claim that it is not difficult for CEOs to cut positions, that is not how CEOs feel. For them, cutting an LT position is akin to the nuclear option because it sends a signal that the function or unit the LT position represented is no longer valued. Furthermore, it may force them to change reporting relationships and organizational structure because LT membership reflects that structure.

Thus, our focus in the actionable insights that follow is on helping you determine whether adding another position to your LT will truly add value and tips on how to manage an LT when it has grown to a size that feels unwieldy.

Actionable Insight No. 1: Determining Whether You Should Add a Position to Your LT

"CEOs operate in a world where there are no perfect answers, just tough choices" is a saying that certainly applies to CEOs facing the decision of whether to add a new position to their LT.[43] To help you make the necessary trade-offs, here are five criteria we put on the table when discussing this matter with CEOs.

CRITERION NO. 1: WHICH VOICES DOES YOUR BUSINESS MODEL DICTATE YOU NEED AROUND THE TABLE?

An understanding of your business model reveals what activities are critical to delivering your value proposition to customers and what voices should be represented on your top team.

For example, in recent years, cement companies have recognized that their business model rests on a social, and not only a regulatory, license to operate since public concern over pollution could lead government officials to restrict their activities. It is no surprise then when they add a chief environmental or sustainability officer.

And even a superficial examination of a bank's business model will tell you that effective risk management is critical to its success, which explains why banks have a chief risk officer. Contrast this with management consultancies, where risk is a lesser concern because it is difficult for a client to establish a causal link between the advice they receive from a consultancy and the damages suffered from following it. Thus, a chief risk officer is not a position you expect to find on a consulting firm's LT.

Remember that each new addition to your LT that is not dictated by your business model makes managing your team more complex and means voices that are truly strategic have less airtime.

CRITERION NO. 2: IS THE NEW POSITION MEANT TO ADDRESS A SHORT-TERM OR AN ONGOING ISSUE?

When you are faced with an important, ongoing issue, such as risk at a bank, naming an LT member to address it makes perfect sense. However, it may not if the issue is a short-term one, as demonstrated by a CEO we know who hired a COO to address a glitch in operations.

This COO fixed the glitch in a matter of months. For this, his colleagues were very grateful. They were less grateful when he then searched around for a new mandate and launched a series of Six Sigma initiatives to improve business processes that none of them felt were a priority. The COO was eventually dismissed, ostensibly because of conflicts he was deemed to have instigated with LT colleagues. But one can argue that he was fired because he had ceased to add value commensurate with his salary once he fixed the problem he had been hired to fix, something that was foreseeable the day he was named.

When the issue you want to address can be fixed in the short term, consider a less permanent solution than adding a position to your LT, such as hiring someone on a short-term contract.

CRITERION NO. 3: ARE YOU NAMING SOMEONE TO YOUR LT TO SET UP A NEW FUNCTION OR TO LEAD AN EXISTING ONE?

Setting up a function requires more subject-matter *expertise* than it does leadership *experience*, while it is the opposite for managing an existing function.

While this is an oversimplification, it serves to highlight two mistakes we see organizations make. The first was manifest when a company we were involved with experienced a rise in long-term injuries after installing equipment from a new manufacturer and it hired an expert to their LT to set up a new health and safety function. After she finished this work a year later, which all agreed she had done well, she was forced to leave because complaints from staff regarding her poor leadership were piling up.

"How could someone who was so brilliant last year have turned into such a dud the next?" one LT colleague asked. The answer is simple: the task of setting up a function is very much like a consulting assignment. It requires expertise in areas such as needs analysis, structure, and process design. It also takes a strong project manager, which this head of health and safety, a former consultant, certainly was. But project management expertise is not the same as the leadership experience required to guide an existing function.

> *Setting up a function requires more subject matter expertise than it does leadership experience, while it is the opposite for managing an existing function.*

The second mistake organizations make is the mirror image of the one above, and we have seen it committed when organizations hire their first chief diversity officer. In one case we observed, the diversity and inclusion officer in question had strong leadership experience but lacked the subject matter expertise to distinguish diversity-promoting measures that were effective from those that were not. As a result, they promoted measures that were not only ineffective but harmful to the critical diversity cause they had been recruited to serve.

Setting up a function and leading an established one require very different skill sets. Hire accordingly.

CRITERION No. 4: Is Naming a New LT Member the Best Way to Support a New Strategic Priority?

It seems to have become a knee-jerk reaction to appoint a new LT member whenever an organization wishes to signal its commitment to a new issue or strategic priority. If your goal is to do more than signal, you might do well to consider other options.

This would be the case, for example, when the issue or priority requires the full engagement of all LT members. In such instances, it might be best if you, as CEO, became the standard bearer.

Another option would be to assign the issue to one of the more powerful members of your LT, a strategy some have called "double hatting."[44] But when using this approach, CEOs need to remember that some issues or functions do not make good bedfellows. For example, it would be unwise to put risk under the CFO, as the CFO might be tempted to hush up risks that could have sizable financial consequences.

As a rule of thumb, do not put functions together when they are on opposing ends of the classic strategic dualities, such as those represented in Table 1.1.

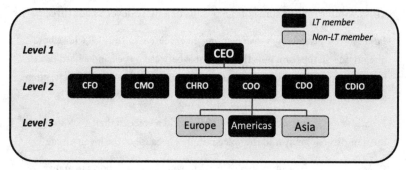

FIGURE 5.1. Illustration of an LT with Three Hierarchical Levels

Criterion No. 5: Avoid Adding a Third Hierarchical Level to Your LT

The vast majority of LTs have only two hierarchical levels: the CEO sits on the first, and the CEO's direct reports sit on the second. An LT has three levels when a CEO adds an executive who reports to an LT member sitting on level 2, as depicted in Figure 5.1.

One reason a CEO might do this is to groom an executive in anticipation of a future promotion since the CEO can then directly assess if that executive "has what it takes," as one leader put it to us. Another reason may be to further organizational alignment. By having the new executive participate in LT discussions, they understand and commit more thoroughly to decisions, which places them in a better position to align their staff.

Both reasons—grooming and alignment—explain why a CEO we worked with added Jorge, the head of the company's largest business unit, to his top team. Jorge reported to the company's COO, Sheila, and it was thought he might take over for her when she retired.

Jorge's fate exposes the downsides of naming someone to your LT when their boss is already an LT member. Indeed, upon Sheila's retirement, the CEO asked our opinion regarding her successor. When the conversation turned to Jorge, the CEO exclaimed: "No way I name him COO. He's been on my LT for more than a year now and he never has an opinion."

Having sat in on the company's LT meetings, we knew this to be true. However, we also knew it was Jorge's loyalty to Sheila that prevented him from expressing his opinion when it differed from hers. However, our CEO chose to interpret Jorge's loyalty to Sheila as a lack of courage, and he was passed over for the COO job. Humiliated, he resigned, and the company lost one of its most successful leaders.

This example reveals some of the pitfalls of a three-level LT for three parties:

- *Pitfall for the person promoted*: Naming an executive to your LT whose boss already sits on the team puts that executive between a rock and a hard place because it may oblige the member to contradict his or her boss publicly, often a career-limiting move and not one loyal executives often make.

- *Pitfall for the organization*: CEOs hoping to add a voice to their LT for alignment or diversity may find the voice is muted because of the loyalty issue.

- *Pitfall for the CEO*: Adding an executive to your LT who reports to an existing LT member reinforces the latter's power because their direct report will likely support them in whatever they wish to do, including creating a common front to thwart initiatives the CEO deems important. This is certainly an advantage that Sheila benefited from when Jorge was named to the LT.

These pitfalls are not insurmountable, which is why a three-level LT can nonetheless thrive, notably when CEOs institute measures that promote psychological safety. How some have done this is discussed in Chapter 6.

Actionable Insight No. 2: Think Twice before Adding an LT Position
If You Already Have Five Members

As we saw in Chapter 1, much of the tension on LTs is due to the fact that LT members represent specific strategic imperatives or "causes" that clash with those defended by their colleagues.

Such conflicts are less intense on small LTs because their members are obliged to take a more holistic, less siloed view of the company and thus must defend multiple causes. For example, on an LT with four members but no CHRO, all members will need to defend staff by paying attention to engagement levels because there is no HR executive to do so.

In our experience, it is when a CEO adds a sixth member to their LT that members cease to take a holistic vision of the company and focus more exclusively on the cause associated with their position. We surmise it is because at that moment, LT members see more clearly the strategic imperatives their colleagues are defending and they react by defending their own more strongly.

While we readily admit that there is no scientific study to validate this observation, we share it as a word of caution to those CEOs who are currently sitting with five LT members.

*Actionable Insight No. 3: Get Alignment on the Type of COO
or CMO You Need before Searching for One*

We have discussed how many people assume that all COOs play the same role. The same can be said about CMOs such that when a CEO discusses the hiring of a COO or CMO, it is rare that everyone around the table shares a common definition of what those roles entail. Such discussions are rarely fruitful.

To help one European organization avoid this, we sent it the *Harvard Business Review* article we referred to earlier after it expressed the need to hire a COO. It describes seven different types of COOs: the Executor, the Change Agent, the Mentor, the Other Half, the Partner, the Heir Apparent, and the MVP. We then asked those gathered which one they thought they needed. Interestingly, the conversation led them to realize that hiring a COO would not resolve their problems, and they called their search firm to say the search for a COO was off.

To help a company that wanted to hire a CMO, we adopted a slightly different approach, although our objective was similar in that we wanted to surface everyone's expectations regarding the new CMO's role. We alerted them to the payback period paradox described in the first section of this chapter by drawing a continuum on a sheet of paper with the words "Sales—Today" at one end, and "Market/Client trends—3 years" at the other. We then asked the CEO and one other member to pinpoint where on that continuum they wanted their new CMO to sit. The discussion that ensued led them to realize they wanted their new CMO to deliver sales more rapidly than what was inferred in the job description HR had drawn up for the position.

Actionable Insight No. 4: What to Do If Your LT Feels Too Big

If you sense your LT has become so big that it has become ineffective, beware of a common reflex identified by Cross and Katzenbach: "When confronting the performance of the top group of executives, as in any other major change effort, CEOs and other senior leaders often leap to the role of architect. They move boxes and lines around on an organization chart and redesign the formal incentive structures and workflow."[45]

To "play architect" should be a last resort because adding, moving, or removing members on an LT has far more consequences than on a nonexecutive team because LT membership mirrors organizational structure. We propose three less disruptive options.

Option 1: Create an Executive Team Subcommittee

To be clear, we are not speaking about disbanding a large LT and replacing it with a smaller one. We are speaking about creating a formal LT subcommittee that deals with certain recurring issues that do not concern a good number of LT members.

A discussion of this option can be found in the last Actionable Insight in Chapter 4. We refer you to it for more detail.

Option 2: Enlist a Right-Hand Person to Form
a Dynamic Duo at the Top

On several effective LTs, we notice that the CEO has what we would call a strong right-hand person. That person has been, at times, an LT member, a CFO or COO, but not always. It may also be someone who is not always considered a full-fledged member of the team such as a chief of staff or a strategy director.

Some of these right-hand people are men, some women, some young, others old, such that we would be hard pressed to define traits they had in common. However, the relationship they shared with their CEO had three common characteristics.

The first is its *complementariness*, which we define using the words from the authors of a study that lends support to our view that organizational performance is supported by having what we call a "dynamic duo at the top."[46] These authors state that for the duos they identified, the "pair incorporated different world views, as indicated by differences in functional background and industry experience."

The second characteristic of the CEO/right-hand person relationship is *respect*. Although the dynamic duos we observe fight intensely, their task-related conflict never morphs into relationship conflict, and we never hear either party criticize the other behind their backs.

Finally, there is *trust*. What leads to the development of such trust is open to interpretation, but we think there are two contributing factors. The first is that the right-hand person has no hope of taking over the CEO position or, alternatively, has made it abundantly clear that he or she does not want the job. Another is that the right-hand person has repeatedly shown a willingness and capacity to set aside personal and unit interests for the greater good.

These right-hand persons play a mix of two roles that mirror the LT's critical roles of decision making and alignment. The first is as a sounding board. As one often hears, CEOs feel quite lonely at the top because they are ultimately held responsible for all strategic decisions. CEOs lucky enough to have a true right-hand person feel less lonely because they can run decisions by that person before pulling the trigger, and that person, if he or she is the right one, stands by the CEO no matter how that decision turns out.

The second right-hand person role is an alignment role. It may be even more critical than the first because, as we explained in Chapter 3, CEOs spend most of their time leading their LT in Hub-and-Spoke mode and must play the three bridging roles if they want their LT to remain aligned. But all three bridging roles are difficult for the CEO to play alone, especially if the LT is large and its members geographically dispersed.

> *A good right-hand person has no hope of taking over the CEO position or, alternatively, has made it abundantly clear that he or she does not want the job.*

Thus, for example, CEOs may let a conflict between LT members fester because they have no time to play the mediator-bridging role or simply because they never find out about the conflict in the first place. Or the CEO may not have time to ensure that LT members socialize their projects with colleagues before presenting to colleagues at LT meetings. This is an alignment task that the chief of staff played on the highly effective seventeen-person LT we mentioned previously, and it was her ability to do so that greatly contributed to this LT's effectiveness.

While very little research has been done on dynamic duos at the top, based on our experience we encourage CEOs to think about who might become their right-hand person and test them by tasking them explicitly with certain of tasks such the one described here.[47] Or it could be any one of the tasks associated with the three CEO bridging roles we described at the end of Chapter 3.

Based on how indispensable CEOs who have a chief of staff have told us they were, we would strongly encourage LT leaders to consider hiring one to play this role.

OPTION 3: IMPROVE YOUR LT PROCESSES

One of the least effective LTs we encountered had seventeen members, but so did one of the most effective. The reason for the latter's effectiveness was the presence of a chief of staff who played the two right-hand person roles described in option 2 above, as well as the measures they implemented so the LT could benefit from its diversity.

We discuss these measures in Chapter 6.

The Chapter in a Nutshell

- CEOs face constraints in removing members and feel pressure to add members. The questions answered in this chapter thus are "Should I add an CXO to my LT?" and "Is my LT too big and, if so, what can I do about it?"

What the Evolution of LT Roles Can Teach You about Your LT Today

- There has been an explosion of new CXO positions pushed by what has been named the "fast fashion industry of CXOs."

- The evolution of the following positions offers lessons to CEOs who are thinking of adding these and other CXO positions to their LTs:

  - Chief operation officer (COO)

  - Chief financial officer (CFO)

  - Chief strategy officer (CSO)

  - Chief talent officer (CTO)

  - Chief information technology officer (CITO)

  - Chef marketing officer (CMO)

  - Chief diversity and inclusion officer (CDIO)

How Big or Small Should Your LT Be?

- There is no evidence that a small LT promotes organizational performance. Those making such claims focus an LT's decision-making role but overlook the evidence that a larger LT supports an LT's critical alignment role.

- Led by influential CEOs such as GE's Jack Welch, the trend is to ever larger LTs. This has made the debate over the optimal LT size largely a theoretical one. Indeed, by the time CEOs become concerned by their LT's size, it has climbed into double digits, and telling them they should cut positions is not realistic in practice.

- Most CEOs are better served by advice on whether they should add a new CXO position to their team and how to manage a large LT.

Summary of Actionable Insights

1. Consider the following criteria when wondering whether to add a new CXO position:

   - Criterion no. 1: Understand what LT positions your business model dictates.

   - Criterion no. 2: Determine if you are creating a new position to address a short-term or an ongoing issue.

   - Criterion no. 3: Consider different options if you are you naming someone to set up a new function or to lead an existing one.

   - Criterion no. 4: Determine if creating a new LT position will best support a new issue or priority.

   - Criterion no. 5: Avoid adding a third hierarchical level to your LT.

2. If you are sitting at five members, think carefully before adding another LT position.

   - Adding a sixth position may have a more significant impact on your team's dynamics than you would imagine.

3. Get alignment on what type of COO or CMO you need before starting your search for this position.

4. Options to consider if your LT feels too big

   - Option 1: Create one or more subcommittees.

   - Option 2: Enlist a right-hand person to form a dynamic duo at the top.

   - Option 3: Improve LT processes.

$$\left(\; 6 \;\right)$$

ASSESS YOUR LEADERSHIP TEAM

AND FIX IT

"Frustrated. Just plain frustrated" was Joanna's response when we asked her how she felt about her LT.

Promoted to CEO a year earlier from her position as VP of operations, she had vowed to manage her team differently than her predecessor, Marcus. It was Marcus's divide-and-conquer leadership style, in her opinion, that had been the obstacle to cross-unit synergies that could have delivered much-needed growth. Marcus was now out. Joanna, known as a team player, was in.

Because her former colleagues, now her LT members, also felt that Marcus was responsible for collaboration-inhibiting silos, Joanna was confident they would support her efforts to build a new culture of cooperation.

Things had started off promisingly. Three months into her tenure, Joanna organized a two-day LT retreat. She hired a team-building consultant who had each of them fill out a Myers-Briggs Personality Type Indicator (MBTI) personality assessment, and they kicked things off by discussing how their personal styles affected team dynamics.[1] They also explored the benefits of teamwork and engaged in an outdoor scavenger hunt demonstrating how teamwork led to better results.

"It was the greatest retreat we'd ever had. We had so much fun! Things improved. The mood was better. We had better discussions and, when things got tense, someone would joke that it was because we had too many ENTJs around the table," she laughed.[2] "But a couple of months later, the silos and the politics were back. I felt betrayed because the team told me they hated silos and politics!"

A year into her tenure, Joanna invited us to observe one of her LT meetings. The agenda included an investment discussion led by a business unit head who was asking for the lion's share of the firm's capital expenditures budget. Joanna introduced the topic by saying, "Remember: I want everyone to think of what's best for the organization, not for your unit."

"Do you feel that saying that made any difference?" we asked her afterward.

"Yes … well, maybe … Oh, I don't know!," she exclaimed, which is when she admitted she was "frustrated, just plain frustrated."

Joanna's story illustrates two common strategies CEOs use to address their dysfunctional LT. The first, reflected by Joanna's two-day retreat, is the **Team Benefits / Mind-set approach**. It consists of gathering LT members for a "team-building" offsite, hoping things will improve if executives explore the benefits of teamwork through data, discussion, and case studies. They may even experience those benefits firsthand with games and simulations. Personality assessments and other tools are also used to promote a "collaborative mind-set."

Many LT programs simply assume that executives will adopt the correct behaviors if they understand their benefits. If this were true, we would all be exercising daily.

While these programs often improve behavior in the short term, they rarely lead to lasting change, and for good reason: their short duration does not provide sufficient practice and repetition for team skills and mind-sets to become habit. The assumption behind these programs is that people will adopt the correct behaviors if they understand their benefits. If this were true, we would all be going to the gym and eating greens daily.

The second common strategy to address dysfunctional LTs is what we call the **Just-Do-It strategy**, as illustrated by Joanna's "think of what's best for the organization" comment. We also hear CEOs use "leave your unit hat at the door" and other such phrases exhorting executives to sacrifice their unit's interests for the greater good.

Leaving aside that executives who regularly sacrifice their unit's interests rarely keep their jobs (see why in Chapter 1), CEOs who adopt the Just-Do-It approach implicitly assume that their LT's dysfunctionality stems from their executives' personal failings (e.g., they are selfish or lack courage). If we accept this assumption, we would need to conclude that selfishness and a lack of courage are the dominant traits of all executives, including those reading this book, because LTs everywhere experience similar dysfunctionalities.

But there is no evidence that executives are any more selfish or lacking in courage than the general population. Thus, it is more logical to conclude that LT dysfunctionality is rooted not in executives' personalities but in structural factors common to all LTs. These structural factors are the ones we explored earlier: LT members' dual role (Chapter 1), power (Chapter 2), and Hub-and-Spoke functioning (Chapter 3). They are what make executives, even the bravest and most selfless, emphasize their unit's interests, which is why telling them to set these interests aside is ineffective. Intuitively, CEOs know this. As such, Just-Do-It is less a strategy than an admission that they are at a loss to fix their LT's dysfunctionality.

If the bad news is that the Team benefits / Mind-Set and the Just-Do-It approaches continue to be promoted as panaceas despite their limited effects, the good news is that an effective approach does exist. We describe this approach, which we label the POP, in this chapter. It produces results rapidly, typically within three or four months and is the most durable method to improve LT teamwork we have come across because it leverages the science of habit formation.

A description of the POP approach comes in the second section of this chapter, because first you need to assess if making the effort to improve your LT is worth it. It may not be. For LTs, the dimensions you need to pay attention to are set out in the first section:

- Constructive conflict

- Productive collaboration

- Strategic alignment

Reading our description of these dimensions will already give you many ideas regarding how to improve your LT before you move on to the POP framework which comes in the second section of this chapter.

At the end of the chapter, we offer answers to questions frequently asked by CEOs embarking on a journey to improve their LTs. If you do not find your own questions addressed there, please send them to leadershipteamalignment@insead.edu. We will do our best to answer as many as we can.

Assess Your LT's Effectiveness: The Three Dimensions

Want to improve your LT? Start with assessing its current effectiveness.

Meetings offer a good opportunity to do so, as highlighted by Harvard professor Julie Battilana and her colleague at Rotman, Tiziana Casciaro, who explain that those who pay attention in meetings, no matter how dull,

> gain invaluable insights by carefully noting other attendees' behavior, verbal and nonverbal, and analyzing interactions: who defers to whom; what alliances seem to emerge; which conflicts lurk beneath the surface; who is gaining influence and who is losing it.[3]

How CEOs can use meetings to assess their team was illustrated by an offsite we observed during which Gianpiero, a chief marketing officer (CMO), presented his new marketing plan for validation. As he did so, we noticed his CEO was paying little attention to him. Instead, she was watching her other LT members.

When Gianpiero finished presenting his plan, he asked his teammates, "Any questions or feedback?" Silence. "Well, okay then," he said, disappointed that no one bothered to respond. "I'll be reaching out to all of you individually to discuss your role in phase 1." And then the team moved on to the next topic.

After the meeting, we asked the CEO why she had been observing the members of her team while Gianpiero presented. She answered, "Before the meeting, I asked each of them, one-on-one, about Gianpiero's marketing plan. They all told me they liked it. But when I saw their faces during the meeting, I could see many didn't. Now I know I need to do something about it or Gianpiero's plan has no chance."

We learned a lot from this CEO and many others about how meetings provide information about LT effectiveness that, ironically, is not always easy for CEOs to get in one-on-one discussions or, to use a Chapter 3 expression, in Hub-and-Spoke mode.

But, of course, you must know what you are looking for. We next describe the three dimensions you need to focus on: constructive conflict, productive collaboration, and continuous alignment.

Dimension No. 1: Constructive Conflict

Constructive conflict, which some prefer to call "constructive debate," is the first dimension of LT effectiveness: It is **an LT's ability to engage in <u>task-related conflict</u> at the <u>right time</u> and leaves LT members feeling the <u>process was fair</u>**. It is the foundation of quality strategic decision making. which, along with alignment, is a key LT role, as discussed in Chapter 4.

Constructive conflict supports decision making by surfacing assumptions and biases and preventing groupthink. It is what enables a team to benefit from its diversity. It also increases the likelihood that LT members will align with a decision, even when they disagree with it.[4]

Based on complaints that executives have shared with us, very few LTs master constructive conflict, meaning they are incapable of putting tough issues on the table.[5] Instead, tough issues get dealt with by the CEO behind closed doors in hub-and-spoke mode.

Nothing could be less effective as LT members line up outside their CEO's door to complain about colleagues, fomenting distrust and leaving CEOs with time for little else than conflict resolution, prompting one CEO we met to say: "I often feel like the CMO—chief mediation officer—not the CEO."

A word about each of the three elements we underlined in our definition: task-related conflict, at the right time, and fair process.

Task-Related Conflict

Also called cognitive conflict, task-related conflict involves the expression of different viewpoints, ideas, and opinions. It is opposed to relationship conflict, which is characterized by tension, annoyance, and animosity among team members.[6]

Many LTs fear putting tough issues on the table because task conflict easily morphs into relationship conflict, as many of you may have experienced.[7] To prevent this, effective LTs take concrete steps such as the ones we detail in the second section of this chapter. Ineffective LTs rely on their LT members' goodwill in accordance with the Just-Do-It strategy.

At the Right Time

As seen in Chapter 4, truly strategic decisions get made over weeks, if not months. This means a strategic topic (e.g., a plan, an investment decision) can make it to the LT's agenda more than once. But on ineffective LTs, strategic topics make it to the agenda only at the very end of the decision-making process when a decision has, for all intents and purposes, already been taken. It is then too late for LT members to contribute significantly. When an LT lets this happen, it is no wonder it experiences more destructive conflict.

Process Was Fair

A fair process provides psychological safety that enables LT members to express themselves freely, without concern for the power factors discussed in Chapter

2. It also gives them assurance their voice has been heard and their perspective considered, even if their opinion did not win the day.

Dimension No. 2: Productive Collaboration

Productive collaboration, the second key dimension of LT effectiveness, **is collaboration between the right LT members where the benefits outweigh the costs**.

Few LT members can achieve their objectives without their colleagues' collaboration. An absence of collaboration not only leads to conflict among LT members; it also impedes collaboration between managers and employees below and thus becomes an organizational problem.[8] This is why strong CEOs do not let poor relationships among LT members fester.

The importance of collaboration is so widely accepted that "more collaboration" is often what CEOs respond when we ask them, "What is your main objective in bringing your team together for an offsite?" The assumption is that if a little collaboration is a good thing, more must be better. Unfortunately, that is not the case.

This is something LT leaders like Anand, CEO of a multinational service provider we worked with for years, understood well. Informed that his regional heads were complaining that he was blocking their collaboration to create a key account structure that would facilitate sales across their regions, Anand's response was, "But I *don't* want them to collaborate."

Surprised that a CEO would actively discourage collaboration, we asked him why.

"It's simple," he replied. "Market growth inside each of their regions is projected at 10 to 12 percent. If each of my regional heads captures just half that growth in their region, we meet our targets. But instead, they are wasting their time developing cross-regional sales, which are ten times more complicated to develop and coordinate than sales within their regions. They need to stop wasting time collaborating and focus on their own backyards."

This exchange illustrates how strong CEOs are careful not to let their LT members fall into the many collaboration traps identified by collaboration specialist Morten Hansen.[9] It also underscores the two elements of the definition of productive collaboration that we underlined:

BENEFITS OUTWEIGH THE COSTS

Collaboration between LT members does not necessarily improve organizational performance.[10] *Productive* collaboration does. Ideally, LT members would recognize this. Often they do not. Thus, CEOs must ensure their most highly paid executives spend their time wisely. Among the traps CEOs need to look out for include these:

- Collaboration between LT members on an initiative that is not strategic.

- Collaboration on an initiative that is strategic but so ill managed by the LT member who "owns" it that he or she wastes their LT colleagues' time by making them sit through poorly planned meetings, interviews, and workshops.

- Collaboration that is overkill. As we explored in Chapter 4, it is neither possible nor desirable to involve all LT members in every decision-making process. Effective LTs ensure that LT members are involved only when their collaboration creates more value than is lost from taking them away from their day-to-day responsibilities.

BETWEEN THE RIGHT LT MEMBERS

To assess collaboration on an LT, it's important to know which LT members need to work together closely based on your organization's business model.

This is something a CEO of an industrial manufacturing firm we supported clearly lost sight of when we asked her to rate the collaboration on her LT. "Well, it's pretty good," she answered. "Of course, no team is perfect, so I would say we're an 8 out of 10." To justify her rating, she added: "Most everyone on the team gets along. Many go out for drinks after work. So, yeah, it's a solid 8."

"What would it take to bump that 8 up to a 10?" we asked. She paused and then said, "Well, if Paul and Magda got along better."

Paul and Magda were, respectively, the CEO's purchasing and supply chain directors. When Paul was hired, he had made the mistake of giving Magda advice on how to do her job. Magda had not taken it kindly. Since then, their relationship had deteriorated to the point that they barely spoke outside meetings. During meetings, their exchanges were frosty.

When we reminded the CEO that she had told us that cooperation between Paul and Magda's departments was critical, she looked pained. "Well, yes, I did say that … OK then, so maybe our team's collaboration isn't as good as I thought … Maybe it's closer to a 4 or 5."

This story reflects what we notice on all dysfunctional LTs: collaboration is dictated by personal relationships. On effective LTs, it is the organization's business model that dictates who collaborates with whom, not who gets along.

> *On effective LTs, it is the organization's business model that dictates who collaborates with whom, not who gets along.*

Dimension No. 3: Continuous Alignment

It is said that "strategy is a commodity; execution is an art," a phrase attributed by many to management guru Peter Drucker. The implication is that the ingredients of good execution are hard to define. While true, we do know that one of those ingredients is LT members who act on a common set of priorities.[11] This is why alignment, and more specifically *continuous* alignment, is our third dimension.[12]

We define continuous alignment as **the ability to develop two types of alignment—<u>vertical</u> and <u>horizontal</u>—and a <u>process to maintain them</u>**.

Once more, let us take a closer look at the underlined elements of this definition.

VERTICAL ALIGNMENT

Vertical alignment exists if each LT member's unit or functional priorities reinforce a set of organizational priorities that are often captured in a broader strategy. Said more simply, vertical alignment exists when each LT member's priorities align with their CEO's.

One might think vertical alignment is common. It is not. We rarely find it when we assess LTs, to the great dismay of their CEOs, most of whom believe their teams are perfectly aligned. Our findings are far from uncommon.[13]

HORIZONTAL ALIGNMENT

Horizontal alignment is alignment across units and functions. It exists when LT members meet their individual objectives in ways that complement, rather than impede, their colleagues' efforts to achieve their own objectives. It further requires that LT members receive support from colleagues when needed.

Horizontal alignment is as rare as the vertical type. In one study, less than 10 percent of leaders interviewed felt they could rely on the support of colleagues in other functions or units. And while the great majority of companies studied had at least one formal system for managing commitments across silos, only 20 percent of leaders believed these systems worked well all or most of the time.[14]

A PROCESS TO MAINTAIN THEM

Ineffective LTs rely on their members' willingness to maintain vertical and horizontal alignment. Their CEO expects them to "just do it." Effective LTs take systematic steps in a process to maintain them because both types of alignment insidiously erode over time for two reasons. The first is that an organization's strategy must evolve but LT members' priorities do not always evolve accordingly. This is because some executives view strategic planning as a two-step, sequential process: you develop the strategy, and only then do you implement it. If only it were that linear and simple.[15] The reality is that your strategy will change after it has been formally defined as competitors, clients, and regulators react to it, and other elements in the environment develop. A strategy rarely remains static.

While this seems obvious, many organizations do not have formal practices enabling LT members to adapt their personal objectives over the course of the year. When we asked one CEO why, he replied, "That would make working out year-end bonuses a nightmare." The moment he said it, he realized this was no reason to let his LT members pursue outdated objectives.

The second reason alignment erodes is that LT members interpret their organization's priorities through their function or unit lens. Over time, they begin to confound the organization's priorities with their own. Thus, for example, we have seen a CFO's priority to improve earnings before taxes, depreciation, and amortization (EBITDA) margin eventually become, in her mind, *the* priority, which in turn led her to block expenses other LT members needed to make for organizational success.

Thus, unless CEOs institute practices to maintain alignment, they can be 99 percent certain that their members will become misaligned over time, even if all of them are "great team players."

But Does Your LT Need Fixing?
A Tool to Assess It

Given the consensus that LT effectiveness is critical to your firm's performance, you might think organizations would routinely evaluate it. But few bother to assess their top team. As a former CEO and member of many boards told us, "It's just not done." When asked why, he said, "I honestly don't know."

We heard much the same from a private equity firm partner. She explained, "When we want to invest in a company, we'll evaluate the individual track record of its executives. We want all-stars. But assessing how those individuals work together *as a team?* No, we don't do that." Upon reflection, she added, "But we do take those executives out to dinner to see if they get along," the implication being that this was a sound team evaluation methodology.

Leaving aside that executives know to "get along" when observed, LT members who get along too well may be the last thing CEOs want since it reduces their willingness to challenge each other and makes them prone to groupthink.[16] As renowned LT expert Donald Hambrick writes:

> Of course, outright acrimony is almost always harmful in a group, but we seldom see chumminess at the top executive level. It rarely occurs in the best of teams; it's not sought; it's not needed.[17]

But if observing how executives get along over dinner is not an appropriate methodology, what is? There are several assessment tools on the market. Some are supported by sound science. Many are not. Even some of the sounder tools suffer from a flaw: they yield numerical scores whose seeming precision obscures the challenge of measuring something as complex as the human interactions on an LT, or any other team for that matter.

But the bigger problem may be that precise measures are not always helpful for a reason highlighted by Michael Lewis, author of the best-seller *Moneyball*: "Numbers start out as tools for thinking [but] they wind up replacing thought."[18]

In recognition of this, we present a tool that is not designed to give you a definite measure of your LT's effectiveness. What it gives you is something that executives tell us they want: a quick and noncostly way to think about their LT effectiveness and determine if it warrants attention. Although it is meant to be used by CEOs because they are the ones who ultimately decide if they want to invest time improving their LT's effectiveness, LT members and consultants can use it as well.

The tool is composed of ten statements addressing elements that can be observed when an LT meets. And while observing how LT members behave during a meeting can never tell the whole story, it can offer quite a bit about an LT's dynamics, as the anecdote at the start of this chapter can attest. Furthermore, the alternative of trying to understand team dynamics solely through questionnaires or individual interviews is fraught with obvious methodological pitfalls.

The ten statements that follow are linked to the three LT effectiveness dimensions we presented. Each statement may touch on more than one dimension because the dimensions are mutually supportive: affect one (positively or negatively), and there is a domino effect on the other two.

You can use the tool after any regular or offsite meeting. However, because the meeting you choose may be atypical, we suggest you spread your assessment across two or three meetings.

Methodology

Table 6.1 sets out the ten statements.

Step 1: Read each statement, and put an X in one of the columns to the right of the statement:

- Put your X in the column labeled Green if you completely agree with the statement.
- Put your X in the column labeled Yellow if you somewhat agree with the statement.
- Put your X in the column labeled Red if you completely disagree with the statement.

Step 2: When you are done, add up the number of Xs in each column.

Step 3: Discuss your results. To help you with this, appendix A offers a summary guide of what to look for and hints at best practices that can increase your LT's effectiveness.

It is worth reiterating that this tool is designed to spur and structure a discussion about your LT's effectiveness and not to deliver a precise measure of that effectiveness. To reinforce this point, it uses a "traffic light" assessment (green, yellow, and red) instead of a numerical assessment, thus reducing the temptation to argue over a precise number.

The discussion should culminate with an answer to a very simple question: Does my LT need to improve its effectiveness? We suggest you discuss this with a member of your inner circle (one of the LT members you trust the most) or with a trusted outside adviser (e.g., a board member or consultant, or even with your partner).

The discussion might be short if all your Xs are in the green column in which case you might well be justified in thinking your LT is functioning quite well.

The discussion may be just as short if all your Xs are in the red column

TABLE 6.1. Ten Statements to Assess your LT during Any Meeting

Statement	GREEN Completely Agree	YELLOW Somewhat Agree	RED Completely Disagree
No strategically important topics were missing from the agenda.			
All LT members seized the opportunity to network with colleagues either immediately before or immediately after the LT meeting—or both.			
LT members referred to the organization's strategy or strategic priorities over the course of the meeting.			
All topics presented during the meeting were followed by a discussion.			
When a topic was addressed to obtain LT member feedback, there was no "illusion of inclusion"; in other words, the LT member asking for feedback showed sincere interest in their colleagues' opinions.			
During discussions, all LT members had the opportunity to express themselves freely and were made to feel that their opinion was heard when they spoke.			
Task conflict did not morph into relationship conflict.			
When a plan or course of action was presented during the meeting, those most affected by it were not silent or visibly upset.			
All LT members paid attention to every topic on the agenda and were not busy doing something else.			
The follow-ups from the previous LT meeting were on the agenda.			
TOTAL			

because it would be hard not to conclude that your LT is dysfunctional (but this probably comes as no surprise if you have read all previous chapters of this book.)

The more likely scenario is that you will have a few Xs in each of the columns. This tells you that your LT is doing some things right, but that it is also raising some red flags. This alone does not mean you should devote time and energy to addressing them. We have come across LTs that were "in the red" on many of the statements and yet their organization was performing quite well judging from key performance indicators (e.g., revenue growth, margin). In such instances, who are we to tell the CEO there was a problem?

However, if your assessment raises several red flags *and* your organization is not performing well, improving your LT'S effectiveness may well be the place to start to get your organization back on track.

Add POP to Fix Your LT

"Does your LT exist outside of your LT meetings?"

We ask all CEOs this question because so many LTs do not exist outside their meetings. By this we mean that as soon as they leave the meeting room, members throw off their organizational leader hat and grab their function or unit leader hat to focus exclusively on their so-called individual objectives.

> *LT members must take their organizational leadership responsibilities seriously, inside meetings and outside them.*

Such behavior is encouraged by those who describe an executive's LT member role—their organizational leadership role—as a "part-time job." This invites executives to complain, "Let me do my *real* job," when asked to do work that does not directly contribute to their unit's performance, such as preparing for LT meetings or offsites or collaborating with LT colleagues who ask for support. These executives enjoy the status that comes with an LT position but shirk the related responsibilities.

So let us be clear: if CEOs want a well-functioning LT and firm, they must ensure LT members take their organizational leadership responsibilities seriously, not only inside meetings but outside as well. But as one CEO asked, "I can see if my executives behave as a team and take their organizational leadership responsibilities seriously when I have them in front of me, but what can I do when they are out of sight?"

We have provided answers to this question throughout this book. The POP framework presented here provides a further, systematic answer. POP stands for Purpose-Outcomes-Process. In short, it is a template that LT members must fill out and submit to their CEO if they want to add an item to an LT meeting's agenda.

Now, after reading the above sentence, you may be recoiling in horror like the subject in Edvard Munch's painting *The Scream*, thinking: "Wait a minute. This is a trap! You told us this chapter was about improving my LT, but it's really about improving meetings?!"

Yes and no. The POP will improve your meetings. But its primary purpose is to improve your LT's effectiveness, both inside and outside meetings. It does so by leveraging the science of habit formation.

This science tells us that good habits, whether they are related to teamwork, a healthy lifestyle. or anything else, require certain conditions. These include *regular prompts, repetition*, and *short-term benefits* that ingrain the desired behavior. We also know that good habits will not develop if they demand extraordinary willpower or the mastery of *complex skills*.[19]

The POP covers these conditions because it operates through LT meetings:

- First, meetings governed by POP offer regular prompts to adopt team behaviors and provide the repetition that enable these behaviors to become a habit both inside and outside the meeting room for reasons we will show. As the head of HR of an industrial firm who adopted the POP told us at the time we were writing this chapter:

    Last week, Jonathan [the company's chief legal officer] and I were discussing a real estate deal with a few staff members. In the past, we would have just launched into the discussion without clarifying what everyone's goals were, and this often led to conflict. And even if there wasn't conflict, we wasted a lot of time before we got everyone on the same page. But Jonathan immediately said, "Here are my outcomes." Everyone understood he was referring to the POP and that prompted us to align on what we were there to do. It made a huge difference.

- Second, a meetings-based approach delivers an obvious and sizable short-term benefit: your meetings will be more effective. But when we asked a CEO who used the POP what benefits her team gained, she emphasized something quite different: "It forced some of my executives who did not necessarily like each other to speak outside of meetings. They had no choice. But not only that, the discussions it enabled us to have increased our readiness to implement the plans the team brought to the table."

- The POP accomplishes this without requiring LT members to master complex skills because these skills are embedded in the POP framework.

To explain what the POP is, we begin by providing an example of an actual POP in Table 6.2. Here is some context leading to its development:

- It was developed by a strategy VP tasked with identifying acquisition targets. In doing so, he singled out ABC Inc. as a good bet. His CEO agreed but wanted his LT's feedback before pulling the trigger.

- Rather than consult his colleagues one-on-one, our strategy VP thought it would be quicker to obtain their feedback by presenting a business case for ABC Inc.'s acquisition at their next meeting.

- Thus, when the CEO's executive assistant sent an email asking for agenda items for that meeting, he emailed back what you find in the left column of Table 6.2 (labeled "Original Agenda Item"), which is how we routinely see LT agenda items presented.

- The CEO insisted he rework the agenda item using the POP framework the team had recently adopted. The strategy VP complied and later submitted the POP you find in the right column.

Purpose: The Why

To introduce the POP's first element, the Purpose statement, we hark back to a meeting we attended late one November many years ago. At this meeting, LT members discussed many critical strategic topics but never spent more than fifteen minutes on any one of them. Yet at the end of the meeting, the team spent forty-five minutes discussing the company's upcoming Christmas dinner—including whether chicken or salmon should be served.

That the company's senior executives would spend so much time discussing yuletide logistics did not appear to strike anyone as absurd. Some around the table even seemed happy when the meeting ended with a decision all could rally around. (They would serve chicken *and* salmon.)

You may smile at this anecdote, thinking that this could never happen on your LT. And you may well be right. However, very few LTs do not, at one time or another, waste time on nonstrategic topics, which points to a need for guardrails. This is where the POP's Purpose statement comes in.

TABLE 6.2. ABC Inc. Acquisition: The Before and After Agenda Items

Original Agenda Item (Before)	Revised Agenda Item Using POP Framework (After)
Subject: ABC Inc. acquisition	Purpose: Advance our objective of achieving 8% in nonorganic revenue growth by year end.
Type: For decision	Outcomes: 1. A list of the top reasons that we should acquire ABC Inc.
Time: 60 min.	2. Concerns about the acquisition we need to plan for if we go ahead with it.
	Process: 1. Presentation: the business case for acquiring ABC Inc.—10 min. 2. Discussion in subgroups—10 min. • What are the 3 top reasons we should acquire ABC Inc.? • What are your main concerns about the acquisition? 3. Plenary share of the subgroup work—20 min. 4. Next steps—2 min.

The Purpose statement forces the person who wants a topic added to the agenda to succinctly express why it warrants the LT's attention. It is not the output you are hoping for but the reason the topic needs to be discussed There are only two potential purposes:

1. To advance a strategic priority.

2. To address a problem that is an obstacle to achieving a strategic priority.

In the ABC Inc. acquisition example in Table 6.2, the Purpose statement, "Advance our objective of achieving 8% in nonorganic revenue growth by year end," is, of course, an example of the first.

Requiring that an agenda topic have a Purpose statement ensures that addressing it supports your strategy. That does not mean operational topics are banned from the agenda. These can be included if they meet one of the two purposes outlined above.

Here is how defining a Purpose for every LT agenda item supports the three LT effectiveness dimensions described earlier, both inside and outside meetings:

How Purpose Statements Support Constructive Conflict

Purpose statement support constructive conflict by obliging LT members to refer to their organization's strategic priorities thus offering a regular reminder of the organization' strategy, that is, the common ground on which LT members stand. As seen in Chapter 1, common ground is a precondition for constructive conflict both outside and inside meetings.

How Purpose Statements Support Productive Collaboration

As our Christmas dinner chicken versus salmon story attests, topics with little strategic relevance often make it to an LT's agenda simply because its members propose them. One CEO defended this practice by saying, "Well, it's their meeting, not just mine." That may well be, but CEOs are responsible for ensuring their highest-paid executives spend their time productively. The Purpose statement prompts CEOs to ensure they do.

Furthermore, by reminding LT members of a topic's strategic relevance, the Purpose statement reminds everyone that the topic is not only the topic owner's priority but the entire team's, encouraging them to contribute to it during the meeting. If the POP is sent out with the agenda ahead of the meeting, it will encourage the team members to contribute to the agenda item before the meeting as well and serves as a reminder that LT duties extend outside the meeting room.

Finally, by highlighting the strategic nature of a topic, we have found that a Purpose statement contributes to more productive discussions by keeping LTs out of the operational weeds.

How Purpose Statements Support Continuous Alignment

By forcing LT members to link an item they want tabled to a strategic priority, a Purpose statement obliges LT members to ask, "Do we *have* strategic priorities?" Do not laugh. After adopting the POP, many CEOs discover that theirs are not as clear as they thought or that none of their LT members can name them. Obliging LT members to define a Purpose statement for LT agenda topics surfaces this immediately.

Furthermore, Purpose statements address a far more common problem illustrated by an exchange we had with an operations VP who wished to launch a Six Sigma initiative at an LT meeting. We noticed his POP for this agenda item lacked a Purpose statement. When we pointed this out, he said, "Oh, I don't need one. Everyone knows why we need to talk about this. It's so obvious."

"Then shouldn't writing your Purpose statement be easy?," we asked.

He hesitated. Eventually he admitted his reason for not writing one. While his initiative would contribute to the organization's strategic priorities as defined earlier that year, he surmised those priorities had changed, since the company had missed earnings in the previous quarter. Since then, a change in the organization's priorities had never been explicitly discussed around the LT table, but if he was right, it was not the right time to launch a Six Sigma program with its significant upfront costs. Nonetheless, he felt compelled to do so because the program was included in his individual objectives.

Prompted by the POP, our operations VP met with his CEO to discuss the relevance of embarking on a Six Sigma journey at that moment. They agreed it could wait and so ensured that LT members could focus their efforts on more urgent matters.

Could this discussion have happened without the POP? Of course. But in practice, it often does not, and LT members are left clinging robotically to objectives and priorities despite a changing environment or, alternatively, redefining priorities alone, in their silo, something we saw many LTs do in the months following the 2020 COVID-19 pandemic.

By requiring that LT members refer to their organization's strategic priorities regularly, the POP's Purpose statement inevitably leads them to ask: "Are these priorities, and my own, adapted to our current circumstances?"

Table 6.3 summarizes the benefits of having LT members define Outcomes for LT agenda items.

Outcomes: The What

Outcomes define what the LT should be left with after an agenda item has been addressed. They replace the "For decision," "For discussion," and "For information" categorization touted as a team best practice but is ill suited to LTs for reasons tied to the three LT effectiveness dimensions:

How Outcomes Support Constructive Conflict

Many LT members mistakenly suppose LT meetings are where decisions should always be taken (see Chapter 4). As such, it leads to an overutilization of the "For decision" label, notably in two situations: when a topic is not ripe for decision and when a decision presented before the LT has, for all intents and purposes, already been taken but the pretense is made that it has not (what we referred to earlier as the "illusion of inclusion.")

In these two situations, the "For decision" label harms team trust because

TABLE 6.3. How a Purpose Statement Supports the Three LT Effectiveness Dimensions

	Purpose Defined • *Why a topic warrants the LT's attention (1 sentence)* • *Two options: advance a strategic priority / address a strategic problem*
Constructive conflict	• Reminds LT members of the common ground they stand on.
Productive collaboration	• Prompts CEOs to assess the relevance of a proposed topic. • Reminds LT members why a topic warrants their participation. • Maintains discussion at a strategic level.
Continuous alignment	• Confirms you have common strategic priorities. Some LTs don't. • Assesses if LT members know these priorities. • Obliges LT to reflect on their priorities' ongoing relevance.

LT members feel manipulated by the topic owner. This does little to encourage constructive debate, and the frustration it fuels leads to relationship conflict.

Specifying measurable outcomes avoids such trouble by forcing topic owners to assess if their topic is ripe for decision. It also precludes the illusion of inclusion by obligating them to be transparent about their reasons for adding their topic to the agenda.

> *"Outcomes" replace the "For decision" and "For discussion" categorization that is ill suited to LTs.*

Another problem with the "For decision" label is that it feeds the misconception that LT members are decision takers rather than decision makers, as discussed in Chapter 4—said differently, that they have a veto over whatever decision is on the table. With the POP, there is no such misconception because Outcome statements clarify the contribution LT members are expected to make.

To use our ABC Inc. acquisition example from Table 6.2, recall that the initial wording of the agenda item was "ABC Inc. Acquisition—For decision." Such wording left the impression that LT members still had a say in the decision to acquire ABC Inc. despite the open secret that a date to sign the deal had already been set.

The CEO nevertheless wanted the deal brought onto the LT table so all LT members understood the rationale behind the deal so they could explain it to their teams. He also wanted to ensure the due diligence process had been thorough. Both were achieved when the strategy VP used the POP format and specified the Outcomes of the planned discussion as:

- "A list of the top reasons we should acquire ABC Inc."

- "Concerns about the acquisition we need to plan for, if we go ahead with it."

TABLE 6.4. How Outcomes Support the Three LT Effectiveness Dimensions

Outcomes Defined • *The What: Specific, measurable goals to be achieved via an agenda item* • *Replace ill-suited "For decision / discussion / information" framework*

Constructive conflict	• Avoid harming team trust and prevent the illusion of inclusion. • Prevent the blurring of the decision-taker versus decision-maker roles.
Continuous alignment	• Encourage raising topics well before a decision has been taken.
Productive collaboration	• Reduce frustration by providing a natural end to a discussion. • Encourage LT members to focus on what they like about a proposal. • Enable LT members to better prepare.

How Outcomes Support Continuous Alignment

Continuous alignment is better served by defining outcomes rather than using the "For decision" label because the latter invites LT members to bring topics to the table only at the end of the decision-making process when there is little room left for LT colleagues to contribute. While bringing a topic to the table at the very end of the decision-making process is often better than not bringing it at all, it is not optimal. The less space LT members have to contribute, the less they understand and commit to a decision, the two key ingredients for alignment.

How Outcomes Support Productive Collaboration

If specific Outcomes are better than the "For decision" label, they are also better than tagging a topic "For discussion."

When topics are "For discussion," there is no natural end to them. Thus, they run overtime and oblige someone, usually the CEO, to shut down the discussion. This does little to promote team potency, leaving LT members feeling they did not get sufficient airtime or that their team is unable to achieve anything tangible. This is hardly productive.

In the ABC Inc. acquisition example from Table 6.2, the Outcomes proposed by the strategy VP specify a clear end to the discussion: when the team had drawn up a list of the top reasons for acquiring ABC Inc. and when the major concerns about the acquisition had been surfaced.

Another reason to avoid labeling a topic "For discussion" is because, based on what we observe in LT meetings, it incites LT members to focus exclusively on what they dislike about whatever idea is proposed to them. Unsurprisingly, topic owners react poorly to such "feedback." The result is that trust and the team's belief in its ability to collaborate suffer, which impedes productive collaboration outside the meeting room.

One last advantage of specifying Outcomes is they let LT members know what to prepare for, something that the "For decision" or "For discussion" labels do only in the vaguest of ways.

The points made above are summarized in Table 6.4.

Process: How the Outcomes Will Be Achieved

The last element of the POP, the Process, is how the outcomes will be achieved in the allotted time.

The benefits of having LT members think about process become obvious the first time they try. We recall an HR VP who had been given twenty-five minutes to present her rollout of a staff engagement survey. She knew that most of her fifteen colleagues thought the survey was a bad idea.

When we asked her how she would proceed, she said: "Well, I'll need at least twenty minutes to present my rollout plan." When we pointed out that this left just five minutes for feedback—a mere twenty seconds for each of her colleagues—she recognized, "Okay, I can see how that might not be realistic."

Her recognition, which came about only because she had to prepare a POP, prevented her and her LT colleagues from engaging in a foreseeably conflictual discussion that would have wasted the team's time during the meeting and afterward, when the HR VP would have struggled to find support to run her survey.

The right process is necessary for psychological safety.

But having LT members recognize when their timing is unrealistic is low-hanging fruit. With the right Process, a more important goal can be achieved, psychological safety, which allows LT members to share their information and opinions freely and provides CEOs with the truth very few receive otherwise, for reasons described in Chapter 2.

Ironically, the term *psychological safety* may itself be an obstacle to its implementation because, for some, it implies that executives are fragile beings who need protection. As one CEO told us, half-mockingly: "If my executives need to feel psychologically safe, then maybe I need braver executives." Implicit is that a lack of courage is what prevents executives from telling the truth.

But as explored in Chapter 2, executives who withhold the truth are rational, not cowardly. So, creating psychological safety is not about coddling the faint-hearted. It is about creating conditions that make it worth their while to speak up.

The points made above are summarized in Table 6.5.

TABLE 6.5. How Process Supports the three LT Effectiveness Dimensions

	Process Defined • *How the topic owner proposes to achieve outcomes*
Productive collaboration	• At the most basic level, ensures an agenda item's timing is realistic. • Promotes the free expression of opinion (i.e., psychological safety). • Provides LT members with information to participate intelligently.
Constructive conflict	• Presenting a proposal avoids a go/no-go confrontation. • Subgroups enable introverts to have a voice and prevent task conflict from morphing into emotional conflict.
Continuous alignment	• Clarifies what the questions are so all are on the same page. • Recap and closure ensure no misunderstandings when all leave the room.

The generic Process we propose next is designed to do just that, and implementing it does not require a psychology degree or expert skills. It can be adapted to any topic on an LT's agenda, no matter how much time is allotted to it. (The timing we propose is simply meant to provide an idea of the percentage of time to allocate to each of its steps.)

We describe these steps summarily here. Details are in appendix B for two reasons. First is that you may be reading this on a plane, a train, a beach, or possibly in your bed. and the details are superfluous at this time. Second is that if you are a CEO, you do not need to know the details of the process. You only need to know enough about the process to own it. On effective LTs we have observed, CEOs delegated Process details to their chief of staff or to an LT member selected because they had an interest and a talent for managing process.

So, what follows is all you need to know about the Process steps:

PRELIMINARY STEP: PRESENTING THE TOPIC AS A PROPOSAL

Topic owners should avoid presenting the ideas they wish to validate at a meeting as a plan, a strategy, or anything resembling a final product. When they do this, it sets the conditions for a go/no-go confrontation with colleagues. It is best to present ideas as a proposal, which increases the likelihood of discussion and feedback.[20]

STEP 1: INTRODUCING THE TOPIC (5–10 MINUTES)

LT members are reminded of the topic's POP so all LT members understand:

• Why the topic warrants their attention and to serve as a reminder of organizational priorities (i.e., the Purpose).

- What the Outcomes are, so all know what is expected of them and when the topic ends.

- How the topic will be addressed – the Process – including the specific questions they will be asked.

The topic owner then provides sufficient background information for all LT members to participate. (Effective LTs never assume all LT members will have time to study prereads).

Step 2: Individual or Subgroup Reflection (2–10 minutes)

If you want all LT members to participate freely in plenary, have them first address the issue individually or, better yet, in subgroups. This gives introverts the time to formulate their thoughts and creates psychological safety by giving all LT members a place to try out ideas. Using subgroups also prevents task conflict from morphing into relationship conflict because it softens the language executives may initially use to criticize their colleagues' ideas.

But beware: the most powerful and extraverted LT members will often want you to skip the subgroup step, ostensibly to "save time." Give in to them, and you pave the way for them to monopolize the plenary discussion.

Step 3: Plenary Discussion—Produce a List of Pros and Con(cern)s (15–20 minutes)

To kick off a good plenary discussion, you need a good question. "Any questions or comments?" does not qualify. If, as suggested, topic owners present their topic as a proposal, two questions rarely fail to provoke discussion:

- "What benefits will this proposal bring to our organization?" sets the tone for constructive conflict and lets topic owners know what elements of their proposal they can proceed with.

- "What concerns do you have about the proposal?" also supports constructive conflict and adds a dose of productive collaboration.

Step 4: Recap and Closure (3–5 minutes)

Postmeeting conflict often stems from LT members having misunderstood what was accomplished or agreed to during the meeting. This can be avoided by having the topic owner recap and the CEO then provide closure by specifying next steps.

Such a simple step can make your LT much more effective outside the meeting and, conversely, leads to much conflict outside of your meetings when it is overlooked.

Actionable Insights

This book, like many others in its category, may give the impression that fixing your LT is simply a matter of following a recipe. Of course, it is not. Every LT is different, and thus the CEOs we support generally have many questions.

In this section, we present the ones that come up most frequently and provide our answers to them as our actionable insights. Our focus is on meetings because, as indicated earlier, the fastest way to improve your LT's effectiveness is by improving its meetings. If done well, it will lead to the right behavior both inside *and* outside meetings. If your questions are not here, we invite you to send them to us using leadershipteamalignment@insead.edu. We will answer as many as we can.

Actionable Insight No. 1: What Are the Topic Owner's Responsibilities?

Answer: The topic owner must prepare.

This answer may appear blindingly obvious. However, those who have sat in an LT meeting know how few topic owners truly prepare and the result is that most organizations institutionalize the wasting of time of its highest paid people.

Despite this, CEOs let many LT members get away with not having prepared their topics adequately. Sometimes this is because CEOs do not take their own meetings seriously, but it may also be because they are unsure how to tell LT members to prepare.

The POP offers a simple and standard solution to this problem. Having topic owners fill out a POP should be the minimum expected of topic owners. Furthermore, when an LT member is proposing any type of plan or strategy to colleagues at a meeting, CEOs must insist topic owners reach out to their colleagues who will be most affected—what we call "LT stakeholders "affected— to socialize their ideas beforehand in yet another example of how the POP provokes teamwork outside meetings. (See the last section of Chapter 4 for a discussion on LT members' obligation to socialize their ideas prior to meetings).

When CEOs do not insist that topic owners socialize their ideas with LT stakeholders before a meeting, the in-meeting impact is easily foreseeable: a plenary discussion that is monopolized by these stakeholders who feel blindsided by the topic owner. Meanwhile, the other LT members are left checking emails wondering when they can get back to their "real job." This is hardly a good use of anyone's time and something that proves detrimental to your LT as LT members' belief in their team's effectiveness erodes.

Prework between topic owners and stakeholders is so critical that one of the most effective LTs we have observed wove it into their own custom POP template. We share this template (see Table 6.6) to illustrate how your LT can adapt the POP template to your own needs.

In this example, the agenda item addresses an acquisition of a company called Unicorn Inc. As you will note, this template does not use the words *purpose, outcomes,* and *process,* but their equivalents can be found at items 7, 9, and 5, respectively.

We highlight item 10 of this custom POP framework because it obliges the topic owner to identify the topic's main stakeholders. In this case, the topic owner, strategy VP John Doe, has identified three:

- The leader of the China business unit who will absorb Unicorn Inc.

- The operations leader who will need to train Unicorn Inc.'s technical personnel

- The HR leader rresponsible for general onboarding

This template requires that the topic owner go a step further and assess the level of interest each of these stakeholders has in the topic (high or low) and their influence on the final decision (high or low). This assessment is then expressed in a 2 × 2 matrix.

By requiring all topic owners to identify their stakeholders explicitly, a CEO makes sure that the owner has kept them in mind when developing their proposal, which supports horizontal alignment.

A CEO can also check if the topic holder has reached out to these stakeholders before the meeting so that less time is wasted during the meeting. However, in the LTs we have worked with, this can also be delegated to a chief of staff or to the LT member given responsibility for LT meetings.

On one occasion that we observed the LT who developed this template, a topic owner admitted he had not reached out before the meeting to the stakeholders he had identified. The CEO gently but forcefully cut him off, saying the topic would not be dealt with that day. And on to the next topic.

On another LT we observed, a topic owner who had not done her stakeholder homework was allowed to proceed. However, when the plenary discussion she was leading was soon monopolized by two stakeholders upset about her proposal, she was the one who interrupted the discussion this time. She apologized

TABLE 6.6. Example of a Customized POP Template

Request Sheet for Agenda Item

1. Name of proposer:	John Doe, Strategy VP
2. Meeting (date)	Oct. 16, 2023
3. Proposed topic	Unicorn Inc. acquisition
4. Guest speaker	Julie Paul , Dir. of Strategy
5. Time / process	1. Presentation – 10 min. 3. Plenary – 25 min. 2. Subgroups – 10 min 4. Conclusion – 2 min.
6. Proposed prereads	• Unicorn Inc. financial statements • Unicorn Inc. key figures sheet
7. How topic links to our strategic priorities	Unicorn Inc. was identified as the best target in response to strategic priority no. 3 to grow through merger or acquisition in 2023.
8. The issue in brief	Over the 2020–2022 period, our organic growth slowed by 10% annually. In response, we made inorganic growth a priority in 2023. In our 6-month search led by our Dir. of Strategy, we focused on market extension targets rather than product extension targets. Unicorn Inc. rose to the top of the list as a means to accelerate our entry into Asian markets.
9. Specific question(s) to be discussed	1. Reasons it makes sense to acquire Unicorn. 2. Concerns about the acquisition we need to plan for should we go ahead with it.
10. Main stakeholders	

to both stakeholders, but also to the rest of her colleagues, recognizing that she had wasted their time by not having done what she called her "homework" before the meeting. She vowed to meet with both stakeholders shortly after the meeting. This was a great example of leadership maturity on her part and of LT effectiveness more generally.

Actionable Insight No. 2: Who Should Be Responsible for Developing Your LT Meeting Agenda?

Answer: The CEO needs to own it but can get help from a chief of staff or LT member.

In most organizations we have worked with, the CEO oversees the development of the LT meeting agenda, but many do so passively. For example, they delegate the canvassing of LT members for agenda topics to an executive assistant who has little power to block topics that are not strategic.

LT expert David Nadler suggests that CEOs adopting such a passive approach may do so to avoid appearing autocratic. But they are making a mistake and confuse two distinct dimensions of leadership illustrated in Figure 6.1:

- The participative dimension, which covers the extent to which CEOs allow LT members to participate in decision making

- The agenda and process dimension, which addresses how directive CEOs are about the choice of topics and how those topics will be addressed

As a result, Nadler says CEOs often begin in quadrant 2 of Figure 6.1, giving little or no direction about the agenda or process to LT members before meetings and giving their LT members a lot of room to participate during the meeting. But, as he notes, "This frequently leads to ill structured and non-productive work sessions and a drift toward not very effective management by consensus."[21] Some CEOs may then overreact and move to quadrant 4: they take control of the agenda and are much more forceful about presenting their viewpoints during meetings, the very thing they wanted to avoid in the first place.

Nadler says it is better for CEOs to start, and remain, in quadrant 1. To do this in practice, we suggest that they do the following two things, for which they can get support from a chief of staff or an LT member.

TAKE CONTROL OF THEIR LT's MEETING AGENDA

CEOs can take control of the agenda by reaching out to LT members for topics they want to add to the agenda and discarding those whose Purpose neither

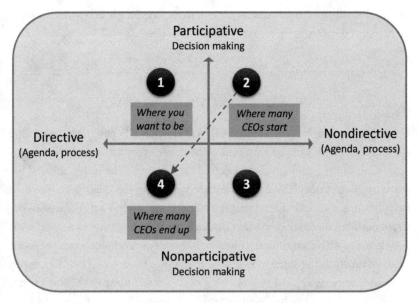

FIGURE 6.1. Nadler's Two Dimensions of LT Leadership

advances a strategic priority nor addresses a problem that poses an obstacle to a strategic priority.

They can also add topics to the agenda of their own if they gauge there is misalignment, vertical or horizontal, on their LT. For example, we once suggested to a CEO that he get his human resources VP, who had been working on a new compensation and benefits package without any input from his LT colleagues, to add this topic to the next LT meeting so this VP could present his preliminary thoughts for feedback. We suggested to another CEO that she ask her R&D VP to present the rationale behind each of the projects this VP had prioritized to make sure those initiatives responded to client needs as identified by his LT colleagues.

CEOs must make sure they control the agenda because, as the discussion in Chapter 2 notes, he or she who controls the agenda controls the LT.

ASK EACH TOPIC OWNER TO FILL OUT A POP TEMPLATE AND REVIEW IT WITH THEM BEFORE THE MEETING

By reviewing the POP with the LT member who develops it, CEOs can ensure that the agenda item's Purpose is strategically relevant, the Outcomes are appropriate, and the Process will achieve the outcomes. They can also evaluate if the topic owner has correctly identified the stakeholders and reached out to them before the meeting to ensure none of them feels blindsided when the topic is introduced, a common occurrence on ineffective LTs.

Actionable Insight No. 3: Does the Order in Which You Address Meeting Topics Matter?

Answer: Definitely.

The order of topics is something CEOs of effective LTs pay attention to. One seasoned CEO we worked with told us he made every effort to group topics according to the mind-set each required. For example, he never allowed his team to discuss people issues immediately after having dealt with business performance issues. He found that the dispassionate mind-set required to address performance issues made it difficult for his LT members to deal with people issues with compassion. However, if there was no choice to address both types of topics in the same meeting, he made sure there was a break between the two. The same applied to topics that required solutions in the short term: "exploit" topics, to use his wording, versus "explore" topics, which required long-term thinking.

CEOs also need to pay attention to how their meetings begin. Although you want LT members to address tough issues when they are fresh, kicking things off with tough issues is rarely a good idea because this may cause tension that sets the tone for the entire meeting. Nor should tough issues be the last issues on the agenda because they may leave a bad taste in the mouths of some LT members, which then have an impact on how they relate to colleagues outside of the meeting.

Paying attention to agenda architecture is an easy but often-overlooked aspect of LT effectiveness.

Actionable Insight No. 4: What Meeting Follow-Ups Should Be Done?

Answer: At minimum, keep a running list of post-meeting to-dos.

Although there are many meeting follow-up practices, we discuss only one because we see many effective LTs adopt it. In fact, this practice largely contributes to their being effective inside and outside of meetings. It consists of keeping a list of the to-dos coming out of every meeting and kicking off each new meeting with a review of that list to ensure that LT members have implemented the actions they committed to. These reviews are always short—anywhere between five and ten minutes and never more than fifteen.

On one team we worked with, one LT member read through the list and ex-

TABLE 6.7. Two Options for Delivering the To-Do List Review

	Pros	*Cons*
Option 1 One LT member reviews the to-do list	• Speed. Review rarely goes overtime.	• Designated LT member has big burden.
Option 2 Each to-do owner speaks up	• CEOs can discover much that would not come out otherwise.	• Risk that review runs overtime.

plained the follow-ups that had been done—or not—for every item. On another LT, the topic owner accountable for each item stood up to provide an update.

The advantage of the first option is speed. Because the one executive leading the review is not responsible for the to-dos, he or she will not linger over any of them. The disadvantage is that this person has the burden of reaching out to all their LT colleagues before each meeting to update the list. (See Table 6.7).

With respect to the second option, the risk is that the review runs overtime as the topic owners who have not done what they promised attempt to justify their inaction. However, a considerable advantage of this second approach is that it provides the CEO the opportunity to learn many things that they would not otherwise learn. One CEO told us, "If two people were responsible for getting a task done, but it did not get done, I find out a lot just by paying attention to which one speaks first and then watching the other's body language."

The Chapter in a Nutshell

- Two traditional approaches to improving LT effectiveness—the Benefits / Mind-Set and the Just-Do-It approaches—rarely produce long-lasting effects.

- A third, based on the POP framework, does because it leverages the science of habit formation.

- But the first question you need to ask is: Do you need to improve your LT's effectiveness? Start by assessing it.

Assessing LT Effectiveness

There are three dimensions you need to pay attention to:

- Dimension no. 1: *Constructive conflict*. An LT's ability to engage in task-related conflict at the right time and leaves LT members feeling the process was fair.

- Dimension no. 2: *Productive collaboration*. Collaboration between the right LT members where the benefits outweigh the costs and which does not depend on who gets along but on what your business model dictates.

- Dimension no. 3: *Continuous alignment* is the ability to develop two types of alignment—vertical and horizontal—and a process to maintain them. Vertical alignment exists when each LT member's priorities align with their CEO's. Horizontal alignment exists when LT members meet their individual objectives in ways that complement, rather than impede, their colleagues' efforts to achieve their own objectives.

Observing an LT meeting provides a great low-cost, low-effort opportunity to assess these dimensions. Use our simple assessment tool at Table 6.1 to see if your LT raises red flags that warrant your attention.

Adding POP to Your Meetings to Improve LT Effectiveness

- The POP framework improves LT effectiveness in a way that lasts because it leverages the science of habit formation.

- It is a framework to structure agenda items for LT meetings, but it is designed to support LT effectiveness both inside and outside meetings.

- Think of it as proposal template that anyone wishing to add a topic to the agenda (the topic owner) must prepare with these elements:

  - Purpose: to explain why the topic warrants the LT's attention, which is either to advance a strategic priority or address a challenge that prevents you from advancing a strategic priority.

  - Outcomes: what the LT should be left with after a topic has been addressed, that is, the specific outputs from the topic.

  - Process: how the outcomes will be achieved.

- POP replaces the "For decision"" For discussion," and "For information" categorization that is touted as a team best practice but is ill suited for LTs.

Summary of Actionable Insights

Our focus is on meetings because the fastest way to improve your LT's effectiveness is by improving its meetings in a way that provokes the right behavior outside of meetings.

1. *What should the topic owner's responsibilities be?* Prepare by filling out a POP and reaching out before the meeting to colleagues who have a major stake in the topic you will be presenting. No surprises.

2. *Who and how should you develop your LT meeting agenda?* The "who" is the CEO. CEOs need to take a more active role in crafting LT agendas because whoever controls the LT's agenda controls the LT. On effective LTs we have observed, the CEO is often supported by a chief of staff of LT member with an interest and the competence to do so.

3. *Does the order in which you address meeting topics matter?* Yes. Group topics should be arranged by the mind-set LT members must adopt to tackle them and do not put tough topics first or last.

4. *What meeting follow-ups should be done?* All effective LTs begin by reviewing the to-do list coming out of the previous meeting.

CONCLUSION

How the two of us met reflects in many ways the three LT dimensions discussed in this book: the relationship began with a potential conflict that transitioned to collaboration and then to alignment.

It was back in 2019. Each of us had been asked to teach a half-day class on power and politics in a top EMBA program. Appearing in the morning, Jacques offered a practical perspective on the topic in his capacity as an LT adviser, and former executive. Frédéric, as the seasoned academic, was to complete the picture in the afternoon, presenting power and politics models to push participants to assess how they used power in their current positions.

In theory, there should have been no overlap.

It was not until Frédéric arrived in class at 1:45, fifteen minutes before he was due onstage, that he saw Jacques' summary slide, still onscreen from the morning session, and sensed the overlap might be considerable. Jacques walked in at that moment to retrieve a coat he had left behind.

While Frédéric could have been upset, he simply introduced himself, explained the situation, and Jacques rapidly ran through what he had covered that morning. Class began a minute later, and Frédéric adjusted his presentation on the fly.

Two weeks later, we received participants' evaluations and discovered that they had felt the transition had been seamless and that the material had been rated quite highly. We decided to meet formally to celebrate over beers. The discussion soon turned to how little practical material was available to help those who reached the top team and how hungry all of them, rookies and veterans alike, were for insights into how LTs really worked. When the pandemic hit, we began writing down the insights that became this book.

Two years later, shortly before we handed in the final manuscript to our editors at Stanford University Press, Frédéric was asked to speak at the senior executive offsite of an international food and beverages conglomerate held at a countryside resort not far from the company's headquarters. Over dinner, the CEO of one of the group's European subsidiaries asked him for advice. She was having trouble getting the members of her LT to open up. She explained how techniques she had used to great effect with her team just months before when she was still the organization's CFO seemed to have lost their magic when she used them with her LT. What should she do? Her LT was unlike any other team she had managed before, and although she had sat on an LT, it was only now that it hit her to what extent an LT was unlike other teams.

Frédéric asked whether she had posed her question to colleagues sitting nearby, many of whom had years of experience leading LTs. She shrugged the question off, not unexpectedly. Few executives enjoy asking for help once they reach the top for a good reason: they do not want to appear foolish or seem to lack the understanding of LT dynamics they need to succeed. So not unlike teenagers who pretend to understand all there is about the birds and the bees, many executives fumble around for years before they learn.

Our goal was to speed up the learning process by laying out LT fundamentals, beginning in Chapter 1 with the paradoxical task LT members face when they must combine their role as members of the top team with their role as spokespersons for their divisions, groups, units, and so on. It is this foundational duality that provokes much of the power games and politics evoked in Chapter 2 and why LTs often get stuck in Hub-and-Spoke mode, the most maligned and misunderstood of the LT modes we discuss in Chapter 3 but the one CEOs must master if they wish to lead an effective team.

Having dealt with the fundamentals, we next dug into the key questions CEOs and LT members alike ask us, starting in Chapter 4 with, "What role should my LT play if I want it to support, rather than undermine, my organization's success?" Such a straightforward question turns out to be anything but. In Chapter 5, we provided criteria to help CEOs face off against the fast-fashion industry of CXOs to decide if the latest CXO position to pop up in the popular press is one their organization truly needs. We also discussed options for CEOs who feel their LT has grown too big. We completed that discussion in Chapter 6 with material to help assess and fix your LT, notably using the POP framework.

Several themes weave their way throughout these chapters. We return to them briefly here to underline their importance for executives, but also for the consultants and academics with whom we also wanted to share our work.

The first is the structural nature of many LT issues that, unfortunately, are often misdiagnosed as the result of clashing personalities. And while it would be foolish to deny that personalities contribute to some LT issues, ignoring the structural element underlying the most acute issues explains why many LTs never shake the dysfunctionality that plagues them.

The second is a related point. Many equate a well-functioning LT with harmonious relations and the absence of power games. As those familiar with LTs acknowledge, an effective LT has more to do with effective processes and engagement that minimize power games than naive efforts to eradicate them altogether. Making harmonious relations the prime goal of an LT "team-building" intervention is not only to misplace focus, but it may ultimately harm your LT.

The last issue we stress is the importance of diversity in its many guises because an LT can be truly effective only if its diversity can be expressed and expanded.

With these thoughts, we wish you all the best in your careers. We look forward to your feedback so that we can take it into account in our future efforts to demystify the workings of top teams and support your endeavors to become more effective LT leaders and members.

APPENDIX A

Assess Your Leadership Team: What to Look For When Doing the Ten-Statement Assessment

The material in this appendix is meant to assist you in using the assessment tool in table 6.1.

Statement	*What to Look For*
1. No strategically important topics missing from the agenda.	An effective LT can put difficult issues on the team table because it has developed a capability for constructive conflict. Strategically important topics require this capability because they often involve making the trade-offs that the strategic dualities discussed in Chapter 1 require.
	When there are no strategically important topics on the agenda, this can be the sign that a CEO is not confident that the LT can address such topics in Team mode, and so they are only addressed in Hub-and-Spoke mode. While there is nothing wrong with addressing certain strategic issues in Hub-and-Spoke mode, as discussed in Chapter 3, a healthy LT does not function exclusively in this mode.
	To set the agenda for an LT meeting, ask yourself: What are your organization's most important strategic issues? Start with your strategic priorities and see if there are issues related to them that should have been addressed, even in a cursory manner. If so, you must determine if these were left off the agenda for a valid reason or simply because the LT did not have the capability to address it in Team mode.

Statement	What to Look For
2. All LT members seized the opportunity to network with colleagues either immediately before or immediately after the LT meeting—or both.	Unless your organization is a conglomerate, your LT members need to communicate with each other often to achieve their objectives. Furthermore, the more LT members communicate with each other, the more they get to know each other and the less they succumb to the naive realism discussed in Chapter 1, a major source of negative conflict on many LTs.

The time immediately before or immediately after a meeting offers a prime opportunity for LT members to interact. If none grab this opportunity, it may be that they already discussed what they needed to discuss, or that they are sufficiently familiar with each other that there is no need for small talk.

However, if you know that your LT members do not often run into each other outside of meetings, the absence of networking immediately before or immediately after a meeting may be a sign of "silofication" that needs to be addressed. |
| 3. LT members referred to the organization's strategy or strategic priorities over the course of the meeting. | Your strategy and strategic priorities should be the driving force behind most proposals and topics put forward by your LT members during LT meetings. When these are explicitly linked to your strategy or strategic priorities, it contributes to alignment and offers an opportunity to validate it. Furthermore, when LT members invoke your strategy or strategic priorities, they remind everyone of the common ground on which all stand which in turn contributes to both constructive conflict and productive collaboration.

At an LT meeting when no one invokes the strategy or strategic priorities, this can be a sign that the team is misaligned because LTs invariably become misaligned over time. |

Statement	What to Look For
4. All topics presented during the meeting were followed by a discussion.	LT meetings are forums that should reinforce the two LT roles discussed in Chapter 4: decision making and alignment. It follows that topics should make it to the agenda because they warrant the LT's input or they require LT members to understand and be committed to a course of action tied to that topic. Both goals are hard to achieve via one-way communication, and lengthy presentations by topic owners detract from them. Discussion is required. As a rule of thumb, we tell CEOs that the ratio of presentation to discussion should be, at worse, 50 percent to 50 percent. Ideally, it would be closer to 33 percent presentation, 66 percent discussion.
	A lack of discussion is often a sign that the topic owner did not truly want discussion, either consciously or not. Or it may be that LT members did not have sufficient information to contribute to the topic or that the topic was not worthy of the LT's time. Whatever the case may be, an absence of discussion is often the sign of an ineffective LT.
5. When a topic was addressed to obtain LT member feedback, there was no "illusion of inclusion" or, in other words, the LT member asking for feedback showed sincere interest in their colleagues' opinions.	We discussed the illusion of inclusion in Chapter 4, which refers to the pretense of asking LT members for feedback on an idea, strategy, or plan but with little intention to take that feedback into account.
	Common indications of this are topic owners who (a) use the "formula" (see Chapter 3), (b) do not ask clarifying questions when someone offers feedback, (c) fail to take notes on the feedback they receive, or (d) argue with those providing feedback rather than accepting it.
	The illusion of inclusion has a negative impact on trust between LT colleagues and thus should be heartily discouraged.

Statement	What to Look For
6. During discussions, all LT members had the opportunity to express themselves freely and were made to feel that their opinion was heard when they spoke.	An LT benefits from its diversity only if that diversity can be freely expressed and, furthermore, when LT members are made to feel their opinions have been considered. This is another way of saying that an LT must create psychological safety for its members. When it does not, a host of unfortunate outcomes can be expected, such as lowered trust, groupthink, and low commitment to decisions taken.

An obvious sign that psychological safety does not exist is aggressive behavior that shuts down discussion. Another is a topic owner or CEO who summarizes a discussion but ignores the opinions of those they disagree with. More subtle signs we have observed in meetings are LT members whose body language screams out that they have something to say and yet are not invited to speak. |
| 7. Task conflict did not morph into relationship conflict. | Of the ten statements to assess an LT, this may be the easiest to assess because it does not take a psychology degree to discern when a task conflict transforms into relationship conflict (both of these terms are defined in Chapter 6). When this transformation begins to happen, effective LTs have the skill to get the discussion back on the rails.

Ineffective LTs do not have this skill, and the discussion continues to derail or, in many instances, the CEO or the topic owner quickly shuts down the discussion and suggests that it be taken "offline." When this happens, it affects the rest of the meeting, and the ill will often spills over outside the meeting room, hindering productive collaboration, all of which further erodes the team's belief that it can handle tough topics as a team. |

Statement	What to Look For
8. When a plan or course of action was presented during the meeting, those most affected by it were not silent or visibly upset.	When LT members are visibly upset by a proposed plan or course of action, it is often because they have been taken by surprise. This does not happen on effective LTs where members who propose a plan or course of action will have socialized it with what we called the main LT stakeholders (see Chapter 6).
	When such socialization does not occur and these stakeholders express their frustration openly, it leads to unproductive discussions, with many LT members sitting on the sidelines . When stakeholders do not express their frustration but remain silent, it may be no better because one can easily guess that they will not collaborate when the time comes to implement the plan or course of action.
9. All LT members paid attention to every topic on the agenda and were not busy doing something else.	When LT members are not engaged in every topic on an LT meeting's agenda, it may be for many reasons, including that the process to address the topic was poorly designed, LT members are not taking their role as organizational leaders seriously (i.e., they do not consider it their "real job"), or the agenda was poorly planned and certain topics should never have been added to it.
	Whatever the case may be, when LT members are not paying attention or, worse, are openly doing email on their computers, this is a clear sign of an ineffective LT. As one CEO told his LT members during a meeting we observed: "If you're going to sit on this LT, all the topics should interest you, whether they concern you directly or not."

Statement	What to Look For
10. The follow-ups from the previous LT meeting were on the agenda.	We have yet to see an effective LT whose meetings did not result in some action items. Effective LTs make sure there is agreement on what those action items are and who is accountable for them, and then follow up on them explicitly in subsequent meetings, as discussed in actionable insight no. 4 at the end of Chapter 6. If there is no agenda item entitled "Follow-ups from last meeting" or something of the sort, this implicitly means that what is discussed at LT meetings is of no consequence. There is no more telltale sign of ineffectiveness than this.

APPENDIX B

Details of the POP's Process

The appendix provides details on the Process of the POP process described in Chapter 6.

The steps we propose can be adapted to any topic on an LT's agenda, no matter how much time is allotted to it. Thus, the timing we propose is simply to provide an idea of the proportion of time to allocate to each of its steps.

Preliminary Step: Present the Topic as a Proposal

Topic owners do themselves few favors when they present the idea(s) they wish to validate with colleagues as a plan, a strategy, or anything that resembles a final product. Doing so creates the conditions for a go/no-go confrontation with colleagues, a mistake for three reasons:

- Conflict is not likely to be constructive when LT members feel a gun has been put to their heads. This is often how they feel when they are implicitly given only two options: approve or reject. Things are made worse when the time allotted for such discussions is short, as it often is.

- Productive collaboration also goes out of the window because go/no-go scenarios invariably have everyone focusing on what is wrong with a proposal for fear it will be approved without consideration of their concerns.

- Alignment is affected because the discussion will likely end without a clear decision.

It is best for topic owners to present their ideas as a proposal they would like their colleagues to consider. The topic owner should do so explicitly by stating at the start, "This is a proposal." This increases the likelihood of discussion and feedback.

Step 1: Introducing the Topic (5-10 Minutes)

The introduction to a topic should have two parts: the POP and the background information.

The POP

The POP's Purpose statement is read to remind everyone why the topic warrants their attention. Although it can be presented by the topic owner, it is most powerful if the CEO reads it.

Having the CEO, rather than the topic owner, do the introduction emphasizes that the topic is meant to advance the organization's strategy, not simply the topic owner's agenda. Productive collaboration is enhanced because it is the CEO (everyone's boss) who is asking them to participate in a discussion that is deemed important. And, of course, continuous alignment is reinforced by the reminder of a strategic priority. The impact of this symbolic role played by the CEO should not be underestimated.

Reviewing the Purpose statement should be quick. If we take the ABC Inc. acquisition example we presented in Chapter 6, the CEO or topic owner could simply say, "The next topic on our agenda today is a proposal from your colleague in strategy that we consider acquiring ABC Inc. This project fits in with our third strategic priority: to develop our nonorganic growth."

The Outcomes and Process are presented to ensure the discussion immediately starts down the right path and there is no doubt what will and will not be discussed. It prevents what we observe too often in LT meetings: an LT member responding to a colleague's comment by saying, "But that's not what we are discussing at all!" LT members then waste time debating what the discussion is or should be about, which adds an emotional layer to the discussion that does not favor constructive conflict.

Presenting the outcomes and process can be done by topic owner or by a facilitator—another LT member chosen by the topic owner—who will help the topic owner run the process and achieve the outcomes. We do not recommend the CEO play the facilitator role for reasons discussed in Chapter 2.

Background Information

It is impossible for LT members to participate competently unless they have sufficient background information. That is why topic owners often post a preread. The problem is that many LT members will never open it.

Most LTs address this problem by adopting a ground rule that "all LT members must study preread documents," a solution very much in line with the Just-Do-It philosophy, which assumes that LT members do not do their LT homework because they are lazy. Whether they are or not changes nothing to the following: we have yet to see an LT where this solution works.

The most effective solution we have observed is when the topic owner takes anywhere between 5 and 10 minutes—no more—to expose the minimum information LT members need to participate. This enables those who had no time to review prereads to participate.

While we recognize that some may feel this "rewards" LT members who show up to meetings unprepared, the benefits of a summary far outweigh the downsides:

- It obliges the topic owner to think about what is truly relevant and what is not. Absent this obligation, topic owners will often make lengthy PowerPoint presentations that leave no time for discussion. Furthermore, they will also send fifty slide prereads that discourage colleagues from preparing for meetings.

- Topic owners who have a clear idea of what information is truly relevant often devise a better implementation plan.

- Kicking off a discussion with a short summary means the facts are fresh in everyone's mind.

While we believe that having topic owners present a short summary of the facts is a best practice, Jeff Bezos at Amazon has adopted a very different approach with his famous six-page summary. We have been told by Amazon executives that it works quite well. While we have no doubt it does, it requires effort that most LTs have little appetite for it. Nevertheless, we are leaving a link for those who are interested in exploring this practice further.[1]

Step 2: Individual or Subgroup
Reflection (2–10 Minutes)

If your goal is to have all LT members participate freely in plenary, have them first reflect on the issue individually or, better, in subgroups. Depending on the size of your LT, the subgroups can be pairs, trios, or larger.

Subgroups gives the introverts on your LT the time to formulate their thoughts. Furthermore, it is one of the key ingredients for creating psychological safety because a subgroup is a safer space to try out ideas than plenary. When those ideas are later brought into plenary, they are not immediately associated with the person who expressed them but with the subgroup that puts it on the table. Furthermore, it becomes harder for an LT member in plenary to say they have no opinion because the topic owner or CEO can immediately respond: "Well, tell us what you discussed in your subgroup."

Perhaps the most important benefit of subgroups is that they offer a critical mechanism to prevent task conflict from morphing into the relationship conflict that is harmful to team performance. This is because LT members may use harsh language when they first comment on a colleague's ideas. When this happens directly in plenary, it can be perceived as a personal attack.[2] But when harsh language is used in a subgroup, subgroup members will, in our experience, reformulate those words in a more constructive manner when they bring them back into plenary.

Despite the obvious benefits of subgroups, some executives prefer to skip this step. These executives may be extraverts who find it easy to speak up in plenary within seconds of being asked and who have no inkling that this is not everyone's preference. Making them aware that introverted colleagues may not be as comfortable as they are may be enough to get them to accept the subgroup step.

A second group of executives who often want to skip subgroups are the most powerful LT members who experience fewer downsides when they express their opinions immediately in plenary. When these executives are also skeptical of the benefits of getting everyone's input, they exert their power to jump straight to plenary, ostensibly to "save time" but also because they intuitively know they can monopolize the conversation.

If time is truly of the essence—and in some cases it may be—then, by all means, skip the subgroup step. However, we find there are very few instances where an LT cannot afford to take the few minutes required for the subgroup step and so benefit from the decision-making quality and alignment advantages that subgroups contribute to.

Step 3: Plenary Discussion: Producing a List of Pros and Con(cern)s (15–20 Minutes)

Want to have a good plenary discussion?

You will need a good question to kick it off. Asking "Any questions or comments?" rarely does the trick, as many of you will have experienced, especially if the question is asked at the end of a meeting when everyone is watching the clock.

However, if a topic owner follows the recommendation in the preliminary step and presents their idea—whether it be a plan, a strategy, or something else—as a proposal, two simple questions immediately make sense.

- *"What benefits will this proposal bring to our organization?"* Alternatively, you could ask "What benefits will this proposal, as presented today, bring to our organization?" or, simply, "What do you like about this proposal?."

  This sets the tone for constructive conflict and, just as important, enables topic owners to find out what elements of their proposal their LT colleagues support. When LT members skip this question, the topic owner is often left wondering what, if anything, in their proposal they can act on after the meeting.

  To further the chances a discussion will ensue, we suggest that topic owners specify that the reason for the question is not to garner pats on the back but to ensure that they retain elements of their proposal that their colleagues appreciate.

  We have noticed that some LT members often want to skip this first question because they are in a rush to deliver their criticism. The only reason you would is if you do not care about creating the conditions for constructive conflict.

- *"What concerns do you have about the proposal?"* Note that the question is not, "What drawbacks do you see to this proposal?" or, as one masochistic executive once proposed in a meeting we observed, "What do you dislike about my proposal?" Such a question does not provoke constructive conflict or productive collaboration. Asking about concerns will.

Ultimately, these two questions lead to two outcomes: a list of pros and a list of concerns. If the pros overwhelmingly outscore the concerns, a decision to go ahead with the proposal can often be made on the spot, subject to the concerns being addressed by the topic owner.

Step 4: Recap and Closure (3–5 Minutes)

Too often a topic ends with LT members wondering what was accomplished, and they disperse with very different interpretations of what was agreed to. This inevitably causes conflict outside the meeting room. Having the topic owner recap what they heard solves this problem.

After the recap, the CEO provides closure. By having the last word, the CEO can add any elements the topic owner may have omitted in the recap, Furthermore, once a topic is addressed, it often means next steps for several people in the room. Since the topic owner has no authority to tell their colleagues what they must do, the CEO must step in.

If, as suggested, the topic has been presented as a proposal, the follow-up is quite simple. Using our example of the ABC Inc. POP at Table 6.2, you can imagine the CEO closing off by saying:

> Thank you all for your feedback. I see many of you see some quite positive things about the ABC acquisition. But at the same time, some of you expressed concerns. Your colleague in strategy and I will now work to see how these can be addressed. We will get to you about this at our next meeting."

Or more simply, the CEO can say: "I will get back to you with next steps after speaking with [topic owner]."

NOTES

Introduction

1. "Crickets" is a British idiom meaning "no reply or reaction at all" (https://dictionary.cambridge.org/dictionary/english/crickets).

2. Louis Hébert et al., *Paroles de PDG: comment 75 grands patrons du Québec vivent leur métier* (Montreal: Les Éditions Rogers Ltée, 2014).

3. Donald Sull, Charles Sull, and James Yoder, "No One Knows Your Strategy—Not Even Your Top Leaders," *MIT Sloan Management Review* 59, no. 3 (2018).

4. Natasha Bergeron, Aaron de Smet, and Liesje Meijknecht, "Improve Your Leadership Team's Effectiveness through Key Behaviors," *McKinsey Quarterly* (2020), https://www.mckinsey.com/business-functions/organization/our-insights/the-organization-blog/improve-your-leadership-teams-effectiveness-through-key-behaviors.

5. José Luis Alvarez and Silviya Svejenova, *The Changing C-Suite: Executive Power in Transformation* (Oxford: Oxford University Press, 2022).

6. Many academic and nonacademic sources allude to this question with a broad variety of competing views—for example, Henry Kissinger, *World Order* (New York: Penguin, 2014), https://books.google.fr/books?id=NR5oAwAAQBAJ.

7. David N. Berg, "Senior Executive Teams: Not What You Think," *Consulting Psychology Journal: Practice and Research* 57, no. 2 (2005).

8. "Creativity has become a necessity for many organizations because it may help them thrive in uncertain environments: F. C. Godart, S. Seong, and D. J. Phillips, "The Sociology of Creativity: Elements, Structures, and Audiences," *Annual Review of Sociology* 46 (2020): 489510. Diversity is one way to achieve creativity at the organizational level."

9. Alice Cahill, *Are You Getting the Best Out of Your Leadership Team?* (Greensboro, NC: Center for Creative Leadership, March 31, 2020). Nearly all the senior ex-

ecutives in the study (97 percent) agreed that "increased effectiveness of my executive team will have a positive impact on organizational results." EgonZehnder, *The CEO: A Personal Reflection* (Zurich: EgonZehnder May 11, 2018), 34: "As most executives know, a new CEO cannot and will not succeed without a strong team."

10. EgonZehnder, *The CEO*. 34

11. As Sigal G. Barsade et al., "To Your Heart's Content: A Model of Affective Diversity in Top Management Teams," *Administrative Science Quarterly* 45, no. 4 (2000), 826, https://journals.sagepub.com/doi/abs/10.2307/2667020, write: "Also, as J. Richard Hackman, "Designing Work for Individuals and for Groups," in *Perspectives on Behavior in Organizations*, ed. J. Richard Hackman, E. E. Lawler, and L. W. Porter (New York: McGraw-Hill, 1983), 257, pointed out, "Too often managers or consultants attempt to 'fix' a group that has performance problems by going to work directly on obvious difficulties that exist in members' interpersonal processes. And, too often, these difficulties turn out not to be readily fixable because they are only symptoms of more basic flaws in the design of the group or in its organizational context."

12. Richard Leblanc and Mark S. Schwartz, "The Black Box of Board Process: Gaining Access to a Difficult Subject," *Corporate Governance: An International Review* 15, no. 5 (2007), 843, https://doi.org/10.1111/j.1467-8683.2007.00617.x.

13. For example, see Donald C. Hambrick, "Top Management Teams," in *Wiley Encyclopedia of Management*.

14. This quote is often attributed to Albert Einstein, although it has also been attributed to many others, including New York Yankee baseball player Yogi Berra. According to the website "Quote Investigator," there is no substantive reason to credit either of them, and the expression may have originated with a student writing in a Yale student publication in the 1880s (https://quoteinvestigator.com/2018/04/14/theory/ accessed September 19, 2022). However, this is not something we have verified.

15. Peter Cappelli, Monika Hamori, and Rocio Bonet, "Who's Got Those Top Jobs?," *Harvard Business Review* 92, no. 3 (2014).

16. Including Yazmina Araujo-Cabrera, Miguel A. Suarez-Acosta, and Teresa Aguiar-Quintana, "Exploring the Influence of CEO Extraversion and Openness to Experience on Firm Performance:The Mediating Role of Top Management Team Behavioral Integration," *Journal of Leadership and Organizational Studies* 24, no. 2 (2017), 210, https://doi.org/10.1177/1548051816655991, https://journals.sagepub.com/doi/abs/10.1177/1548051816655991, and Scott Keller and Mary Meaney, "Attracting and retaining the right talent," *McKinsey Global Institute study* (2017). who write that 90 percent of investors think the quality of the management team is the most important nonfinancial factor when evaluating an IPO.

Chapter 1

1. Wendy K. Smith, Marianne W. Lewis, and Michael L. Tushman, "'Both/and' Leadership," *Harvard Business Review* 94, no. 5 (2016).

2. Jonathan Schad et al., "Paradox Research in Management Science: Looking Back to Move Forward," *Academy of Management Annals* 10, no. 1 (2016).

3. David N. Berg, "Senior Executive Teams: Not What You Think," *Consulting Psychology Journal: Practice and Research* 57, no. 2 (2005).

4. Emily Pronin, Daniel Y, Lin, and Lee Ross, "The Bias Blind Spot: Perceptions of Bias in Self versus Others," *Personality and Social Psychology Bulletin* 28, no. 3 (2002); Lee Ross and Andrew Ward, "Naive Realism in Everyday Life: Implications for Social Conflict and Misunderstanding," in *Values and Knowledge*, ed. Edward S. Reed, Elliot åTuriel, and Terrance Brown (Hillsdale, NJ: Erlbaum, 1996).

5. Wendy K. Smith, "Dynamic Decision Making: A Model of Senior Leaders Managing Strategic Paradoxes," *Academy of Management Journal* 57, no. 6 (2014).

6. Cheryl A. Picard, *Mediating Interpersonal and Small Group Conflict* (Saskatchewan: Dundurn, 2002).

7. Santiago Madrid Liras, "Why A Fourth Mediation Model: Opportunities and Integration of the Insight Mediation Model," *Revista de Mediación* 10, no. 2 (2017).

8. Robert J. Robinson et al., "Actual versus Assumed Differences in Construal: `Naive Realism' in Intergroup Perception and Conflict," *Journal of Personality and Social Psychology* 68, no. 3 (1995).

9. For example, Berg, "Senior executive Teams: Not What You Think"; Amy C. Edmondson, Michael A. Roberto, and Michael D. Watkins, "A Dynamic Model of Top Management Team Effectiveness: Managing Unstructured Task Streams," *Leadership Quarterly* 14, no. 3 (2003); Ann C. Mooney and Allen C. Amason, "In Search of the CEO's Inner Circle and How It Is Formed," in *The Handbook of Research on Top Management Teams*, ed. Mason A. Carpenter (Northhampton, MA: Elgar, 2011); Smith et al., "'Both/and' Leadership."

10. Charles Galunic and Jacques Neatby, "Order in the Strategy Court," *Harvard Business Review* (November 16 2013).

11. Ivanka Mihaylova, "Well Prepared for Conflict in Organizations? A Manager's Self-Assessment of Their Conflict Management Knowledge," *Knowledge International Journal* 42, no. 1 (2020).

12. *Game of Thrones* is an American fantasy TV show created for HBO and first aired in 2011 that became synonymous with political intrigue and often murderous and destructive attempts to seize power. *House of Cards* (created for Netflix in 2013) is also an American TV show. Although it is not unlike *Game of Thrones* when it comes to murderous attempts to seize power, it takes place in contemporary America, not in a fantasy world.

13. Éloi Lafontaine-Beaumier, Jacques Neatby et Louis Hébert, «Émergence de la publicité native: la Société Radio-Canada face à la transformation de l'industrie publicitaire (The Canadian Broadcasting Corporation and the upheaval of the advertising industry),» *Revue internationale de cas en gestion / International Journal of Case Studies in Management* 18, no. 1 (2020). which is why it can be used without being disguised.

14. Rufus E. Miles, "The Origin and Meaning of Miles' Law," *Public Administration Review* 38, no. 5 (1978).

15. Jon R. Katzenbach, *Teams at the Top: Unleashing the Potential of Both Teams*

and Individual Leaders (Boston: Harvard Business Press, 1998); Patrick Lencioni, *The Five Dysfunctions of a Team: A Leadership Fable* (San Francisco: Jossey-Bass, 2002).

16. See https://www.hoganassessments.com/blog/big-five-personality-characteristics-behind-hogan-personality-tests/ (accessed September 19, 2022)

17. Amy E. Colbert, Murray R. Barrick, and Bret H. Bradley, "Personality and Leadership Composition in Top Management Teams: Implications for Organizational Effectiveness," *Personnel Psychology* 67, no. 2 (2014).

18. Adam Galinsky and Maurice Schweitzer, *Friend and Foe: When to Cooperate, When to Compete, and How to Succeed at Both* (New York: Currency, 2015) write: "To succeed in life and at work, being either fundamentally cooperative or fiercely competitive won't get you the best outcomes. In fact, they explain that humans are hardwired to do both, and learning how to strike the right balance between the two is the best way to improve long-term relationships both at work and at home and to get more of what you want."

19. F. Scott Fitzgerald, *The Crack-Up: With Other Uncollected Pieces* (New York: Edmund Wilson/New Directions, 1945).

20. David Fubini, *Hidden Truths: What Leaders Need to hear But Are Rarely Told* (Hoboken, NJ: Wiley, 2021).

21. Perel used the phrase while interviewed by Wharton professor Adam Grant in episode 22 of his podcast, *Work Life*, which first aired on March 30, 2020.

22. Roger Fisher, William L. Ury, and Bruce Patton, *Getting to Yes: Negotiating Agreement without Giving In* (New York: Penguin, 2011; originally published in 1981). Subsequent editions came out in 1991 and then 2011, when Bruce Patton was added as coauthor. Roger Fisher, William L. Ury, and Bruce Patton. *Getting to Yes: Negotiating Agreement without Giving In* (New York: Penguin, 2011).

23. Donald Sull, Charles Sull, and James Yoder, "No One Knows Your Strategy—Not Even Your Top Leaders," *MIT Sloan Management Review* 59, no. 3 (2018).

Chapter 2

1. Amy C. Edmondson, Michael A. Roberto, and Michael D. Watkins, "A Dynamic Model of Top Management Team Effectiveness: Managing Unstructured Task Streams," *Leadership Quarterly* 14, no. 3 (2003): 305: "Scholars have argued that power plays a more central role in strategic decision-making within top teams than in the tasks performed by other work groups." See also Jose Luis Alvarez and Silviya Svejenova, *Sharing Executive Power: Roles and Relationships at the Top* (Cambridge: Cambridge University Press, 2005), 57ff., and Deborah G. Ancona and David A. Nadler, "Top Hats and Executive Tales: Designing the Senior Team," *MIT Sloan Management Review* 31, no. 1 (1989).

2. Jeffrey Pfeffer, *Leadership BS: Fixing Workplaces and Careers One Truth at a Time* (New York: HarperCollins, 2015), 23–24.

3. Joshua Rothman, "Shut Up and Sit Down: Why the Leadership Industry Rules," *New Yorker*, February 29, 2016, argues that it is precisely by "decoupling" leadership and power that the leadership industry has been able to thrive.

4. Rosabeth Moss Kanter, "Power Failure in Management Circuits," *Harvard Business Review*, no. 57 (July/August 1979): 65.

5. See Chapter 5 of David Nadler and Janet L. Spencer, *Executive Teams* (San Francisco: Jossey-Bass, 1998). The term "moose on the table" is an expression that Nadler and Spencer (99–100) attribute to D. N. T. Perkins, "Ghosts in the Executive Suite: Every Business Is a Family Business" (Branford, CT: Syncretics Group,1988). They speak of four such moose: the distribution of power between the CEO and members of the team; succession; the relative power among LT members; and failure (of individuals or projects).

6. Kathleen M. Eisenhardt and Mark J. Zbaracki, "Strategic Decision Making," *Strategic Management Journal* 13, no. S2 (1992): 26.

7. Linda Hill and Kent Lineback, "Stop Avoiding Office Politics," *Harvard Business Review*, November 2, 2011.

8. For example, Anthony C. Fletcher, Georges A. Wagner, and Philip E. Bourne, "Ten Simple Rules for More Objective Decision-Making" (San Francisco: Public Library of Science 2020).

9. Michelle K. Duffy, Daniel C. Ganster, and Milan Pagon, "Social Undermining in the Workplace," *Academy of Management Journal* 45, no. 2 (2002): 332.

10. David J. Gavin, Joanne H. Gavin, and James Campbell Quick, "Power Struggles within the Top Management Team: An Empirical Examination of Follower Reactions to Subversive Leadership," *Journal of Applied Biobehavioral Research* 22, no. 4 (2017).

11. A blowhard, according to the Cambridge online dictionary, is a person who likes to talk about how important they are (https://dictionary.cambridge.org/dictionary/english/blowhard).

12. This is something we observe on all LTs we work with and has been observed by others such as Theresa J. B. Kline, *Teams That Lead: A Matter of Market Strategy, Leadership Skills, and Executive Strength* (London: Psychology Press, 2020). See also Markus Menz, "Functional Top Management Team Members: A Review, Synthesis, and Research Agenda," *Journal of Management* 38, no. 1 (2012), who writes: "Despite the sparse empirical research, the literature indicates that functional TMT members' effectiveness is contingent upon the quality of their relationships with the CEO."

13. The lengths to which some LT members will go to show they have a special relationship with their CEO illustrate how important this currency is. In one company we worked with, an LT member had noticed that their new CEO came in every morning at the exact same time and went straight to the coffee machine. He started mimicking this behavior and would later pepper his conversation with his colleagues with phrases that often began, "When I was having coffee with [CEO's name] this week, he was telling me that ..." and ended with an insinuation that the CEO supported whatever he was doing. In another company, the CEO had offered his summer cottage for the weekend to one member of his team to use. When the executive arrived there, he immediately called two of his colleagues who, as he had anticipated, asked him where he was. This enabled him that he was at their boss's cottage, thus leaving the impression they were close friends.

14. Alvin W. Gouldner, "The Norm of Reciprocity: A Preliminary Statement," *American Sociological Review* 25, no. 2 (1960); Robert B. Cialdini, "The Science of Persuasion," *Scientific American* 284, no. 2 (2001).

15. Steven Lukes, *Power: A Radical View* (New York: Palgrave Macmillan, 2005). Peter Bachrach and Morton S. Baratz, "Two Faces of Power," *American Political Science Review* 56, no. 4 (December 1962).

16. Anne Smith et al., "Power Relationships among Top Managers: Does Top Management Team Power Distribution Matter for Organizational Performance?," *Journal of Business Research* 59, no. 5 (2006): 623.

17. Leo Lewis, "Collision Course : The Sensational Downfall of Carlos Ghosn," *Financial Times*, July 16, 2021: "That first press conference, conducted by Nissan's CEO, made it plain that Ghosn's downfall had been precipitated through collaboration between Nissan executives and prosecutors."

18. Jeffrey Pfeffer, "Teaching Power in Ways That Influence Student' Career Success: Some Fundamental Ideas" (working paper 3839), Stanford University Graduate School of Business, November 25, 2019.

19. Wei Shen and Albert A. Cannella Jr., "Power Dynamics within Top Management and Their Impacts on CEO Dismissal Followed by Inside Succession," *Academy of Management Journal* 45, no. 6 (2002).

20. Shen and Cannella, "Power Dynamics."

21. Alvarez and Svejenova, *Sharing Executive Power.*

22. In the year after Ghosn's arrest on November 18, 2018, Nissan's share price lost one-third of its value on the Tokyo Stock Exchange. The share price was 1010.0 the week of November 11, 2018. It was down to 681.5 the week of November 10, 2019 (https://www.investing.com/equities/nissan-motor-co.-ltd.-historical-data). It was much the same for Renault. Its share price fell by almost a third on the Paris Stock Exchange from the week prior to Ghosn's arrest, falling from 64.45 the week of November 11, 2018, to 44.45 the week of November 10,2019 (https://www.investing.com/equities/nissan-motor-co.-ltd.-historical-data).

23. Jeffrey Immelt, "How I Remade GE and What I Learned along the Way," *Harvard Business Review* (September–October 2017).

24. Although the benefits of shared leadership are obvious, interesting work has been done on the limits of such sharing and how CEOs need to maintain a measure of final control over decision making to maintain unity of command. See, for example, R. Krause, R. Priem, and L. Love, "Who's In Charge Here? Co-CEOs, Power Gaps, and Firm Performance," *Strategic Management Journal* 36, no. 13 (December 2015).

25. For the Apple data presented here, see https://www.ibtimes.com/infographic-apple-ipods-contribution-companys-revenue-2002-2796171, accessed September 19, 2022.

26. Adam Grant, *Think Again: The Power of Knowing What You Don't Know* (New York: Viking Press, 2021).

27.Julie Battilana and Tiziana Casciaro, *Power, for All: How It Really Works and Why It's Everyone's Business* (New York: Simon and Schuster, 2021), 39. We encourage you to read the following chapter in this book, "Power Can Be Dirty, But It Doesn't Have to Be," to discover more insights on how to minimize the damaging impact of power games on your LT.

28. An emphasis on a common strategy is a recurrent theme throughout the power and politics literature, as illustrated by Said Elbanna, "Strategic Decision-Making: Process Perspectives," *International Journal of Management Reviews* 8, no. 1 (2006), where the author asks how managers can overcome the negative effects of political tactics and cites "common goals" as one of the fundamental elements (see p. 14). See also Kathleen M. Eisenhardt, "Strategy as Strategic Decision Making," *Sloan Management Review* 40, no. 3 (1999).

29. https://www.aboutamazon.com/news/company-news/2016-letter-to-shareholders accessed January 30, 2022.

30. Daniel Kahneman, Olivier Sibony, and C. R. Sunstein, *Noise* (London: HarperCollins UK, 2022).

31. Lucy A. Arendt, Richard L. Priem, and Hermann Achidi Ndofor, "A CEO-Adviser Model of Strategic Decision Making," *Journal of Management* 31, no. 5 (2005). "Ashford, Blatt, and VandeWalle … argued that those occupying the highest levels in a hierarchy likely receive less spontaneous feedback from others and, thus, have a greater instrumental need to seek feedback proactively. Moreover, high contextual uncertainty—almost universal for CEOs—also increases their instrumental motive for feedback seeking" (694).

32. T. J. Peters and R. H. Waterman, *In Search of Excellence* (New York: Harper, 1982).

33. Theodore Kinni, "Why Wandering Works Wonders for Managers, Strategy and Business," August 2, 2018,

34. I. Davis and T. Dickson, "Lou Gerstner on Corporate Reinvention and Values," *McKinsey Quarterly* 3 (2014).

35. Mintzberg, *Managing*, 54.

36. William Oncken Jr. and Donald L. Wass, "Management Time: Who's Got the Monkey?" *Harvard Business Review*, no. 12 (November–December 1999).

37. For a full account of the Boeing 737 Max fiasco, see Joseph Herkert, Jason Borenstein, and Keith Miller, "The Boeing 737 MAX: Lessons for Engineering Ethics," *Science and Engineering Ethics* 26, no. 6 (December 1, 2020).

38. Abraham Carmeli, John Schaubroeck, and Asher Tishler, "How CEO Empowering Leadership Shapes Top Management Team Processes: Implications for Firm Performance," *Leadership Quarterly* 22, no. 2 (2011).

39. Harvard Business case no. 9-494-055, Rudi Gassner and the Executive Committee of BMG International (A), 1995, 10.

40. Maria Guadalupe, Hongyi Li, and Julie Wulf, "Who Lives in the C-Suite? Organizational Structure and the Division of Labor in Top Management," *Management Science* 60, no. 4 (2014).

Chapter 3

1. Michael L. Tushman, Wendy K. Smith, and Andy Binns, "The Ambidextrous CEO," *Harvard Business Review* 89, no. 6 (2011).

2. Henning Bang et al., "Effectiveness in Top Management Group Meetings: The Role of Goal Clarity, Focused Communication, and Learning Behavior," *Scandinavian Journal of Psychology* 51, no. 3 (2010): 253.

3. Tushman et al., "The Ambidextrous CEO."

4. Lucy A. Arendt, Richard L. Priem, and Hermann Achidi Ndofor, "A CEO-Adviser Model of Strategic Decision Making," *Journal of Management* 31, no. 5 (2005): 681. As scholars familiar with social network analysis terminology will recognize, the Hub-and-Spoke and Team models are just another way to describe brokerage and closure structures, respectively. Leaders must dynamically balance both structures to maximize group and individual performance. F. C. Godart, F. Cavarretta, and M. Thiemann, M. (2016). "Task Complexity and Shared Value Orientation: Exploring the Moderators of a Social Dilemma in Team Social Networks," *Industrial and Corporate Change* 25 (2016): 739–56.

5. Arendt et al., "A CEO-Adviser Model ," 684.

6. Arendt et al., "A CEO-Adviser Model of Strategic Decision Making, " 681.

7. See Ann C. Mooney and Allen C. Amason, "In Search of the CEO's Inner Circle and How It Is Formed," in *The Handbook of Research on Top Management Teams*, ed. Mason A. Carpenter (Northampton, MA: Elgar, 2011): 37: "Given the size of the TMT in most large organizations, along with the breadth of tasks and responsibilities with which this group must deal, it is rare that the full TMT would gather often to collectively identify strategic issues and make strategic decisions."

8. Arendt et al., "A CEO-Adviser Model," 687.

9. Arendt et al., "A CEO-Adviser Model," 688.

10. Occam's razor is the principle according to which "given two explanations of [some] data, all other things being equal, the simpler the explanation is preferable." Anselm Blumer et al., "Occam's Razor," *Information Processing Letters* 24, no. 6 (1987): 377.

11. Bart A. De Jong, Kurt T. Dirks, and Nicole Gillespie, "Trust and Team Performance: A Meta-Analysis of Main Effects, Moderators, and Covariates," *Journal of Applied Psychology* 101, no. 8 (2016): 1136.

12. Donald D. Hambrick, "Top Management Groups: A Conceptual Integration and Reconsideration of the 'Team" Label,'" in *Research in Organizational Behavior*, ed. B. Staw and L. L. Cummings (Greenwich, CT: JAI Press, 1994).

13. Ronald S. Burt, Martin Kilduff, and Stefano Tasselli, "Social Network Analysis: Foundations and Frontiers on Advantage," *Annual Review of Psychology* 64 (2013): 529: "Network models of advantage use structure as an indicator of how information is distributed in a system of people. The models build on two facts established in social psychology during the 1940s and 1950s ... : a) People cluster into groups as a result of interaction opportunities defined by the places where people meet; and b) communication is more frequent and influential within than between

groups such that people develop similar views. People tire of repeating arguments and stories explaining why they believe and behave the way they do. Within a group, people create systems of phrasing, opinions, symbols, and behaviors defining what it means to be a member."

14. This is a phenomenon called "homophily" in sociology: we like people who are like us. Miller McPherson, Lynn Smith-Lovin, and James M. Cook, "Birds of a Feather: Homophily in Social Networks," *Annual Review of Sociology* 27 (2001).

15.   https://www.thebalance.com/the-great-recession-of-2008-explanation-with-dates-4056832 - accessed September 19, 2022, See under "Key Points"

16. See https://www.library.hbs.edu/hc/lehman/exhibition/lehman-brothers-timeline (accessed September 19, 2022).

17. Lehman Brothers would file for bankruptcy only some nine months later, on September 15, 2008: https://www.investopedia.com/articles/economics/09/lehman-brothers-collapse.asp.

18. Shenghui Ma and David Seidl, "New CEOs and Their Collaborators: Divergence and Convergence between the Strategic Leadership Constellation and the Top Management Team," *Strategic Management Journal* 39, no. 3 (2018), https://onlinelibrary.wiley.com/doi/abs/10.1002/smj.2721: "Comparing group and dyadic advice interactions, Garg and Eisenhardt (2017) find that dyadic interactions with individual board members allow the CEO to obtain a better quality of advice by enabling an in-depth exchange of thoughts and encouraging closer consideration of the director's ideas. These dyadic interactions also help the CEO preserve his or her discretion or influence in the decision process, whereas the effects of group-based advice interactions during board meeting can be more difficult to control." See Sam Garg and Kathleen M. Eisenhardt, "Unpacking the CEO–Board Relationship: How Strategy Making Happens in Entrepreneurial Firms," *Academy of Management Journal* 60, no. 5 (2017). Although they are writing about board of director dynamics, the same reasoning applies to LTs.

19. David Nadler and Janet L. Spencer, *Executive Teams* (San Francisco: Jossey-Bass, 1998), 102.

20. "'Bridging' roles are what social network theorists would call 'brokerage' roles, although some do use the term bridging" Seok-Woo Kwon et al., "Network Brokerage: An Integrative Review and Future Research Agenda," *Journal of Management* 46, no. 6 (2020). These authors, like us, believe bridging roles are required in a closed circle of people who, although they are connected, may not be aware of what the others are up to. They write: "Thus, even in a closed triad, there may be opportunities for brokerage behavior and third-party influence, that is, situations where one actor has the time, ability, or motivation to learn more about the other two than they know (or care to know) about each other." This article also highlights how brokering/bridging can be viewed as behavior (versus a structure) and that a broker/bridge builder can adopt both brokering and closure behavior within a closed network. These three roles are inspired most notably by roles found in Roberto Fernandez and Roger Gould, "The Dilemma of State Power: Brokerage and Influence in the National Health Policy Domain," *American Journal of Sociology* 99 (1994). The disseminator role is one identified

by management guru Henry Mintzberg in his "The Manager's Job: Folklore and Fact," *Harvard Business Review* 53, no. 4 (1975).

21. William Oncken and Donald L. Wass, "Management Time: Who's Got the Monkey?" *Harvard Business Review* (1999; originally published December 1974).

22. Abraham Carmeli, John Schaubroeck, and Asher Tishler, "How CEO Empowering Leadership Shapes Top Management Team Processes: Implications for Firm Performance," *Leadership Quarterly* 22, no. 2 (2011): 408: "There are situations, particularly those involving the allocation of scarce resources, which place the motives of individual TMT members at odds with one another. If the top executive fails to recognize these situations and does not serve as a strong facilitator in such discussions, the team is likely to become demoralized."

23. Kwon et al., "Network Brokerage," 1098: "Finally, an emerging stream of brokerage behaviors focuses on cultural brokerage. Emphasizing the role of context, Pachucki and Breiger (2010) argue that a broker crosses boundaries not just between social circles (i.e., across structural holes in a network), but also across different cultural communities ('cultural holes'). Actors bridging across a structural hole have access to diverse information, but the information they access may be hard to interpret and absorb (Aral and Van Alstyne, 2011). A cultural broker with the ability to interpret information and translate to others can bridge these cognitive gaps (Carlile, 2004) or 'thought worlds" (Dougherty, 1992)."

24. Silviya Svejenova and José Luis Alvarez, "Changing the C-Suite: New Chief Officer Roles as Strategic Responses to Institutional Complexity," in *New Themes in Institutional Analysis*, ed. Georg Krücken et al. (Northampton, MA: Elgar, 2017).: "Finally, we propose that this variety and expansion of C-suite roles strengthens the role of the CEO as opposed to being a symptom of flattening, decentralisation and democratisation of hierarchical power. The CEO takes on more supremacy as a result of the contests between direct reports and more leeway in the design of the structure and the selection of candidates for his or her team."

Chapter 4

1. Ruth Wageman and J. Richard Hackman, "What Makes Teams of Leaders Leadable?," in *Handbook of Leadership Theory and Practice*, ed. Nitin Nohria and Rakesh Khurana (Boston: Harvard Business School Press, 2010).

2. Wageman and Hackman, "What Makes Teams of Leaders Leadable?," 486.

3. Wageman and Hackman, "What Makes Teams of Leaders Leadable?," 486.

4. We encourage you to perform this experiment with members of your own organization. To do so, simply reproduce the questions at the top of this chapter and send them to the people you believe are on your organization's LT. If you want to share these collated responses with us (not raw data, please!), we would be delighted. You can email them to leadershipteamalignment@insead.edu with the title "Survey: The Size of Our Leadership Team." Do not hesitate to share your insights with us. Of course, should we decide to do anything with your information, we will contact you first and ask for your permission.

5. An example is Patrick Lencioni, *The Five Dysfunctions of a Team: A Leadership Fable* (San Francisco: Jossey-Bass, 2002).

6. This example is taken an article in *Forbes* magazine whose author has asked various executives to give their definition of "executive leadership team." See Kimberly A. Whitler, "What Is the Executive Leadership Team? 33 Board and C-Level Leaders Explain," *Forbes*, June 5, 2021, https://www.forbes.com/sites/kimberlywhitler/2021/06/05/what-is-the-executive-leadership-team-33-board-and-c-level-leaders-explain/?sh=21dde7b66dbf.

7. Steven A. Stewart and Allen C. Amason, "Assessing the State of Top Management Teams Research," in *Oxford Research Encyclopedia of Business and Management* (2017).

8. For example, Tony Simons, Lisa Hope Pelled, and Ken A. Smith, "Making Use of Difference: Diversity, Debate, and Decision Comprehensiveness in Top Management Teams," *Academy of Management Journal* 42, no. 6 (1999).

9. Stewart and Amason, "Assessing the State of Top Management Teams Research," 21.

10. Wageman and Hackman, "What Makes Teams of Leaders Leadable?," 485.

11. Jon R. Katzenbach, *Teams at the Top: Unleashing the Potential of Both Teams and Individual Leaders* (Boston: Harvard Business Press, 1998), 46.

12. Carla D. Jones and Albert A. Cannella, "Alternate Configurations in Strategic Decision Making," in *The Handbook of Research on Top Management Teams*, ed. Mason A. Carpenter (Northampton, MA: Elgar, 2011).

13. Wageman and Hackman, "What Makes Teams of Leaders Leadable?," 485.

14. See, for example, David Nadler and Janet L. Spencer, *Executive Teams* (San Francisco: Jossey-Bass, 1998), 93. "Research suggests that the optimal group size for real problem solving and decision-making ranges from seven to nine, yet it is not uncommon to see executive teams with fifteen or twenty members."

15. For example, in their seminal article, Henry Mintzberg, Duru Raisinghani, and Andre Theoret, "The Structure of 'Unstructured' Decision Processes," *Administrative Science Quarterly* 21, no. 2 (1976), 246, define *strategic* as "simply means important, in terms of the actions taken, the resources committed, or the precedents set."

16. See, for example, Amy E. Colbert, Murray R. Barrick, and Bret H. Bradley, "Personality and Leadership Composition in Top Management Teams: Implications for Organizational Effectiveness," *Personnel Psychology* 67, no. 2 (2014), 351–52: "Yet, the complexity of creating and carrying out the strategic decisions of an entire organization demands more skill and effort than a single leader can effectively provide. Instead, it requires the collective ability and motivation of a dominant team of leaders within the firm, See also Sydney Finkelstein and Donald Hambrick, *Strategic Leadership: Top Executives and Their Effects on Organizations* (Eagan, MN: West Publishing, 1996); Donald D. Hambrick and Phyllis Mason, "Upper Echelons: The Organization as a Reflection of Its Top Managers," *Academy of Management Journal* 9, no. 2 (1984); Richard M. Cyert and James G. March, *A Behavioral Theory of the Firm*, vol. 2 (Englewood Cliffs, NJ: Prentice Hall, 1963). Consistent with this view, Hambrick noted,

NOTES

"Leadership of a complex organization is a shared activity": D. C. Hambrick, "The Field of Management's Devotion to Theory: Too Much of a Good Thing?," *Academy of Management Journal* 50 (2007), 334." See also Stewart and Amason, "Assessing the State of Top Management Teams, Research," 2–3 who write: "Central to the examination of TMTs are two general observations. First, while the CEO of an organization is usually the most visible and influential executive, the CEO alone is limited in time and cognitive ability and therefore must rely upon a dominant coalition of executives for a more complete strategic analysis of the environment and organization."

17. Shenghui Ma, Yasemin Y. Kor, and David Seidl, "CEO Advice Seeking: An Integrative Framework and Future Research Agenda," *Journal of Management* 46, no. 6 (2020), 776, https://journals.sagepub.com/doi/abs/10.1177/0149206319885430.,

18. Stewart and Amason, "Assessing the State of Top Management Teams Research," 5.

19. Ravi Kathuria, Maheshkumar P. Joshi, and Stephen J. Porth, "Organizational Alignment and Performance: Past, Present and Future," *Management Decision* 45, no. 3 (2007), 503, https://doi.org/10.1108/00251740710745106, https://doi.org/10.1108/00251740710745106.

20. Allen C. Amason, "Distinguishing the Effects of Functional and Dysfunctional Conflict on Strategic Decision Making: Resolving a Paradox for Top Management Teams," *Academy of Management Journal* 39, no. 1 (1996), 125, https://journals.aom.org/doi/abs/10.5465/256633.

21. See Pikka-Maaria Laine and Eero Vaara, "Participation in Strategy Work," in *Cambridge Handbook of Strategy as Practice*, ed. Damon Golsorkhi, Linda Rouleau, David Seidl, and Eero Vaara (Cambridge: Cambridge University Press, 2015): "Participation is arguably a key issue in strategy process research because it helps to create commitment to strategies and its absence may have a negative impact on the quality of decision-making (Floyd & Wooldridge, 2000)." (Thousand Oaks, CA: Sage, 2000)."

22. Robert J. Bies and Debra L. Shapiro, "Voice and Justification: Their Influence on Procedural Fairness Judgments," *Academy of Management Journal* 31, no. 3 (1988), https://journals.aom.org/doi/abs/10.5465/256465; M. Audrey Korsgaard, David M. Schweiger, and Harry J. Sapienza, "Building Commitment, Attachment, and Trust in Strategic Decision-Making Teams: The Role of Procedural Justice," *Academy of Management Journal* 38, no. 1 (1995).

23. Jaques introduced the concept of organizational culture in Elliott Jaques, ed., *The Changing Culture of a Factory* (London: Tavistock, 1951), 251.

24. Elliott Jaques, "In Praise of Hierarchy," *Harvard Business Review* 68, no. 1 (1990).

25. For example, quotations to this effect are peppered throughout Louis Hébert et al., *Paroles de PDG: Comment 75 grands patrons du Québec vivent leur métier* (Montreal: Les Éditions Rogers Ltée, 2014), 76.

26. Anneloes M. L. Raes, Heike Bruch, and Simon B. De Jong, "How Top Management Team Behavioural Integration Can Impact Employee Work Outcomes: Theory Development and First Empirical Tests," *Human Relations* 66, no. 2 (2013).

27. A distinction he later developed in Charles Galunic, *Backstage Leadership: The Invisible Work of Highly Effective Leaders* (Cham, Switzerland: Springer Nature, 2020), 87.

28. This is the definition of *decision* proposed by Mintzberg et al., "The Structure of 'Unstructured' Decision Processes," 246.

29. See Michael A. Roberto, *Why Great Leaders Don't Take Yes for an Answer: Managing for Conflict and Consensus* (London: FT Press, 2013), 9.

30. Mintzberg et al., "The Structure of 'Unstructured' Decision Processes," 265.

31. Ma et al., "CEO Advice Seeking," 789.

32. John E. Mathieu et al., "Embracing Complexity: Reviewing the Past Decade of Team Effectiveness Research," *Annual Review of Organizational Psychology and Organizational Behavior* 6 (2019), 29.

33. Pontus Wadström, "Aligning Corporate and Business Strategy: Managing the Balance," *Journal of Business Strategy* 40, no. 4 (2019), 45, https://doi.org/10.1108/JBS-06-2018-0099.

34. Kathuria et al., "Organizational Alignment and Performance," 505: "Horizontal alignment refers to coordination of efforts across the organization and is primarily relevant to the lower levels in the strategy hierarchy. Horizontal alignment can be defined in terms of cross-functional and intra-functional integration. Cross-functional integration connotes the consistency of decisions across functions (e.g., level 3) so that activities and decisions across marketing, operations, HR, and other functions complement and support one another. Intra-functional coordination is achieved through coherence across decision areas (level 4) so as to achieve synergy within each function. For successful implementation, decisions within a function (level 4) should be aligned vertically with that function's strategic objectives, as well as laterally—across decision areas within a function."

35. As Prasad Balkundi et al., "Demographic Antecedents and Performance Consequences of Structural Holes in Work Teams," *Journal of Organizational Behavior* 28, no. 2 (2007): 245, report, this bottleneck effect is not uncommon on teams that rely too heavily on one person—bridge builder or broker in social network theory vocabulary—to play the coordinator between disconnected subgroups causing performance issues.

36. The support for the beneficial impact of ground rules is overwhelming and comes from varied sources, including the work of psychological safety expert and the findings from Google's team research: Charles Duhigg, "What Google Learned from Its Quest to Build the Perfect Team," *New York Times,* February 28, 2016, https://www.nytimes.com/2016/02/28/magazine/what-google-learned-from-its-quest-to-build-the-perfect-team.html, and the work of Wageman and Hackman et al., "What Makes Teams of Leaders Leadable?"

37. Euth Wageman et al., *Senior Leadership Teams: What It Takes to Make Them Great* (Boston: Harvard Business Review Press, 2008), 212.

38. Kathleen M. Eisenhardt, Jean L. Kahwajy, and L. J. Bourgeois III, "How Management Teams Can Have a Good Fight," *Harvard Business Review* 75, no. 4 (1997).

39. Although some claim it is better to use rewards rather than sanctions to promote LT effectiveness, we do not have enough evidence to draw unequivocal conclusions regarding this matter. We surmise your organizational culture will dictate which approach will be the more successful.

40. Galunic, *Backstage Leaderships*, 3; Kathleen M. Eisenhardt and Mark J. Zbaracki, "Strategic Decision Making," *Strategic Management Journal* 13, no. S2 (1992).

41. For those wishing to have a quick overview of OKRs, we suggest the YouTube video "The New OKR Crash Course: An Intro to Objectives & Key Results" (https://www.youtube.com/watch?v=EIcpFZ5rbHc). For those wishing for a deeper immersion, another good bet is the YouTube video entitled "Startup Lab %: How Google Sets Goals: OKRs" (https://www.youtube.com/watch?v=mJB83EZtAjc&feature=youtu.be) which lasts a little over an hour (both accessed in February 2022).

42. Donald Sull, Rebecca Homkes, and Charles Sull, "Why Strategy Execution Unravels—and What to Do about It," *Harvard Business Review* 93, no. 3 (2015).

43. Charles Galunic and Immanuel Hermreck, "How to Help Employees 'Get' Strategy," *Harvard Business Review* 90, no. 12 (2012).

44. John Izzo, "Consistency Drives Success at Telus," *Strategy + Business* (2015), https://www.strategy-business.com/article/00360.

45. Roger Fisher, William L Ury, and Bruce Patton, *Getting to Yes: Negotiating Agreement without Giving In* (New York: Penguin, 2011).

46. The CEO in question was French speaking, and the actual question he would ask was, "As-tu attaché ton dossier?" which literally translates as, "Have you tied your initiative?" However, the word *attaché* is better translated as "socialize" because the CEO's goal was to determine if stakeholders were aware of the initiative and were ready to support it.

47. See Longqi Yang et al., "The Effects of Remote Work on Collaboration among Information Workers," *Nature Human Behaviour* (2021). Although not a study about LTs, its results point to remote working's tendency to make collaboration networks more static and siloed, with fewer bridges between disparate parts.

Chapter 5

1. For example, Shenghui Ma and David Seidl, "New CEOs and Their Collaborators: Divergence and Convergence between the Strategic Leadership Constellation and the Top Management Team," *Strategic Management Journal* 39, no. 3 (2018), https://onlinelibrary.wiley.com/doi/abs/10.1002/smj.2721.

2. CEO could also mean chief ecosystem officer, or chief ESG officer—the latter being an intriguing case of nesting acronyms. Erin Albert offers an updated list of trends here: https://erinalbert.medium.com/cxo-2020-the-latest-c-suite-titles-for-2020-58a7d9e651a4 (accessed September 19, 2022).

3. Jenna Goudreau, "C Is For Silly: The New C-Suite Titles," *Forbes*, January 10, 2012.

4. Josh Kovensky, "Chief Happiness Officer Is the Latest, Creepiest Job in Corporate America," *New Republic*, July 22, 2014.

5. https://erinalbert.medium.com/cxo-2020-the-latest-c-suite-titles-for-2020-58a7d-9e651a4 (accessed September 19, 2022).

6. José Luis Alvarez and Silviya Svejenova, *The Changing C-Suite: Executive Power in Transformation* (Oxford: Oxford University Press, 2022), 15.

7. Alvarez and Svejenova, *The Changing C-Suite: Executive Power in Transformation*, 27.

8. S. Crainer and D. Dearlove, *Financial Times Handbook of Management* (Harlow: Financial Times/Prentice Hall, 2004), 959, https://books.google.fr/books?id=R7fMHYTCJdQC.

9. Peter Ferdinand Drucker, *The Practice of Management* (New York: Harper, 1954).

10. Donald C. Hambrick and Albert A. Cannella Jr., "CEOs Who Have COOs: Contingency Analysis of an Unexplored Structural Form," *Strategic Management Journal* 25, no. 10 (2004), 407, https://doi.org/https://doi.org/10.1002/smj.

11. Gary L. Neilson, "The Decline of the COO," *Forbes*, May 20, 2015.

12. David Bendig, "Chief Operating Officer Characteristics and How They Relate to Exploration via Patenting versus Venturing," *Journal of Business Research* 140 (2022), https://www.sciencedirect.com/science/article/pii/S0148296321008080.

13. Nathan Bennett and Stephen Miles, "Second in Command: The Misunderstood Role of the Chief Operating Officer," *Harvard Business Review* 84, no. 5 (2006).

14. Dirk M. Zorn, "Here a Chief, There a Chief: The Rise of the CFO in the American Firm," *American Sociological Review* 69, no. 3 (2004), 354, https://doi.org/10.1177/000312240406900302.

15. Maria Guadalupe, Hongyi Li, and Julie Wulf, "Who Lives in the C-Suite? Organizational Structure and the Division of Labor in Top Management," *Management Science* 60, no. 4 (2014), 829, n. 7.

16. "The Imperial CFO: Chief Financial Officers Are Amassing a Worrying Amount of Power," *Economist*, June 17, 2016.

17. Daniel R. Delmar, "The Rise of the CSO (Organization Design)," *Journal of Business Strategy* 24, no. 2 (2003).

18. Paul Leinwand, Nils Naujok, and Joachim Rotering, "Memo to the CEO: Is Your Chief Strategy Officer Set Up for Success?," *Strategy + Business* (2019).

19. Alvarez and Svejenova, *The Changing C-Suite*, 14.

20. Elizabeth G. Chambers et al., "The War for Talent," *McKinsey Quarterly*, no. 3 (1998).

21. James Suzman, "How McKinsey & Co. Created 'The War for Talent' in 1998 to Propagate a 'Myth of Brilliance,'" *Print*, 2021.

22. Boris Groysberg, L. Kevin Kelly, and Bryan MacDonald, "The New Path to the C-Suite," *Harvard Business Review* 89, no. 3 (2011).

23. Kimberly A. Whitler and Neil Morgan, "Why CMOs Never Last and What to Do about It," *Harvard Business Review* 95, no. 4 (2017).

24. Alvarez and Svejenova, *The Changing C-Suite*, 38, where they cite Kunisch, Menz, and Langan (2010), who "noted that among S&P 1500 companies, the CDO role appeared in 2003 but did not gain traction until 2010."

25. Tuck Rickards, Kate Smaje, and Vik Sohoni, "'Transformer in Chief': The New Chief Digital Officer," *McKinsey Digital* (2015).

26. P. Péladeau and O. Acker, "Have We Reached 'Peak' Chief Digital Officer'" *Strategy + Business* (2019).

27. Scott A. Snyder and Shaloo Kulkarni, "So You Think You Need a Chief Digital Officer?," *Knowledge at Wharton* (2018).

28. Don Knight et al., "Top Management Team Diversity, Group Process, and Strategic Consensus," *Strategic Management Journal* 20, no. 5 (1999): 445: "Diversity supposedly leads to greater variance in ideas, creativity, and innovation, thus generating better group performance (Cox, 1993; Jackson, May and Whitney, 1995). In the popular press, diversity is almost always synonymous with gender or ethnic diversity."

29. Daniel Kahneman, *Thinking, Fast and Slow* (New York: Macmillan, 2011).

30. Saku Mantere and Eero Vaara, "On the Problem of Participation in Strategy: A Critical Discursive Perspective," *Organization Science* 19, no. 2 (2008): 341.

31. Michael A. West, *Effective Teamwork: Practical Lessons from Organizational Research* (Hoboken, NJ: Wiley, 2012), 65, https://books.google.fr/books?id=dmIjlneC3HwC.

32. Ruth Wageman et al., *Senior Leadership Teams: What It Takes to Make Them Great* (Boston: Harvard Business Review Press, 2008): 116

33. Jerayr Haleblian and Sydney Finkelstein, "Top Management Team Size, CEO Dominance, and Firm Performance: The Moderating Roles of Environmental Turbulence and Discretion," *Academy of Management Journal* 36, no. 4 (1993), https://journals.aom.org/doi/abs/10.5465/256761.

34. Wageman et al., *Senior Leadership Teams*, 116–223

35. Geoff Colvin, "For a Time, Jack Welch Was the Most Valuable CEO on Earth," *Fortune*, May 2, 2020, https://fortune.com/2020/03/02/jack-welch-ge-ceo-death/.

36. Andrew Hill, "Axe the Middle Managers at Your Peril," *Financial Times,* May 20, 2018.

37. Jack Welch and Suzy Welch, *Winning* (New York: HarperBusiness, 2005).

38. Guadalupe et al., "Who Lives in the C-Suite?"

39. Guadalupe et al., "Who Lives in the C-Suite?" 825.

40. Guadalupe et al., "Who Lives in the C-Suite?" 825–26.

41. Guadalupe et al., "Who Lives in the C-Suite?" 827.

42. https://www.lefigaro.fr/histoire/retrospective/2013/09/19/26005-20130919ART-FIG00295-quand-napoleon-accordait-des-titres-de-noblesse.php (in French, accessed September 19, 2022).

43. This saying is attributed to C. Mitchell in Wilma J. Slenders, *Chief Executive Officers and Their Trusted Advisor Relationships: A Qualitative Study from the CEO's perspective* (Minneapolis: Capella University, 2010).

44. Gary L. Neilson and Julie Wulf, "How Many Direct Reports?," *Harvard Business Review* 90, no. 4 (2012).

45. Rob Cross and Jon R. Katzenbach, "The Right Role for Top Teams," *Strategy + Business*, no. 67 (2012).

46. Anne Smith et al., "Power Relationships among Top Managers: Does Top Management Team Power Distribution Matter for Organizational Performance?," *Journal of Business Research* 59, no. 5 (2006), https://doi.org/https://doi.org/10.1016/j.jbusres.2005.10.012.

47. Yina Mao, Ching-Wen Wang, and Chi-Sum Wong, "Towards a Model of the Right-Hand Person," *Leadership and Organization Development Journal* 37, no. 4 (2016), https://doi.org/10.1108/LODJ-08-2014-0153.

Chapter 6

1. MBTI is designed to identify a person's personality type. Although its validity and reliability have come under strong criticism, the MBTI is one of the most widely used psychological assessments in the world.

2. ENTJs—with the Extraverted, iNtuitive, Thinking, and Judging traits—is one of the sixteen personality types that emerge from the MBTI. ENTJs are generally seen— by MBTI proponents—as competitive, logical thinkers who are quick to see the shortcomings of any system.

3. Julie Battilana and Tiziana Casciaro, *Power, for All: How It Really Works and Why It's Everyone's Business* (New York: Simon and Schuster, 2021).

4. For a more in-depth examination of these points, we recommend Bill Wooldridge and Birton Cowden, "Strategic Decision-Making in Business," in *Oxford Research Encyclopedia of Business and Management* (2020); Ann C. Mooney, Patricia J. Holahan, and Allen C. Amason, "Don't Take It Personally: Exploring Cognitive Conflict as a Mediator of Affective Conflict," *Journal of Management Studies* 44, no. 5 (2007), https://doi.org/https://doi.org/10.1111/j.1467-6486.2006.00674.x. See p. 734; and W. Chan Kim and Renée Mauborgne, "Fair Process," *Harvard Business Review* 75 (1997).

5. Our experience is far from unique. See, for example, Richard Rosen and Fred Adair, "CEOs Misperceive Top Teams' Performance," *Harvard Business Review* 85, no. 9 (2007).

6. Tony L. Simons and Randall S. Peterson, "Task Conflict and Relationship Conflict in Top Management Teams: The Pivotal Role of Intragroup Trust," *Journal of Applied Psychology* 85 (2000), https://doi.org/10.1037/0021-9010.85.1.102.

7. See Frank R. C. de Wit, Karen A. Jehn, and Daan Scheepers, "Task Conflict, Information Processing, and Decision-Making: The Damaging Effect of Relationship Conflict," *Organizational Behavior and Human Decision Processes* 122, no. 2 (2013), https://doi.org/https://doi.org/10.1016/j.obhdp.2013.07.002, and Carmen Camelo-Ordaz, Joaquín García-Cruz, and Elena Sousa-Ginel, "The Influence of Top Management Team Conflict on Firm Innovativeness," *Group Decision and Negotiation* 24, no. 6 (2015), https://doi.org/10.1007/s10726-014-9424-4.

8. Anneloes M. L. Raes, Heike Bruch, and Simon B. De Jong, "How Top Management Team Behavioural Integration Can Impact Employee Work Outcomes: Theory Development and First Empirical tests," *Human Relations* 66, no. 2 (2013).

9. Morten Hansen, *Collaboration: How Leaders Avoid The Traps, Build Common Ground, and Reap Big Results* (Boston: Harvard Business Press, 2009).

10. Murray R. Barrick et al., "The Moderating Role of Top Management Team Interdependence: Implications for Real Teams and Working Groups," *Academy of Management Journal* 50, no. 3 (2007), https://doi.org/10.5465/amj.2007.25525781.

11. Murat Tarakci et al., "Strategic Consensus Mapping: A New Method for Testing and Visualizing Strategic Consensus within and between Teams," *Strategic Management Journal* 35, no. 7 (2014), https://doi.org/https://doi.org/10.1002/smj.2151.

12. Our "continuous alignment" dimension corresponds closely to the concept of "strategic consensus" in the academic literature; see, e.g., Jorge Walter et al., "Strategic Alignment: A Missing Link in the Relationship between strategic Consensus and Organizational Performance," *Strategic Organization* 11, no. 3 (2013), https://doi.org/10.1177/1476127013481155. However, many CEOs we work with are uncomfortable with the word *consensus*, which they associate with drawn-out debates producing watered-down solutions. However, all were quite comfortable with the word *alignment*, which is why we chose it.

13. See, e.g., p. 7 of Donald Sull, Rebecca Homkes, and Charles Sull, "Why Strategy Execution Unravels—and What to Do about It," *Harvard Business Review* 93, no. 3 (2015). where the authors report that only slightly more than 50 percent of LT members in the typical organization they surveyed agreed on what their organization's strategic priorities were. In another study of thirty-seven organizations by McKinsey & Company, the story was similar: while executives generally agree that aligning on their purpose is critical, only 60 percent of team members reported that they were aligned: Natasha Bergeron, Aaron de Smet, and Liesje Meijknecht, "Improve Your Leadership Team's Effectiveness through Key Behaviors," *McKinsey Quarterly* (2020), https://www.mckinsey.com/business-functions/organization/our-insights/the-organization-blog/improve-your-leadership-teams-effectiveness-through-key-behaviors.

14. Sull et al., "Why Strategy Execution Unravels."

15. Mintzberg was one of the first to denounce this false dichotomy between strategy development and strategy implementation, notably in Henry Mintzberg, "The Design School: Reconsidering the Basic Premises of Strategic Management," *Strategic Management Journal* 11, no. 3 (1990), https://doi.org/https://doi.org/10.1002/smj.4250110302. See also Donald N. Sull, "Closing the Gap between strategy And Execution," *MIT Sloan Management Review* 48, no. 4 (2007).

16. Amy Edmondson, "Psychological Safety and Learning Behavior in Work Teams," *Administrative Science Quarterly* 44, no. 2 (1999), https://doi.org/10.2307/2666999.

17. Donald C. Hambrick, "Corporate Coherence and the Top Management Team," *Strategy and Leadership* (September–October 1997).

18. The quote is from a Lewis' podcast entitled "Field of Ignorance" which can be found at https://www.pushkin.fm/podcasts/against-the-rules (accessed September 19, 2022). The citation for *Moneyball* is Michael Lewis, *Moneyball: The Art of Winning an Unfair Game* (New York: Norton, 2004).

19. For those looking for a highly readable summary of the science of habit formation, you cannot go wrong with Wendy Wood, *Good Habits, Bad Habits: The Science of Making Positive Changes That Stick* (London: Pan Macmillan, 2019).

20. This idea is inspired by the work of Amy Edmondson, widely recognized as the leading expert on psychological safety, and her colleague, Solvay Business School professor Paul Verdin, who invite organizations to think of their strategies as hypotheses rather than as plans. See Amy C. Edmondson, *The fearless organization: Creating psychological safety in the workplace for learning, innovation, and growth* (Hoboken, NJ: Wiley, 2018), 70–71.

21. David Nadler and Janet L. Spencer, *Executive teams* (San Francisco: Jossey-Bass, 1998). See p. 16.

Appendix B

1. For those interested in reading a short piece about the six-page memo, we recommend "Working Backwards: Dave Limp on Amazon's Six Page Memo," in which you find excerpts of a Bezos interview explaining the concept, as well as its implementation by Amazon's SVP of Amazon's devices group. See https://amazonchronicles.substack.com/p/working-backwards-dave-limp-on-amazons February 23, 2022. Another short piece that shows both the pros and cons of the six-pager is Brad Porter, " The Beauty of Amazon's 6-Pager," September 22, 2015, https://www.linkedin.com/pulse/beauty-amazons-6-pager-brad-porter

2. See Bradley George, Truls Erikson, and Annaleena Parhankangas, "Preventing Dysfunctional Conflict: Examining the Relationship between Different Types of Managerial Conflict in Venture Capital-Backed Firms," *Venture Capital* 18, no. 4 (2016), https://doi.org/10.1080/13691066.2016.1224457. This is a wonderful piece in that the authors bring important nuances to the perspective that task conflict is necessarily good for team performance. While task conflict may support the quality of individual decisions, their findings indicate that team performance may suffer from task conflict because the latter is positively associated with affective conflict. This may well explain why the CEOs we know are so wary of putting tough issues on the table. However, these authors also explain how good process can mitigate this risk, and, in our experience, that is exactly what the use of subgroups accomplishes.

REFERENCES

Introduction

Alvarez, José Luis, and Silviya Svejenova. *The Changing C-Suite: Executive Power in Transformation.* Oxford: Oxford University Press, 2022.

Araujo-Cabrera, Yazmina, Miguel A. Suarez-Acosta, and Teresa Aguiar-Quintana. "Exploring the Influence of CEO Extraversion and Openness to Experience on Firm Performance: The Mediating Role of Top Management Team Behavioral Integration." *Journal of Leadership and Organizational Studies* 24, no. 1 (2017). 201–15. https://journals.sagepub.com/doi/abs/10.1177/1548051816655991.

Barsade, Sigal G., Andrew J. Ward, Jean D. F. Turner, and Jeffrey A. Sonnenfeld. "To Your Heart's Content: A Model of Affective Diversity in Top Management Teams." *Administrative Science Quarterly* 45, no. 4 (2000): 802–36. https://journals.sagepub.com/doi/abs/10.2307/2667020.

Berg, David N. "Senior Executive Teams: Not What You Think." *Consulting Psychology Journal: Practice and Research* 57, no. 2 (2005): 107–17.

Bergeron, Natasha, Aaron de Smet, and Liesje Meijknecht. "Improve Your Leadership Team's Effectiveness through Key Behaviors." *McKinsey Quarterly* (2020).

Cahill, Alice. *Are You Getting the Best out of Your Leadership Team?* Greensboro, NC: Center for Creative Leadership, 2020.

Cappelli, Peter, Monika Hamori, and Rocio Bonet. "Who's Got Those Top Jobs?" *Harvard Business Review* 92, no. 3 (2014): 74–77.

EgonZehnder. *The CEO: A Personal Reflection.* Zürich: EgonZehnder, 2018.

Godart, F. C., S. Seong, and D. J. Phillips. «The Sociology of Creativity: Elements, Structures, and Audiences.» *Annual Review of Sociology* 46 (2020): 489–510.

Hackman, J. Richard. "Designing Work for Individuals and for Groups." In *Perspectives on Behavior in Organizations*, edited by J. Richard Hackman, E. E.

Lawler, and L. W. Porter, 242–56. New York: McGraw-Hill, 1983.

Hambrick, Donald C. "Top Management Teams." In *Wiley Encyclopedia of Management*. Hoboken, NJ: Wiley, 2015.

Hébert, Louis, Réal Jacob, Alain Gosselin, Éric Brunelle, and Roman Oryschuk. *Paroles de Pdg: Comment 75 Grands Patrons du Québec Vivent Leur Métier*. Montreal: Les Éditions Rogers Ltée, 2014.

Keller, Scott, and Mary Meaney. "Attracting and Retaining the Right Talent." *McKinsey Global Institute Study*. 2017.

Kissinger, Henry. *World Order*. New York: Penguin, 2014. https://books.google.fr/books?id=NR5oAwAAQBAJ.

Leblanc, Richard, and Mark S. Schwartz. "The Black Box of Board Process: Gaining Access to a Difficult Subject." *Corporate Governance: An International Review* 15, no. 5 (2007): 843–51. https://doi.org/10.1111/j.1467-8683.2007.00617.x.

Sull, Donald, Charles Sull, and James Yoder. "No One Knows Your Strategy—Not Even Your Top Leaders." *MIT Sloan Management Review* 59, no. 3 (2018): 1–6.

Chapter 1

Berg, David N. "Senior Executive Teams: Not What You Think." *Consulting Psychology Journal: Practice and Research* 57, no. 2 (2005): 107.

Colbert, Amy E., Murray R. Barrick, and Bret H. Bradley. "Personality and Leadership Composition in Top Management Teams: Implications for Organizational Effectiveness." *Personnel Psychology* 67, no. 2 (2014): 351–87.

Edmondson, Amy C., Michael A. Roberto, and Michael D. Watkins. "A Dynamic Model of Top Management Team Effectiveness: Managing Unstructured Task Streams." *Leadership Quarterly* 14, no. 3 (2003): 297–325.

Fisher, Roger, William L. Ury, and Bruce Patton. *Getting to Yes: Negotiating Agreement without Giving In*. New York: Penguin, 2011.

Fitzgerald, F. Scott. *The Crack-Up: With Other Uncollected Pieces*. New York: Edmund Wilson/New Directions, 1945.

Fubini, David. *Hidden Truths: What Leaders Need to Hear But Are Rarely Told*. Hoboken, NJ: Wiley, 2021.

Galinsky, Adam, and Maurice Schweitzer. *Friend and Foe: When to Cooperate, When to Compete, and How to Succeed at Both*. New York: Currency, 2015.

Galunic, Charles, and Jacques Neatby. "Order in the Strategy Court." *Harvard Business Review* (November 26, 2013).

Godart, Frederic Manon Frappier, and Brian Henry. "Can Creativity and Commerce Ever Be Reconciled? Raf Simons at Calvin Klein," INSEAD case study 6582 (2020).

Katzenbach, Jon R. *Teams at the Top: Unleashing the Potential of Both Teams and Individual Leaders*. Boston, MA: Harvard Business Press, 1998.

Lafontaine-Beaumier, Éloi, Jacques Neatby, and Louis Hébert. «Émergence de la Publicité Native: La Société Radio-Canada Face à la Transformation de l'industrie Publicitaire (the Canadian Broadcasting Corporation and the Upheaval of the Advertising Industry).» *Revue internationale de cas en gestion/International Journal of Case Studies in Management* 18, no. 1 (2020).

Lencioni, Patrick. *The Five Dysfunctions of a Team: A Leadership Fable.* San Francisco: Jossey-Bass, 2002.

Liras, Santiago Madrid. "Why a Fourth Mediation Model: Opportunities and Integration of the Insight Mediation Model." *Revista de Mediación* 10, no. 2 (2017).

Mihaylova, Ivanka. "Well Prepared for Conflict in Organizations? A Managers' Self-Assessment of Their Conflict Management Knowledge." *Knowledge International Journal* 42, no. 1 (2020): 121–27.

Miles, Rufus E. "The Origin and Meaning of Miles' Law." *Public Administration Review* 38, no. 5 (1978): 399–403.

Mooney, Ann C., and Allen C. Amason. "In Search of the CEO's Inner Circle and How It Is Formed." In *The Handbook of Research on Top Management Teams*, edited by Mason A. Carpenter, 35–48. Northampton, MA: Elgar, 2011.

Picard, Cheryl A. *Mediating Interpersonal and Small Group Conflict.* Saskatchewan: Dundurn, 2002.

Pronin, Emily, Daniel Y. Lin, and Lee Ross. "The Bias Blind Spot: Perceptions of Bias in Self versus Others." *Personality and Social Psychology Bulletin* 28, no. 3 (2002): 369–81.

Robinson, Robert J., Dacher Keltner, Andrew Ward, and Lee Ross. "Actual versus Assumed Differences in Construal: 'Naive Realism' in Intergroup Perception and Conflict." *Journal of Personality and Social Psychology* 68, no. 3 (1995): 404–17.

Ross, Lee, and Andrew Ward. "Naive Realism in Everyday Life: Implications for Social Conflict and Misunderstanding." In *Values and Knowledge*, edited by Edward S. Reed, Elliot Turiel, and Terrance Brown, 103–35. Hillsdale, NJ: Erlbaum, 1996.

Schad, Jonathan, Marianne W. Lewis, Sebastian Raisch, and Wendy K. Smith. "Paradox Research in Management Science: Looking Back to Move Forward." *Academy of Management Annals* 10, no. 1 (2016): 5–64.

Smith, Wendy K. "Dynamic Decision-Making: A Model of Senior Leaders Managing Strategic Paradoxes." *Academy of Management Journal* 57, no. 6 (2014): 1592–1623.

Smith, Wendy K., Marianne W. Lewis, and Michael L. Tushman. "'Both/and' Leadership." *Harvard Business Review* 94, no. 5 (2016): 62–70.

Sull, Donald, Charles Sull, and James Yoder. "No One Knows Your Strategy–Not Even Your Top Leaders." *MIT Sloan Management Review* 59, no. 3 (2018): 1–6.

Chapter 2

Alvarez, Jose Luis, and Silviya Svejenova. *Sharing Executive Power: Roles and Re-*

lationships at the Top. Cambridge: Cambridge University Press, 2005.

Ancona, Deborah G., and David A. Nadler. "Top Hats and Executive Tales: Designing the Senior Team." *MIT Sloan Management Review* 31, no. 1 (1989): 19.

Arendt, Lucy A., Richard L. Priem, and Hermann Achidi Ndofor. "A CEO-Adviser Model of Strategic Decision Making." *Journal of Management* 31, no. 5 (2005): 68099.

Bachrach, Peter, and Morton S. Baratz. "Two Faces of Power." *American Political Science Review* 56, no. 4 (December 1962): 947–52.

Battilana, Julie, and Tiziana Casciaro. *Power, for All: How It Really Works and Why It's Everyone's Business.* New York: Simon and Schuster, 2021.

Carmeli, Abraham, John Schaubroeck, and Asher Tishler. "How CEO Empowering Leadership Shapes Top Management Team Processes: Implications for Firm Performance." *Leadership Quarterly* 22, no. 2 (2011): 399-411.

Cialdini, Robert B. "The Science of Persuasion." *Scientific American* 284, no. 2 (2001): 76–81.

Davis, I., and T. Dickson. "Lou Gerstner on Corporate Reinvention and Values." *McKinsey Quarterly* 3 (2014): 123–29.

Duffy, Michelle K., Daniel C. Ganster, and Milan Pagon. "Social Undermining in the Workplace." *Academy of Management Journal* 45, no. 2 (2002): 331–51.

Edmondson, Amy C., Michael A. Roberto, and Michael D. Watkins. "A Dynamic Model of Top Management Team Effectiveness: Managing Unstructured Task Streams." *Leadership Quarterly* 14, no. 3 (2003): 297–325.

Eisenhardt, Kathleen M. "Strategy as Strategic Decision Making." *Sloan Management Review* 40, no. 3 (1999): 65–72.

Eisenhardt, Kathleen M., and Mark J. Zbaracki. "Strategic Decision Making." *Strategic Management Journal* 13, no. S2 (1992): 17–37.

Elbanna, Said. "Strategic Decision-Making: Process Perspectives." *International Journal of Management Reviews* 8, no. 1 (2006): 1–20. https://onlinelibrary.wiley.com/doi/abs/10.1111/j.1468-2370.2006.00118.x.

Fletcher, Anthony C., Georges A. Wagner, and Philip E. Bourne. "Ten Simple Rules for More Objective Decision-Making." San Francisco: San Francisco Public Library of Science, 2020.

Gavin, David J., Joanne H. Gavin, and James Campbell Quick. "Power Struggles within the Top Management Team: An Empirical Examination of Follower Reactions to Subversive Leadership." *Journal of Applied Biobehavioral Research* 22, no. 4 (2017): e12100.

Gouldner, Alvin W. "The Norm of Reciprocity: A Preliminary Statement." *American Sociological Review* (1960): 161–78.

Grant, Adam. *Think Again: The Power of Knowing What You Don't Know.* New York: Viking Press, 2021.

Guadalupe, Maria, Hongyi Li, and Julie Wulf. "Who Lives in the C-Suite? Organizational Structure and the Division of Labor in Top Management." *Management Science* 60, no. 4 (2014): 824–44.

Herkert, Joseph, Jason Borenstein, and Keith Miller. "The Boeing 737 Max: Lessons for Engineering Ethics." *Science and Engineering Ethics* 26, no. 6 (December 1, 2020): 2957–74. https://doi.org/10.1007/s11948-020-00252-y.

Hill, Linda, and Kent Lineback. "Stop Avoiding Office Politics." *Harvard Business Review,* November 2, 2011.

Immelt, Jeffrey. "How I Remade GE and What I Learned along the Way." *Harvard Business Review* (September–October 2017).

Kahneman, Daniel, Olivier Sibony, and C. R. Sunstein. *Noise.* London: HarperCollins UK, 2022.

Kinni, Theodore. "Why Wandering Works Wonders for Managers." *Strategy and Business,* August 2, 2018. https://www.strategy-business.com/blog/Why-Wandering-Works-Wonders-for-Managers.

Kline, Theresa J. B. *Teams That Lead: A Matter of Market Strategy, Leadership Skills, and Executive Strength.* London: Psychology Press, 2020.

Krause, R., R. Priem, and L. Love. "Who's in Charge Here? Co-CEOs, Power Gaps, and Firm Performance." *Strategic Management Journal* 36, no. 13 (December 2015): 2099–110. https://doi.org/10.1002/smj.2325.

Lewis, Leo. "Collision Course : The Sensational Downfall of Carlos Ghosn." *Financial Times,* July 16, 2021.

Lukes, Steven. *Power: A Radical View.* London: Palgrave Macmillan, 2005.

Menz, Markus. "Functional Top Management Team Members:A Review, Synthesis, and Research Agenda." *Journal of Management* 38, no. 1 (2012): 45–80. https://journals.sagepub.com/doi/abs/10.1177/0149206311421830.

Mintzberg, Henry. *Managing.* San Francisco: Berrett-Koehler, 2011.

Moss Kanter, Rosabeth. "Power Failure in Management Circuits." *Harvard Business Review,* no. 57 (July/August 1979).

Nadler, David, and Janet L. Spencer. *Executive Teams.* San Francisco: Jossey-Bass, 1998.

Neustadt, R. E. *Presidential Power: The Politics of Leadership.* New York: Wiley, 1964.

Oncken, William, Jr., and Donald L. Wass. "Management Time: Who's Got the Monkey?" *Harvard Business Review,* , no. 12 (November–December 1999).

Perkins, D. N. T. *Ghosts in the Executive Suite: Every Business Is a Family Business.* Branford, CT: Syncretics Group, 1988.

Peters, T. J., and R. H. Waterman. *In Search of Excellence.* New York: Harper, 1982.

Pfeffer, Jeffrey. *Leadership BS: Fixing Workplaces and Careers One Truth at a Time.* New York: HarperCollins, 2015.

———. "Teaching Power in Ways That Influence Student' Career Success: Some Fundamental Ideas" (working paper 3839). Stanford University Graduate School of Business, November 25, 2019.

———. "Understanding Power in Organizations." *California Management Review* 34, no. 2 (1992): 29–50. http://www.jstor.org/stable/41166692.

Rothman, Joshua. "Shut Up and Sit Down: Why the Leadership Industry Rules." *New Yorker,* February 29, 2016. http://www.newyorker.com/magazine/2016/02/29/our-dangerous-leadership-obsession.

Shen, Wei, and Albert A. Cannella Jr. "Power Dynamics within Top Management and Their Impacts on CEO Dismissal Followed by Inside Succession." *Academy of Management Journal* 45, no. 6 (2002): 1195–206.

Smith, Anne, Susan M. Houghton, Jacqueline N. Hood, and Joel A. Ryman. "Power Relationships among Top Managers: Does Top Management Team Power Distribution Matter for Organizational Performance?" *Journal of Business Research* 59, no. 5 (2006): 622–29.

Chapter 3

Arendt, Lucy A., Richard L. Priem, and Hermann Achidi Ndofor. "A CEO-Adviser Model of Strategic Decision Making." Journal of Management 31, no. 5 (2005): 680–99.

Bang, Henning, Synne L. Fuglesang, Mariann R. Ovesen, and Dag Erik Eilertsen. "Effectiveness in Top Management Group Meetings: The Role of Goal Clarity, Focused Communication, and Learning Behavior." Scandinavian Journal of Psychology 51, no. 3 (2010): 253–61.

Blumer, Anselm, Andrzej Ehrenfeucht, David Haussler, and Manfred K. Warmuth. "Occam's Razor." Information Processing Letters 24, no. 6 (1987): 377–80.

Burt, Ronald S., Martin Kilduff, and Stefano Tasselli. "Social Network Analysis: Foundations and Frontiers on Advantage." Annual Review of Psychology 64 (2013): 527–47.

Carmeli, Abraham, John Schaubroeck, and Asher Tishler. "How CEO Empowering Leadership Shapes Top Management Team Processes: Implications for Firm Performance." Leadership Quarterly 22, no. 2 (2011): 399–411.

De Jong, Bart A., Kurt T. Dirks, and Nicole Gillespie. "Trust and Team Performance: A Meta-Analysis of Main Effects, Moderators, and Covariates." Journal of Applied Psychology 101, no. 8 (2016): 1134.

Fernandez, Roberto, and Roger Gould. "The Dilemma of State Power: Brokerage and Influence in the National Health Policy Domain." American Journal of Sociology 99 (1994): 1455–91.

Garg, Sam, and Kathleen M. Eisenhardt. "Unpacking the CEO–Board Relationship: How Strategy Making Happens in Entrepreneurial Firms." Academy of Management Journal 60, no. 5 (2017): 1828–58.

Godart, F. C., F. Cavarretta, and M. Thiemann. "Task Complexity and Shared Value Orientation: Exploring the Moderators of a Social Dilemma in Team Social Networks," Industrial and Corporate Change 25 (2016): 739–56.

Hambrick, Donald D. "Top Management Groups: A Conceptual Integration and Reconsideration of the 'Team' Label." In Research in Organizational Behavior, edited by B. Staw and L. L. Cummings, 171–214. Greenwich, CT: JAI Press, 1994.

Kwon, Seok-Woo, Emanuela Rondi, Daniel Z. Levin, Alfredo De Massis, and Daniel J. Brass. "Network Brokerage: An Integrative Review and Future Research Agenda." Journal of Management 46, no. 6 (2020): 1092–120.

Ma, Shenghui, and David Seidl. "New CEOs and Their Collaborators: Divergence and Convergence between the Strategic Leadership Constellation and the Top Management Team." Strategic Management Journal 39, no. 3 (2018): 606–38. https://onlinelibrary.wiley.com/doi/abs/10.1002/smj.2721.

McPherson, Miller, Lynn Smith-Lovin, and James M. Cook. "Birds of a Feather: Homophily in Social Networks." Annual Review of Sociology 27 (2001): 415–44.

Mintzberg, Henry. "The Manager's Job: Folklore and Fact." Harvard Business Review 53, no. 4 (1975).

Mooney, Ann C., and Allen C. Amason. "In Search of the CEO's Inner Circle and How It Is Formed." In The Handbook of Research on Top Management Teams, edited by Mason A. Carpenter, 35–48. Northampton, MA: Elgar, 2011.

Nadler, David, and Janet L. Spencer. Executive Teams. San Francisco: Jossey-Bass, 1998.

Oncken, William jr, and Donald L. Wass. Management Time: Who's Got the Monkey? Reprint Service, Harvard business review, 1974.

Roberto, Michael A. "The Stable Core and Dynamic Periphery in Top Management Teams." Management Decision 41, no. 2 (2003).

Svejenova, Silviya, and José Luis Alvarez. "Changing the C-Suite: New Chief Officer Roles as Strategic Responses to Institutional Complexity." In New Themes in Institutional Analysis, edited by Georg Krücken, Carmelo Mazza, Renate E. Meyer, and Peter Walgenbach. Northampton, MA: Elgar, 2017.

Tushman, Michael L., Wendy K. Smith, and Andy Binns. "The Ambidextrous CEO." Harvard Business Review 89, no. 6 (2011): 74–80. F. C. Godart, F. Cavarretta, and M. Thiemann, M. (2016). "Task Complexity and Shared Value Orientation: Exploring the Moderators of a Social Dilemma in Team Social Networks," Industrial and Corporate Change 25 (2016): 739–56

Chapter 4

Amason, Allen C. "Distinguishing the Effects of Functional and Dysfunctional Conflict on Strategic Decision Making: Resolving a Paradox for Top Management Teams." Academy of Management Journal 39, no. 1 (1996): 123–48. https://journals.aom.org/doi/abs/10.5465/256633.

Balkundi, Prasad, Martin Kilduff, Zoe I. Barsness, and Judd H. Michael. "Demographic Antecedents and Performance Consequences of Structural Holes in Work Teams." Journal of Organizational Behavior: International Journal of Industrial, Occupational and Organizational Psychology and Behavior 28, no. 2 (2007): 241–60.

Bies, Robert J., and Debra L. Shapiro. "Voice and Justification: Their Influence on

Procedural Fairness Judgments." *Academy of Management Journal* 31, no. 3 (1988): 67685. https://journals.aom.org/doi/abs/10.5465/256465.

Colbert, Amy E., Murray R. Barrick, and Bret H. Bradley. "Personality and Leadership Composition in Top Management Teams: Implications for Organizational Effectiveness." *Personnel Psychology* 67, no. 2 (2014): 351–87.

Cyert, Richard M., and James G. March. *A Behavioral Theory of the Firm*. Englewood Cliffs, NJ: Prentice Hall, 1963.

Duhigg, Charles. "What Google Learned from Its Quest to Build the Perfect Team." *New York Times*, 2016. https://www.nytimes.com/2016/02/28/magazine/what-google-learned-from-its-quest-to-build-the-perfect-team.html.

Edmondson, Amy C. *The Fearless Organization: Creating Psychological Safety in the Workplace for Learning, Innovation, and Growth*. Hoboken, NJ: Wiley, 2018.

Eisenhardt, Kathleen M., Jean L. Kahwajy, and L.J. Bourgeois III. "How Management Teams Can Have a Good Fight." *Harvard Business Review* 75, no. 4 (1997): 77–86.

Eisenhardt, Kathleen M., and Mark J. Zbaracki. "Strategic Decision Making." *Strategic Management Journal* 13, no. S2 (1992): 17–37.

Finkelstein, Sydney, and Donald Hambrick. *Strategic Leadership: Top Executives and Their Effects on Organizations*. Eagan, MN: West Publishing, 1996.

Fisher, Roger, William L. Ury, and Bruce Patton. *Getting to Yes: Negotiating Agreement without Giving In*. Penguin, 2011.

Floyd, Steven W., and Bill Wooldridge. *Building Strategy from the Middle: Reconceptualizing Strategy Process*. Thousand Oaks, CA: Sage, 2000.

Galunic, Charles. *Backstage Leadership: The Invisible Work of Highly Effective Leaders*. Cham, Switzerland: Springer Nature, 2020.

Galunic, Charles, and Immanuel Hermreck. "How to Help Employees 'Get' Strategy." *Harvard Business Review* 90, no. 12 (2012): 24–24.

Hambrick, D. C. "The Field of Management's Devotion to Theory: Too Much of a Good Thing?" *Academy of Management Journal* 50 (2007): 1346–52.

Hambrick, Donald D., and Phyllis Mason. "Upper Echelons: The Organization as a Reflection of Its Top Managers." *Academy of Management Journal* 9, no. 2 (1984): 193–206.

Hébert, Louis, Réal Jacob, Alain Gosselin, Éric Brunelle, and Roman Oryschuk. *Paroles de Pdg: Comment 75 Grands Patrons du Québec Vivent Leur Métier*. Montreal: Les Éditions Rogers Ltée, 2014.

Izzo, John. "Consistency Drives Success at Telus." *Strategy + Business* (August 31, 2015). https://www.strategy-business.com/article/00360.

Jaques, Elliott, ed. *The Changing Culture of a Factory*. London: Tavistock, 1951.

———. "In Praise of Hierarchy." *Harvard Business Review* 68, no. 1 (1990): 127–33.

Jones, Carla D., and Albert A. Cannella. "Alternate Configurations in Strategic Decision Making." In *The Handbook of Research on Top Management Teams*, ed. Mason Carpenter, 15–34. Northampton, MA: Elgar, 2011.

Kathuria, Ravi, Maheshkumar P. Joshi, and Stephen J. Porth. "Organizational Alignment and Performance: Past, Present and Future." *Management Decision* 45, no. 3 (2007): 503–17. https://doi.org/10.1108/00251740710745106.

Katzenbach, Jon R. *Teams at the Top: Unleashing the Potential of Both Teams and Individual Leaders.* Boston: Harvard Business Press, 1998.

Korsgaard, M. Audrey, David M. Schweiger, and Harry J. Sapienza. "Building Commitment, Attachment, and Trust in Strategic Decision-Making Teams: The Role of Procedural Justice." *Academy of Management Journal* 38, no. 1 (1995): 60–84.

Laine, Pikka-Maaria, and Eero Vaara. "Participation in Strategy Work." In *Cambridge Handbook of Strategy as Practice*, 616–31. Cambridge: Cambridge University Press, 2015.

Lencioni, Patrick. *The Five Dysfunctions of a Team: A Leadership Fable.* San Francisco: Jossey-Bass, 2002.

Ma, Shenghui, Yasemin Y. Kor, and David Seidl. "CEO Advice Seeking: An Integrative Framework and Future Research Agenda." *Journal of Management* 46, no. 6 (2020): 771–805. https://journals.sagepub.com/doi/abs/10.1177/0149206319885430.

Mathieu, John E., Peter T. Gallagher, Monique A. Domingo, and Elizabeth A. Klock. "Embracing Complexity: Reviewing the Past Decade of Team Effectiveness Research." *Annual Review of Organizational Psychology and Organizational Behavior* 6 (2019): 17–46.

Mintzberg, Henry, Duru Raisinghani, and Andre Theoret. "The Structure of 'Unstructured' Decision Processes." *Administrative Science Quarterly* 21, no. 2 (1976): 246–75.

Nadler, David, and Janet L. Spencer. *Executive Teams.* San Francisco: Jossey-Bass, 1998.

Raes, Anneloes M. L., Heike Bruch, and Simon B. De Jong. "How Top Management Team Behavioural Integration Can Impact Employee Work Outcomes: Theory Development and First Empirical Tests." *Human Relations* 66, no. 2 (2013): 167–92.

Roberto, Michael A. *Why Great Leaders Don't Take Yes for an Answer: Managing for Conflict and Consensus.* London: FT Press, 2013.

Simons, Tony, Lisa Hope Pelled, and Ken A. Smith. "Making Use of Difference: Diversity, Debate, and Decision Comprehensiveness in Top Management Teams." *Academy of Management Journal* 42, no. 6 (1999): 662–73.

Stewart, Steven A., and Allen C. Amason. "Assessing the State of Top Management Teams Research." In *Oxford Research Encyclopedia of Business and Management.* 2017.

Sull, Donald, Rebecca Homkes, and Charles Sull. "Why Strategy Execution Unravels—and What to Do about It." *Harvard Business Review* 93, no. 3 (2015): 57–66.

Wadström, Pontus. "Aligning Corporate and Business Strategy: Managing the

Balance." *Journal of Business Strategy* 40, no. 4 (2019): 44–52. https://doi.org/10.1108/JBS-06-2018-0099.

Wageman, Ruth, and J. Richard Hackman. "What Makes Teams of Leaders Leadable?" In *Handbook of Leadership Theory and Practice*, edited by Nitin Nohria and Rakesh Khurana. Boston: Harvard Business School Press, 2010.

Wageman, Ruth, Debra A. Nunes, James A. Burruss, and J. Richard Hackman. *Senior Leadership Teams: What It Takes to Make Them Great*. Boston: Harvard Business Review Press, 2008.

Whitler, Kimberly A. "What Is the Executive Leadership Team? 33 Board and C-Level Leaders Explain." *Forbes*, June 5, 2021. https://www.forbes.com/sites/kimberlywhitler/2021/06/05/what-is-the-executive-leadership-team-33-board-and-c-level-leaders-explain/?sh=21dde7b66dbf.

Yang, Longqi, David Holtz, Sonia Jaffe, Siddharth Suri, Shilpi Sinha, Jeffrey Weston, Connor Joyce, et al. «The Effects of Remote Work on Collaboration among Information Workers.» *Nature Human Behaviour* 6, no. 1 (2021): 1–12.

Chapter 5

Alvarez, José Luis, and Silviya Svejenova. *The Changing C-Suite: Executive Power in Transformation*. Oxford: Oxford University Press, 2022.

Bendig, David. "Chief Operating Officer Characteristics and How They Relate to Exploration via Patenting versus Venturing." *Journal of Business Research* 140 (2022): 297–309.. https://www.sciencedirect.com/science/article/pii/S0148296321008080.

Bennett, Nathan, and Stephen Miles. "Second in Command: The Misunderstood Role of the Chief Operating Officer." *Harvard Business Review* 84, no. 5 (2006).

Chambers, Elizabeth G., Mark Foulon, Helen Handfield-Jones, Steven M. Hankin, and Edward G. Michaels III. "The War for Talent." *McKinsey Quarterly*, no. 3 (1998): 44.

Crainer, S., and D. Dearlove. *Financial Times Handbook of Management*. Harlow: Financial Times/Prentice Hall, 2004. https://books.google.fr/books?id=R7fMHYTCJdQC.

Cross, Rob, and Jon R. Katzenbach. "The Right Role for Top Teams." *Strategy + Business*, no. 67 (2012). https://www.strategy-business.com/article/00103.

Delmar, Daniel R. "The Rise of the CSO (Organization Design)." *Journal of Business Strategy* 24, no. 2 (2003): 8–11.

Drucker, Peter Ferdinand. *The Practice of Management*. New York: Harper, 1954.

Goudreau, Jenna. "C Is for Silly: The New C-Suite Titles." *Forbes*, January 10, 2012, https://www.forbes.com/sites/jennagoudreau/2012/01/10/c-is-for-silly-the-new-c-suite-titles/?sh=2ac432a52a01.

Groysberg, Boris, L. Kevin Kelly, and Bryan MacDonald. "The New Path to the C-Suite." *Harvard Business Review* 89, no. 3 (2011): 60–68.

Guadalupe, Maria, Hongyi Li, and Julie Wulf. "Who Lives in the C-Suite? Organizational Structure and the Division of Labor in Top Management." *Management Science* 60, no. 4 (2014): 824–44.

Haleblian, Jerayr, and Sydney Finkelstein. "Top Management Team Size, CEO Dominance, and Firm Performance: The Moderating Roles of Environmental Turbulence and Discretion." *Academy of Management Journal* 36, no. 4 (1993): 844–63. https://journals.aom.org/doi/abs/10.5465/256761.

Hambrick, Donald C., and Albert A. Cannella Jr. "CEOs Who Have COOs: Contingency Analysis of an Unexplored Structural Form." *Strategic Management Journal* 25, no. 10 (2004): 959–79. https://doi.org/https://doi.org/10.1002/smj.407.

Hill, Andrew. "Axe the Middle Managers at Your Peril." *Financial Times*, May 20, 2018, https://www.ft.com/content/24f2ee84-59dc-11e8-b8b2-d6ceb45fa9do.

Kahneman, Daniel. *Thinking, Fast and Slow.* New York: Macmillan, 2011.

Knight, Don, Craig L. Pearce, Ken G. Smith, Judy D. Olian, Henry P. Sims, Ken A. Smith, and Patrick Flood. "Top Management Team Diversity, Group Process, and Strategic Consensus." *Strategic Management Journal* 20, no. 5 (1999): 445–65.

Kovensky, Josh. "Chief Happiness Officer Is the Latest, Creepiest Job in Corporate America." *New Republic* (January 22, 2014). https://newrepublic.com/amp/article/118804/happiness-officers-are-spreading-across-america-why-its-bad.

Leinwand, Paul, Nils Naujok, and Joachim Rotering. "Memo to the CEO: Is Your Chief Strategy Officer Set Up for Success?" *Strategy + Business* (January 15, 2019).

Ma, Shenghui, and David Seidl. "New CEOs and Their Collaborators: Divergence and Convergence between the Strategic Leadership Constellation and the Top Management Team." *Strategic Management Journal* 39, no. 3 (2018): 606–38. https://onlinelibrary.wiley.com/doi/abs/10.1002/smj.2721

Mantere, Saku, and Eero Vaara. "On the Problem of Participation in Strategy: A Critical Discursive Perspective." *Organization Science* 19, no. 2 (2008): 341–58.

Mao, Yina, Ching-Wen Wang, and Chi-Sum Wong. "Towards a Model of the Right-Hand Person." *Leadership and Organization Development Journal* 37, no. 4 (2016): 520–39. https://doi.org/10.1108/LODJ-08-2014-0153.

Neilson, Gary L. "The Decline of the COO." *Forbes* (May 20, 2015). https://www.forbes.com/sites/strategyand/2015/05/20/the-decline-of-the-coo/?sh=5e0b83447cee.

Neilson, Gary L., and Julie Wulf. "How Many Direct Reports?" *Harvard Business Review* 90, no. 4 (2012).

Péladeau, P., and O. Acker. "Have We Reached 'Peak' Chief Digital Officer." *Strategy + Business* (2019).

Rickards, Tuck, Kate Smaje, and Vik Sohoni. "'Transformer in Chief': The New Chief Digital Officer." *McKinsey Digital* (September 1, 2015).

Slenders, Wilma J. *Chief Executive Officers and Their Trusted Advisor Relationships: A Qualitative Study from the CEO's Perspective.* Minneapolis: Capella University, 2010.

Smith, Anne, Susan M. Houghton, Jacqueline N. Hood, and Joel A. Ryman.

"Power Relationships among Top Managers: Does Top Management Team Power Distribution Matter for Organizational Performance?" *Journal of Business Research* 59, no. 5 (2006): 622–29. https://doi.org/https://doi.org/10.1016/j.jbusres.2005.10.012.

Snyder, Scott A., and Shaloo Kulkarni. "So You Think You Need a Chief Digital Officer?" *Knowledge at Wharton* (November 8, 2018). https://knowledge.wharton.upenn.edu/article/do-you-need-a-chief-digital-officer/.

Suzman, James. "How Mckinsey & Co. Created 'the War for Talent' in 1998 to Propagate a 'Myth of Brilliance.'" *The Print* (2021). https://theprint.in/pageturner/excerpt/how-mckinsey-co-created-the-war-for-talent-in-1998-to-propagate-a-myth-of-brilliance/755705/.

Wageman, Ruth, Debra A. Nunes, James A. Burruss, and J. Richard Hackman. *Senior Leadership Teams: What It Takes to Make Them Great.* Boston: Harvard Business Review Press, 2008.

Welch, Jack, and Suzy Welch. *Winning.* New York: HarperBusiness, 2005.

West, Michael A. *Effective Teamwork: Practical Lessons from Organizational Research.* Hoboken, NJ: Wiley, 2012. https://books.google.fr/books?id=dmIjlneC3HwC.

Whitler, Kimberly A., and Neil Morgan. "Why CMOs Never Last and What to Do about It." *Harvard Business Review* 95, no. 4 (2017): 47-+.

Zorn, Dirk M. "Here a Chief, There a Chief: The Rise of the CFO in the American Firm." *American Sociological Review* 69, no. 3 (2004): 345–64. https://doi.org/10.1177/000312240406900302.

Chapter 6

Barrick, Murray R., Bret H. Bradley, Amy L. Kristof-Brown, and Amy E. Colbert. "The Moderating Role of Top Management Team Interdependence: Implications for Real Teams and Working Groups." *Academy of Management Journal* 50, no. 3 (2007): 544–57. https://doi.org/10.5465/amj.2007.25525781.

Battilana, Julie, and Tiziana Casciaro. *Power, for All: How It Really Works and Why It's Everyone's Business.* New York: Simon and Schuster, 2021.

Bergeron, Natasha, Aaron de Smet, and Liesje Meijknecht. "Improve Your Leadership Team's Effectiveness through Key Behaviors." *McKinsey Quarterly* (2020). https://www.mckinsey.com/business-functions/organization/our-insights/the-organization-blog/improve-your-leadership-teams-effectiveness-through-key-behaviors.

Camelo-Ordaz, Carmen, Joaquín García-Cruz, and Elena Sousa-Ginel. "The Influence of Top Management Team Conflict on Firm Innovativeness." *Group Decision and Negotiation* 24, no. 6 (2015): 957–80. https://doi.org/10.1007/s10726-014-9424-4.

de Wit, Frank R. C., Karen A. Jehn, and Daan Scheepers. "Task Conflict, Information Processing, and Decision-Making: The Damaging Effect of Relationship Conflict." *Organizational Behavior and Human Decision Processes* 122, no. 2 (2013): 177–89. https://doi.org/https://doi.org/10.1016/j.obhdp.2013.07.002.

Edmondson, Amy. "Psychological Safety and Learning Behavior in Work Teams." *Administrative Science Quarterly* 44, no. 2 (1999): 350–83. https://doi.org/10.2307/2666999.

Edmondson, Amy C. *The Fearless Organization: Creating Psychological Safety in the Workplace for Learning, Innovation, and Growth*. Hoboken, NJ: Wiley, 2018.

George, Bradley, Truls Erikson, and Annaleena Parhankangas. "Preventing Dysfunctional Conflict: Examining the Relationship between Different Types of Managerial Conflict in Venture Capital–Backed Firms." *Venture Capital* 18, no. 4 (2016): 279–96. https://doi.org/10.1080/13691066.2016.1224457.

Hambrick, Donald C. "Corporate Coherence and the Top Management Team." *Strategy and Leadership* (September––October 1997): 24–30.

Hansen, Morten. *Collaboration: How Leaders Avoid the Traps, Build Common Ground, and Reap Big Results*. Boston: Harvard Business Press, 2009.

Kim, W. Chan, and Renée Mauborgne. "Fair Process." *Harvard Business Review* 75 (1997): 65–75.

Lewis, Michael. *Moneyball: The Art of Winning an Unfair Game*. New York: Norton, 2004.

Mintzberg, Henry. "The Design School: Reconsidering the Basic Premises of Strategic Management." *Strategic Management Journal* 11, no. 3 (1990): 171–95. https://doi.org/https://doi.org/10.1002/smj.4250110302.

Mooney, Ann C., Patricia J. Holahan, and Allen C. Amason. "Don't Take It Personally: Exploring Cognitive Conflict as a Mediator of Affective Conflict." *Journal of Management Studies* 44, no. 5 (2007): 733–58. https://doi.org/https://doi.org/10.1111/j.1467-6486.2006.00674.x.

Nadler, David, and Janet L. Spencer. *Executive Teams*. San Francisco: Jossey-Bass, 1998.

Raes, Anneloes M. L., Heike Bruch, and Simon B. De Jong. "How Top Management Team Behavioural Integration Can Impact Employee Work Outcomes: Theory Development and First Empirical Tests." *Human Relations* 66, no. 2 (2013): 167–92.

Roberto, Michael A. "Why Great Leaders Don't Take Yes for an Answer." *Management Today* 21, no. 10 (2005): 22–26.

Rosen, Richard, and Fred Adair. "CEOs Misperceive Top Teams' Performance." *Harvard Business Review* 85, no. 9 (2007): 30.

Simons, Tony L., and Randall S. Peterson. "Task Conflict and Relationship Conflict in Top Management Teams: The Pivotal Role of Intragroup Trust." *Journal of Applied Psychology* 85 (2000): 102–11. https://doi.org/10.1037/0021-9010.85.1.102.

Sull, Donald, Rebecca Homkes, and Charles Sull. "Why Strategy Execution Unravels—and What to Do about It." *Harvard Business Review* 93, no. 3 (2015): 57–66.

Sull, Donald N. "Closing the Gap between Strategy and Execution." *MIT Sloan Management Review* 48, no. 4 (2007): 30.

Tarakci, Murat, Nufer Yasin Ates, Jeanine P. Porck, Daan van Knippenberg, Patrick J. F. Groenen, and Marco de Haas. "Strategic Consensus Mapping: A New Method for Testing and Visualizing Strategic Consensus within and between Teams." *Strategic Management Journal* 35, no. 7 (2014): 1053–69. https://doi.org/https://doi.org/10.1002/smj.2151.

Walter, Jorge, Franz W. Kellermanns, Steven W. Floyd, John F. Veiga, and Curtis Matherne. "Strategic Alignment: A Missing Link in the Relationship between Strategic Consensus and Organizational Performance." *Strategic Organization* 11, no. 3 (2013): 304–28. https://doi.org/10.1177/1476127013481155.

Wood, Wendy. *Good Habits, Bad Habits: The Science of Making Positive Changes That Stick*. London: Macmillan, 2019.

Wooldridge, Bill, and Birton Cowden. "Strategic Decision-Making in Business." In *Oxford Research Encyclopedia of Business and Management*. London: Oxford University Press, 2020.

INDEX

team effectiveness, 159; Follow-ups, 177; Informal, 72; Leadership team meetings as forums, 185; Offsites, 5, 46, 86, 158; Order of topics, 177; Post-meeting to-dos, 174; Scheduling, 71; Setting the agenda of a leadership team meeting, 183; Showing up unprepared at, 191
Mind-set: Both/and, 17; Either/or, 17
Mintzberg, Henry, 55, 58, 201, 204, 205, 207, 212
Mode of functioning, 59; CEO-Adviser, 65, 66, 67, 75, 77, 78, 79, 80, 82, 83, 89, 202; Hub-and-Spoke, 9, 59, 62, 63, 64, 65, 67, 68, 70, 71, 72, 73, 75, 79, 80, 82, 83, 84, 85, 89, 109, 111, 112, 149, 180, 183, 202; Team, 63, 67, 73, 75, 76, 77, 78, 79, 80, 82, 83, 84, 85, 86, 110, 111, 183
Monitoring activities, 55, 58, 60, 87, 118
Moss Kanter, Rosabeth, 36, 199
Musk, Elon, 64
Myers Briggs Type Indicator (MBTI), 146, 211

Nadler, David, 172, 173, 198, 199, 203, 205, 213
Naive realism, 17, 184
Neatby, Jacques, 197
Norm of reciprocity, 45

Objectives and key results (OKR), 116, 119, 120, 124, 208
Organizational culture, 32, 103, 206, 208
Organizational performance, 142; And leadership team size, 133

Pfeffer, Jeffrey, 35, 49, 198, 200
Power: Power games, 9, 30, 35, 36, 37, 39, 40, 42, 44, 47, 52, 53, 54, 55, 60, 113, 119, 180, 181, 201; Power-induced silence, 44, 53, 60; Unethical power games, 39, 40, 52
Power and politics, 1, 6, 9, 35, 36, 179, 201
Psychological safety, 29, 52, 113, 150, 166, 167, 168, 186, 192, 207, 213
Purpose-Outcomes-Process (POP) framework, 148, 158, 159, 160, 161, 162, 163, 164, 166, 167, 169, 170, 171, 173, 176, 177, 181, 189, 190, 194

Research and development (R&D), 16, 17
Roberto, Michael, 64, 197, 198
Roosevelt, Franklin D., 54
Ross, Lee, 17, 197

Schultz, Howard, 54
Silos, 2, 9, 62, 63, 67, 72, 73, 75, 85, 86, 88, 89, 112, 121, 124, 146, 154; Oversilofication, 72, 73, 75, 95; Silo-busting, 63, 67; Silofication, 184
Social network analysis: Brokerage, 202, 203, 204; Closure, 202, 203
Social undermining, 42, 43, 55; As a power tactic, 43
Socializing initiatives, 85, 120
Stanford, 17, 35
Starbucks, 18, 54
Strategic dualities, 15, 17, 19, 26, 27, 29, 32, 33, 138, 183; As a principal source of conflict in leadership teams, 16; Conflicts misdiagnosed as interpersonal conflicts, 17; Top line versus bottom line, 16
Strategic Dualities: Exploration versus exploitation, 16; Growth versus risk management, 16
Strategic planning: As two-step process, 154
Suzman, James, 129, 209
Svejenova, Silviya, 195, 204, 209

Team: Team assessment, 8; Team size, 133, 134; Team-building activities, 4, 26, 67, 146, 181
Team accountability, 103, 104, 123
Team solidarity, 104, 108
Trust, 3, 30, 34, 43, 52, 53, 54, 142, 156, 163, 165, 185, 186

Ury, William L., 119, 198, 208

Wageman, Ruth, 94, 98, 113, 133, 204, 205, 207, 210
Wedding question ("The"), 104
Welch, Jack, 134, 144, 210